Queen's Coll
Oxford
June 20 - 1919

THE EVOLUTION OF THEOLOGY IN THE GREEK PHILOSOPHERS.

PUBLISHED BY

JAMES MACLEHOSE AND SONS, GLASGOW,

Publishers to the University.

———

MACMILLAN AND CO., LTD., LONDON.

New York, - - The Macmillan Co.
London, - - - Simpkin, Hamilton and Co.
Cambridge, - - Macmillan and Bowes.
Edinburgh, - - Douglas and Foulis.

———

MCMIV.

The Evolution of Theology

in the

Greek Philosophers

The Gifford Lectures
delivered in the University of Glasgow in
Sessions 1900-1 and 1901-2

By Edward Caird

LL.D., D.C.L., D.Litt.

Fellow of the British Academy; Corresponding Member of the French Academy
Master of Balliol College, Oxford; Late Professor of Moral Philosophy
in the University of Glasgow

Vol. II.

The King's Library

Glasgow
James MacLehose and Sons
Publishers to the University
1904

GLASGOW: PRINTED AT THE UNIVERSITY PRESS
BY ROBERT MACLEHOSE AND CO.

CONTENTS.

LECTURE SIXTEENTH.

THE ORIGIN AND PRINCIPLE OF THE STOIC PHILOSOPHY.

LECTURE SEVENTEENTH.

THE STOIC SYNTHESIS OF PANTHEISM AND INDIVIDUALISM.

CONTENTS

CONTENTS

LECTURE TWENTY-SEVENTH.

THE INFLUENCE OF GREEK PHILOSOPHY UPON CHRISTIAN THEOLOGY.

LECTURE FOURTEENTH.

THE FINAL RESULTS OF THE ARISTOTELIAN PHILOSOPHY.

IN the last lecture I sought to illustrate the doctrine of Aristotle that contemplation is higher than action, and that it is through the former alone that we enter into conscious relation with the divine, by contrasting it with the opposite doctrine of Kant and his disciples, that it is only the postulates of practical reason, the beliefs which are bound up with the consciousness of duty, which free us from the narrow limits of scientific knowledge and cast some light upon the higher destinies of man. And I endeavoured to show that both these doctrines have to be set aside as involving a false abstraction, an attempt to separate elements which are necessarily connected, similar to that which brought condemnation upon the so-called 'faculty psychology.' For the severance of the will from the reason, in whatever sense it may be interpreted, involves a disruption of the organic unity of man's life, and ultimately deprives the factor which is thus disjoined of all its meaning and content.

While, however, this criticism obliges us to condemn equally both the extreme views, it at the same time shows that there is a certain ambiguity in the doctrine that contemplation is higher than action. If we take that doctrine in the sense criticised, namely, in the sense in which the contemplative life excludes the practical, we are obliged to regard it as one-sided and abstract; but it might be taken to mean something very different from this. It might be taken to mean that there is a contemplative consciousness, which may take either a philosophical or a religious form, and in which we are lifted above all the oppositions that affect our natural life, and, in particular, above the opposition of theory and practice. That opposition, indeed, is one that rests on an imperfect view both of the theoretical and the practical consciousness. On the one hand, knowledge cannot be regarded simply as the revelation of an object which is independent of our subjectivity. The bond of object to subject is one that cannot be severed; and if in science we break through the veil of appearances, and so bring to light the reality beneath them, we are at the same time freeing the self from the imperfections of the first form of its consciousness. In penetrating to

the reality of things, the subject is also discovering
his own true nature.   And the converse holds good
of the practical life.   The process by which the
subject seeks to realise his will in the objective
world, cannot be regarded as a mere imposition of
that will upon something which is extraneous and
indifferent to it.   On the contrary, the subject can
do nothing and attain nothing except in conformity
with the nature of the object on which he acts;
and his realisation of himself in it must be a
manifestation of that nature as well as of his own.
Hence the moral world which is built up by the
action of men is no mere product of their particular
subjectivity, but must be regarded as a further
realisation of the same principle which reveals itself
in the natural world.   Thus both the theoretical
and the practical consciousness point back to a
unity which manifests itself in all the relations
of the subject to the objective world, in its action
upon him and in his action upon it.   And both
theory and practice find their completion in a higher
consciousness which is primarily directed to this
unity.

Now, it is the essential characteristic of religion
that it awakes and develops this consciousness, and
makes it the dominating factor both in our theoretical
and in our practical life.   In other words, religion
teaches us to recognise that the ultimate reality,

which knowledge seeks beyond the veil of phenomena, lies in a Being who speaks not only to us but in us; and, on the other hand, that the realisation of the highest end of our will is possible only as that will becomes the organ and vehicle of a divine purpose which is realising itself in the world. Thus to the religious spirit it is no longer the last word of truth that the world acts upon us or that we react upon the world; but rather that God, the ultimate principle of the whole in which both are included, acts in and through both, to make all their agency, whether in conflict or co-operation, the means of realising himself. This, it should be remarked, does not involve any denial of the reality either of the subject or of the object, or the reduction of them to mere appearances. On the contrary, it is only through the relative independence and even conflict of the two terms that the original principle of unity can reveal itself, and without them it would be empty and meaningless. Still, the whole conception of our finite life and of all the discords and antagonisms it displays—especially of this highest antagonism between object and subject—becomes changed and even transformed by the new light thrown upon it, when we realise that in their utmost separation and warfare they cannot break away from the divine principle which holds them together and manifests itself in both.

Thus the central thought of religion is of a peace that is beyond the unrest of life, of a harmony that transcends all its discords, of a unity of purpose which works through all the conflict of the forces of nature and the still more intense conflict of the wills of men.

If we take it in this way, we can find a meaning for the assertion that the contemplative is higher than the practical life which will not imply a false exaltation of thought, as such, above action. For what, on this construction of it, the assertion means, is that we can rise above the one-sidedness of practical endeavour, above the endeavour to "work out our own salvation," to the consciousness of a Power which, in Scripture language, is "working in us to will and to do of his good pleasure." We may thus, as I have indicated, rise above ourselves, and return on a higher level to a contemplative attitude, even in relation to our own interests and actions. Such an attitude does not, indeed, exclude practice any more than it excludes theory; but it raises them both into a higher form and gives them both a new meaning, making the idea of God, as the one principle that manifests itself in the whole system of things, predominant over all sense of division and conflict within that system. Thus religion is not adverse to practical activity any more than to scientific enquiry; but it brings to the latter a consciousness that 'the real is the rational,' which is the anticipative solution of all theoretical difficulties; and it lifts the former above all its doubts and fears by the faith that the battle which it fights with evil is already won. It is, indeed, the great paradox of the religious consciousness, that, as theory, it can foresee the unity of the world with the demands of the intelligence, even when it is most fully conscious of the defects of our actual knowledge; and that, as practice, it can combine the utmost energy in the struggle against evil with the conviction that evil cannot but be overcome, and even that it exists only to be overcome, or made subservient to greater good. In short, religion in its ultimate meaning is just that consciousness of the whole in the parts, of the end in the beginning, which makes the spirit of man strong to face all the apparent materialism of nature and all the deeper materialism of human life, and to detect a spiritual meaning even in natural necessity, and a soul of goodness even in things evil. And what religion thus anticipates or intuitively apprehends, it is the business of philosophy, which is only religion brought to self-consciousness, to work out theoretically, not by withdrawing its eyes from that which is apparently irrational or imperfect, but by reinterpreting all such appearances in view of its highest principle. Hence if we call philosophy contemplation, we must mean by this not that it is merely theoretic, but that it belongs or ought to belong, like religion, to a region of consciousness which is beyond the opposition of theory and practice.

Such an interpretation of the doctrine that contemplation is higher than action is a possible one : but can we ascribe it in any sense to Aristotle ? If we could, it would be possible to agree with those who maintain that the one-sidedness of his philosophy is only apparent, and that, at least in the ultimate results of his speculations, he rises above all dualism. Now I shall not assert that the ambiguity of the doctrine in question is without influence upon Aristotle, or that the higher interpretation of it is always excluded by his words. So long as two senses of a proposition have not been clearly distinguished and set in opposition to each other, it is possible that they may alternate, or even be confused together, in the mind of a philosopher who asserts it. It is, therefore, possible to take the statements of Aristotle in the sense just explained, in spite of all the arguments to the contrary which have been already adduced. Our final decision as to his meaning, however, must be derived from a consideration of his direct statements as to the idea of God, as a pure self-contemplative intelligence. These are to be found mainly in that great theological tractate which is the culminating result of Aristotle's metaphysic,[1] a tractate which unfortunately is very succinct and difficult to interpret, but which has had more influence upon the subsequent history of theology than any other philosophical writing.

The central thought of this tractate is, as I have indicated, that God must be conceived as living a life of pure contemplation. To him, as a being beyond all the limitations of finitude, we can ascribe only an activity, which is free from all unrest, because it is conditioned by no matter, and has no object but itself. Thus God's life is not like man's, a process of development from potentiality to actuality ; it is the out-going of an unimpeded energy, which yet rests for ever in the joy of its own completeness. Such an activity must be purely ideal. It must be νόησις νοήσεως, a pure self-consciousness, which has no need to go out of itself for an object, or, like our intelligence, to come to itself through the consciousness of an external world ; but which is ever self-contained, ever one with itself, —an ἐνέργεια ἀκινησίας, an activity which is without movement or change, a peace which is not death but an infinite self-centred life.

" The life of God," says Aristotle, " is like the highest kind of activity with us : but while we can maintain it but for a short time, with him it is

[1] *Met.*, XII, 6-10.

eternal ; for it is an activity which is at the same
time the joy of attainment. What other reason can
be given for the fact that the modes of our waking
consciousness, sensation and thought, are the keenest
of pleasures, from which also the secondary pleasures
of hope and memory are derived? Now, pure thought
is thinking of that which is essentially good, and the
highest thought has the highest object. And if we
ask what that object is, the answer must be that the
intelligence thinks *itself* when it lays hold of that
which is intelligible : in other words, the intelligence
itself becomes intelligible when it comes into immediate
contact with the intelligible object and thinks it,
so that subject and object are identified. For the
faculty which can receive into itself the intelligible,
which is also the real, is the intelligence, and its
activity implies that it has its object in itself. Hence
it is in this activity rather than in the mere capacity
for it that the intelligence shows its divine nature.
Contemplation is thus the best and happiest of
activities, and if all we could say were that God's
life is like our life in the highest moments of
contemplative thought, it would be worthy of our
admiration : but if it be better with him than with
us, it must be still more worthy of it. And so it
is indeed. In him is life : for the activity of
intelligence is life, and He is that activity. Thus
his essential activity constitutes a perfect and a

blessed life. We speak of God, therefore, as a living being, perfect and eternal : for to him is ascribed a life which is continuous and eternal : or, we might rather say, He is life eternal." [1]

In this conception of God as an eternal activity complete in itself, He is put in direct antithesis to the finite world, which is essentially a world of time and change, of birth and death. For in that world every substance that exists is developed out of a matter, which has the potentiality of it, by the agency of a previously existing substance, as the efficient cause of its development; and, again, every substance finds the end of its own existence in becoming the efficient cause of another substance of the same species. Thus in the process of the universe the same form is reproduced again and again in a succession of individuals, which are connected with each other as causes and effects; and the whole creation moves through a series of changes that continually repeat themselves. We have to observe further that, according to Aristotle, this cycle of changes goes on, not only in the succession of the generations of living things which continually have the same form reproduced in them, but also in the whole movement of the universe up to the circular motions of the heavens. The ebb and flow of human existence, the rise and fall of nations and civilisations, is but one of the phases of the great secular process of

[1] *Met.*, 1072*b*, 15.

'becoming,' which, after a long period, brings back to the same point the cyclical revolution of things : a revolution which has often repeated itself before, and will again and again repeat itself in the future. Thus time, in the language of Plato, becomes the 'moving image of eternity,' and the endless circular movement of the universe exhibits *sub specie temporis* the nearest analogon to the immediate return upon itself or rest in itself of the Absolute Mind, whose ideal activity is above all movement or change. Or perhaps we should rather say that the finite world, in the limitless self-externality of space and the endless succession of time, is the opposite counterpart of the pure self-contained unity and unchanging self-identity of the Eternal Spirit.

But this immediately suggests a problem, which in one form or another has caused much difficulty in the history of philosophy : How can these opposites be connected with each other ? How can a spiritual being who is ever one with himself, be conceived as in any way relating himself to the divided and changeful existence of the world in space and time ? How can an activity which, *ex hypothesi*, must be represented as a pure activity of thought, be at the same time a cause of motion in extended and material substance ? And how, on the other hand, can such substances be supposed to react upon him or to put themselves in any relation to him ? Aristotle in one place seems distinctly to tell us that God can think nothing but himself. To suppose him to think anything lower than himself is to degrade him, and to suppose him to think anything other than himself is to make him dependent. But if God be thus "of purer eyes than to behold" not only 'iniquity,' but even contingency and finitude, and if his whole activity is pure contemplation, how can He have anything to do with the changing finite world? Zeller, the historian of Greek philosophy, maintains that Aristotle has no real answer to this question, that his God, as a purely contemplative Being, is necessarily shut up within himself, so that he can neither act upon the universe nor even take cognisance of it. Zeller further supports this view by pointing out that, though Aristotle speaks of God as the *first mover*, the original cause of all existence, yet when he tries to explain the manner of this movement he is able only to say that God κινεῖ ὡς ἐρώμενον, moves the world by being the object after which the whole creation strives, and not as if it were in any way determined by his action. In other words, it is not that God loves the world, but that the world loves and longs for God. He is the ideal to which all other things are more or less remote approximations; He is the end to which they move; but we are not to conceive of him as acting on or in them.

Now it must be admitted that Aristotle gives considerable grounds for such a view of his doctrine.

In the first place, in his account of the relation of
the world to God, he seems always to move upward
and not downwards. In other words, he seems always
to be showing that the finite world cannot be conceived to be complete and independent, and that its
existence must therefore be referred back to God;
but not that in the nature of God, as he describes
it, there is any necessity or reason for the existence
of the world.   Thus he frequently argues that an
endless series of movements is impossible without a
first mover, and that this first mover must be himself unmoved.   For movement is always of one thing
by another, and a self-mover, as Aristotle urged against
Plato, is *ex vi termini* impossible.   But the idea of
an 'unmoved mover' seems not less liable to objection, unless we can admit the conception of a kind
of action which, without being motion, yet produces
it in other things.   God, then, must be conceived
to move the world by a kind of action which is
not movement.   But what can this mean?   The
only other kind of action we know is the ideal
action of desire and will, in beings that are
capable of such motives.   Now desire is that appe-
tency, directed to particular objects, which belongs
to all sensitive beings; while will is that love and
longing for the universal good, which is peculiar to
beings who are rational and self-conscious.   It is
only in this way that intelligent beings can be

moved or acted upon, namely, in so far as their will
is determined by the object of their thought.[1] But
as God thinks only himself, he can will and love
nothing but himself, and, if we try to conceive of
any influence of the divine Being which goes beyond
himself, it can only be in so far as there is something divine in the world which loves and seeks itself
in God.

It is easy to see that Aristotle has here come to
a kind of dead-lock. The moving and changing
world must be referred back to an unmoving and
unchanging Being as the source of its movement;
the series of causes and effects to a Being who is a
cause without being an effect. But when we come
to this point, we find that the principle which we
have used to reach it is broken in our hands: for a
mover who is not moved has an activity which cannot be conceived as of the nature of motion at all;
a cause that is not an effect cannot be introduced as
a member, even as the first member, of the series
of conditioned causes. We may hide this from ourselves by speaking of a self-mover with Plato, or an
unmoved mover with Aristotle, or a *causa sui* with
Spinoza; but this is only a disguise for the fact
that we have made what Aristotle calls a μετάβασις
εἰς ἄλλο γένος, a change to a quite different category

---

[1] The above is a paraphrase of the beginning of the seventh chapter
of the twelfth book of the *Metaphysic.*

or way of explanation. For in this unmoved mover, we are obliged to assume a kind of action which cannot be described as movement nor as causation, at least in the sense in which we have hitherto been using these words. Instead of a first link in the chain of temporal events—which, if we hold to the idea of movement or cause, is an impossibility—what we have now suggested to us is a kind of cause or mover which is not *in* the chain at all, either as the beginning or as any part of it, but one which is equally related to all its links. Hence Aristotle is obliged to think of the unmoved mover, not as beginning the whole circular movement of the heavens,—indeed, for him it has no beginning—but as continually producing and maintaining it. In other words, He is not a first in time, but a principle which is logically prior to, or presupposed in, all time.

But how are we to represent this new kind of action, this self-determination which is above movement or change? It can only be conceived, as Aristotle admits, as a purely ideal or spiritual movement, such as that by which we set before us an end, and make it the object of our endeavour. Now such self-determination of a spiritual being is easily conceivable, and in imperfect beings, who yet can think of a perfection which they have not attained, it may be conceived as a *transeunt*

activity, that is, as an activity which carries
them beyond themselves to the Being in whom is
the perfection which they seek. In God, however,
as a perfect being, it cannot be so represented; for
there can be no external final cause of his activity.
Hence Aristotle seems forced to think of the ideal
activity, which connects God with the world, as one
which is in the world and not in God. And he
only partly disguises this discrepancy when he
speaks of there being 'something divine' in all
creatures which makes them seek the highest good;
or, again, when he personifies nature, and endows it
with a will for the best which is partly thwarted by
the conditions of its realisation. In this way of conceiving the relation of God to the world there is a
twofold failure; in so far as the action spoken of is
not in God at all, and in so far as it is a kind of
action that can be attributed only to rational beings;
for to speak of a will of nature is to speak of nature
as if it were a rational being. If, indeed, we could
apply to God's presence in the world what Aristotle
says of organisms in general, namely, that the whole,
or the principle of the whole, is in every part, we
might give a more definite meaning to the assertion
of a 'divine something' in the world which loves
and seeks for God; but this would be to attach too
much importance to isolated expressions. And, apart
from this, all that Aristotle has proved is that the

world, as a finite existence in space and time, cannot be conceived as having the principle of its movement and change in itself; but he has not shown how a spiritual being can be conceived as originating such movement and change, or indeed, as relating himself in any way to it.

This conclusion, however, has to be modified by two considerations: first, that, in spite of these difficulties in conceiving God as the active principle in all being, as both its first and its final cause, Aristotle does undoubtedly so conceive Him. His special objection to the Platonic and Pythagorean theories is that they supply no such principle, and even set the world of change in such opposition to the eternal that no connexion can be discerned between them. While, therefore, he declares on the one hand, that there must be something higher than the objects of sense, otherwise there will be no principle of order in the world of sense itself—seeing that every principle that can be set up will have to be referred to a higher principle *ad infinitum* ; on the other hand, he asserts equally that what is wanted cannot be found in the ideas of Plato or the numbers of the Pythagoreans, which are indeed higher than the things of sense, but utterly unconnected with them, and therefore incapable of determining them. His own theory, therefore, he regards as alone supplying a self-determining principle, which can be a determining principle for the world of sense. Further, he thinks that by this conception he has also explained the unity of the world, and bound all that is finite together into one whole by connecting it with one divine cause; and he quotes as against all theories that admit separate and independent spheres of being, Homer's vindication of monarchy: "The rule of many is not good; let one be ruler of all." Aristotle is, therefore, satisfied that his own view, by referring all change and movement of the universe to a spiritual Being—who, as such, is a self-determining activity that is beyond movement and change—has solved the difficulty of explaining the origin of the world. He has thus, he thinks, set up a principle which, as spiritual, is beyond the world, and yet able to act upon it. And he sums up his conception of God, as at once immanent in the universe and transcending it, in what is one of the most striking passages in all the literature of theology.

"If it be asked," he says,[1] "in which of two possible ways the nature of the universe contains the good and the best, whether as something separate, existing independently in itself, or as the order of its parts, the answer is that, as in the case of an army, it must be in both ways at once. For the excellence of an army lies in its order, and it is separately embodied in the general. It lies, however, more in the latter

[1] *Met.*, XII, 10.

than in the former; for the general does not exist
because of the order, but the order because of him.
Now all things in the universe are somehow ordered
together, whatever swims in the sea, or flies in the air,
or grows on the earth, but not all in like fashion
Nothing exists apart and without some kind of relation
to the rest; for all things are ordered in relation to
one end. But it is as in a household, the free
members of which are least of all left to their own
devices, but have all or most of their actions determined beforehand with reference to the general
wellbeing, while the slaves and animals have a few
things prescribed to them with relation to that end,
and for the rest are left to themselves. Thus in each
member of the whole, its own nature manifests itself
as the principle of its actions: and by this I mean
that each has a special sphere allotted to it, while there
are certain other things in which they all contribute
to the good of the whole."

Whatever, therefore, may be the defects of
Aristotle's way of realising his own conception, there
can be no doubt that he means, by referring the
whole order of the natural world to a spiritual and
therefore a self-determining principle, to escape from
the dilemma on one or other horn of which he
supposes all his predecessors to have been impaled.
This dilemma is that either the world of time and
sense has no cause beyond itself (which is self-

contradictory, as such a world cannot be conceived as complete in itself); or that, if it be referred to a cause beyond itself, such a cause is altogether cut off from it, and therefore cannot explain it. But Aristotle's own view does not seem to do what he claims for it: for it does not explain how the conception of the purely ideal self-determination of that divine Being, who lives a life of pure contemplation, can escape from the same censure which he applies to the Platonic theory; in other words, how such pure thought, directed only upon itself, can become a determination of anything else than itself. And his doctrine that it moves the world 'as loved by it,' seems to show at once that he feels the difficulty, and that he can only solve it by an *ignoratio elenchi*. Like many subsequent writers, he seeks to bind the world to God without binding God to the world; nor does he make any use even of the pregnant hint of Plato, that God is good, and that goodness must seek to communicate itself.

At the same time, we must acknowledge that the metaphor of the army and the general contains a suggestion which gives us some help in dealing with the difficulty raised by Aristotle himself, when he says that God cannot think anything lower than or different from himself, and therefore, it would seem to follow, cannot think the finite world, which is full of change and contingency. He can think it,

Aristotle seems to answer, in its order, in the forms or types that are realised in it.   The divine intelligence, therefore, must be conceived, not as an abstract self-consciousness, but as gathering all the ideal forms that are realised in the world into the unity of one thought.   This also seems to be the meaning of another passage,[1] in which Aristotle asks whether the object of the divine reason is simple, or complex and composite.   He answers that it must be simple; for, if the parts of that object were externally put together, reason would be subject to change in passing from one of them to another; and this would imply that it was not altogether immaterial.   Aristotle, then, goes on to illustrate this thought by a comparison of the divine to the human intelligence.   "As the human mind, though it has a complex object, yet at times apprehends it as a unity; not attaining to the good it seeks in each part severally, but finding the *summum bonum* in the whole, and that, in spite of the fact, that the subject here is different from the object it contemplates; so it is with the divine intelligence, whose object is itself, through all eternity."[2]

Thus, according to Aristotle, even the human intelligence, in spite of the complexity in itself and in its object, which is due to the presence of a material element in both, can rise to the perception of the good, not as an attribute of particular things but as

[1] *Met.*, XII, 9.   [2] *Met.*, 1075*a*, 8.

a principle of unity that transcends all their difference. It cannot, however, identify its consciousness of the object with its consciousness of itself as this individual. But the divine intelligence does not need any such process. To it the forms of things are at once present in their ideal nature, free from all matter, and the object is therefore ever in transparent unity with the subject. Thus God must be conceived as having a self-consciousness which is at the same time a consciousness of the ideal order of the world.

From these considerations it seems clear, that the simplicity which Aristotle attributes to the divine intelligence is not the absence of all multiplicity, but a transparent unity in which all difference is taken up and resolved. God's thought is thus represented as embracing all the elements of the whole in one indivisible intuition, just as a great artist sees at one glance the whole work of art in the inter-dependence of all its parts, or as a great scientific man grasps his whole science in one complete thought.[1] In such an intuition there is no possibility of separating the object from the subject, the consciousness of the world from the consciousness of the self. Yet this must not be taken to mean that they are simply merged in one, but only that there is an identity which is above their difference and maintains itself through it. It is true that this view is not as fully

[1] See Vol. I, p. 340.

and distinctly expressed by Aristotle as we might
desire, and that, as has been said, the use of the word
'simple' is apt to produce a misconception, even if
we could be sure that it did not imply one. And
when we find him maintaining that reason in its
perception of the highest truth is beyond judgment,
and therefore incapable of error, because it grasps the
object in an immediate way that is parallel to the
direct perceptions of sense, θιγγάνων καὶ νοῶν, 'touch-
ing it and in the touch having an intellectual intuition of it'; we are obliged to acknowledge that he is
haunted by a false ideal of absolute unity and un-
mingled simplicity, of a unity of the object with the
intelligence which is only a bare identity, and of an
intuition in which all the discourse of reason is
extinguished.

But a still greater difficulty remains. Even if
we put aside such objections and give Aristotle all
the benefit of the above interpretation, it does
not explain how the ideal forms of things can be
realised in matter at all, nor how, as a consequence
of this, the universe can admit contingency and
imperfection, movement and change. The whole
process of the finite—with all its division and fluctua-
tion, the continual conflict of its parts, and the marred
and distorted existences which the conflict produces—
seems to lie beyond the sphere of the contemplative
reason, which cannot see anything but an ideally

complete whole in which every element is in perfect
unity and harmony with every other. The rift which
goes through Aristotle's conception of the life of man,
which reappears in his view of science, and again
in his separation of theory from practice—this rift
is seen finally to take the form of an opposition
between the world in space and time as it is presented in sense-perception, and the world of ideal
forms which is alone capable of being grasped and
understood by reason, and which, therefore, is the
only world that can exist for the divine intelligence.
Nor does Aristotle allow us to take refuge in the idea
that the world of sense and opinion is only the world
as imperfectly apprehended by the developing intelligence, which knows neither the world nor itself as they
really are. This may seem a plausible way out of
the difficulty, but to introduce it into Aristotle would
be to reconstruct his whole philosophy. Nor, indeed,
would it solve the difficulty; for the problem is just
this : to understand how a world conditioned by space
and time, and an imperfect though developing intelligence which apprehends it under such conditions,
should exist at all, or rather how any ground for their
existence can be found in the divine nature. And we
are obliged to acknowledge that in Aristotle's idea
of God no such ground can be discovered, unless we
interpret contemplation in a way for which we can
find no sufficient warrant in his writings.

The subject may be made clearer by raising another question. The object of thought must be distinguished from the thought that apprehends it, else it could not be present to that thought as an object; yet in another aspect it must be one with the thought that apprehends it, else it could not be present to it at all. Now, how are we to discriminate between these two aspects? In what sense is the object of thought only thought itself, and in what sense is it other than thought? Aristotle seems to answer that there is an element in the object which is ideal and therefore can be grasped by reason, and that there is another element in the object which is alien to reason, and which is present to us only through the faculty of sense. Such splitting of the difference, however, will not solve the difficulty; for, if we follow it out logically, it leads us to the result that the ideal element by itself is not objective, and the element which makes it objective is not ideal. But what we want to explain is just how that which is objective should be apprehended by reason, how the ideal world should be also real. Now, from the point of view of Aristotle, the divine or perfect reason cannot apprehend anything but itself, and the objective, as such, must be altogether beyond its reach. It appears, therefore, that the admission into the objective world of any element which, in

Aristotle's sense, is not rational and therefore not explicable by the intelligence, must end in a complete denial of the rationality of the objective world, and in a recoil of the mind upon itself and its own inner consciousness, as that in which alone it can have any real apprehension of truth. The subjective movement of later Greek philosophy, with its concentration upon self-consciousness and its indifference to all knowledge of the world as well as to all the practical bonds of society, is therefore already prefigured in Aristotle.

Now a thorough-going idealism must recognise that thought and reason cannot be confined to itself, that, indeed, it can be conscious of itself only in relation to that which is not itself. For such an idealism there can be no self-consciousness which is not also the consciousness of an objective world. Yet the objective, which is other than itself, must be *its* other, its counterpart; it must be an object in which reason can find itself again, else it could not be presented at all. In other words, thought is possible only as it recognises the distinction between itself and its object, and at the same time transcends this distinction. The neglect of the former of these points leads to a one-sided or merely subjective idealism, while the neglect of the latter gives rise to an irreconcilable dualism; and very often we find philosophical speculation swaying from

one of these extremes to the other.   Thus a dualistic
view of the relation between subject and object is
almost certain to lead to a retreat upon the subjective,
as that which alone is within the compass of the
intelligence ; and a Berkeleian reduction of all objects
to ideas is very apt to raise the thought of another
kind of objects which are not relative to the subject,
and which therefore are altogether beyond the
reach of knowledge.   On the other hand, a thorough-
going idealism will not fear to admit the reality of
that which is other than mind, and even, in a sense,
diametrically opposed to it; for it rests on a perception that these opposites are yet necessarily
related, and that both are different and correlated
aspects of one whole.

Now Aristotle never attains to such a view of
the question, but, so far as we can see, maintains
the existence of a material, and therefore unintelligible, element [1] in the universe, corresponding
to our sense-apprehension of the particular.   Yet
this insight was not very far from him: for it is
not difficult to see that his conception of the finite
world makes it the necessary correlate of his conception of pure self-consciousness, and, therefore, not
really independent of it or separable from it.   The
objective world in its endless difference is not the

---

[1] *Met.*, 1036a, 9, ἡ δ' ὕλη ἄγνωστος καθ' αὑτήν.   Cf. *Met.*, 1039b, 27 :
Phys., 207a, 25.

negation of the unity of pure self-consciousness, but its contrary, not merely other than it, but *its* other. The pure inwardness of the mind is the opposite counterpart of the self-externality of things in space; as also its constant return upon itself is the opposite counterpart of the continual passing away of things in time. And if we apply the Aristotelian principle that the knowledge of opposites is one, we must admit that thought transcends this difference of itself and its object, and that for it the ultimate reality must be found in the unity of its terms. Unfortunately Aristotle seems to deny that this principle holds good for the pure or absolute intelligence,[1] and to assert not that that intelligence transcends all opposition, but that for it the opposition does not exist at all.

I may put this in a still clearer way by connecting it with another aspect of the doctrine of Aristotle to which I have referred above. Aristotle declares that the only practical activity which we can ascribe to a rational being is the activity produced by the love of a good which is the object of his thought. But he is embarrassed by the difficulty that the divine intelligence can find no such good in anything but itself: and in this sense he seems to agree with the saying of Spinoza, that "he who loves God cannot desire that God should love him in return." He, therefore,

[1] See Vol. I, p. 344.

ascribes the movement of the universe to the love of the imperfect creation for God as its perfection. This is the 'something divine' which, in nature, anticipates and points to the perfection it wants, and which, in man, rises into a consciousness of God, and even a participation in his life of contemplation. Thus Aristotle seems to anticipate the doctrine of St. Paul that "the earnest expectation of the creature waiteth for the manifestation of the sons of God"; and that we also, who "have received the first-fruits of the Spirit, we also groan within ourselves, waiting" for the fuller realisation of the divine nature in us. In other words, he anticipates the explanation of the world-process as a process of development towards a higher good, which is implied in its existence from the beginning. This doctrine, however, is a general expression which he does not attempt to work out to its consequences; and the correlative doctrine that the divine love embraces the finite world, and that it is in that world that God is manifested and realised, has no place in his philosophy, unless we are to find some trace of it in the metaphor of the army and its general.

It appears, then, that the question which was raised at the beginning of this lecture as to the meaning of Aristotle's doctrine of the primacy of the intelligence cannot be definitely answered in either way. The general trend and purport of his philosophy is toward

dualism, and towards that abstract opposition of contemplation to action which is the result of dualism.
But, in the first place, we have to admit that the pure
self-contemplation of God is conceived as being at the
same time the contemplation of the intelligible world,
that is, of all the ideal forms realised in the universe.
And, in the second place, we have to recognise that
there are passages in which contemplation seems to be
taken not in an exclusive but in an inclusive sense,
not as meaning a rest of the intelligence in itself
which is the negation of all practical activity, but as
the consciousness of a unity which transcends all
oppositions, even the opposition of the theoretical and
the practical life.   These passages, however, seem to
be little more than the intuitive glimpses of a truth
beyond the range of his explicit system, which we may
find in every great thinker.   Indeed, if we were
allowed to take such glimpses of truth as if they were
equivalent to a clear vision of all that is involved in
them, it would be difficult to prove that there has
been any progress in philosophy or even in human
thought; or that the latest philosopher has gone
beyond the thoughts which presented themselves to
the first men who reflected upon their own nature and
upon the nature of the universe.

LECTURE FIFTEENTH.

THE GENERAL CHARACTER OF THE
POST-ARISTOTELIAN PHILOSOPHY.

IN my previous lectures I have endeavoured to give
a connected view of the development of theological
ideas in Greece up to the time of Aristotle. The
great idealistic movement which culminated in the
philosophies of Plato and Aristotle was the first,
and perhaps the greatest, effort ever made to reach
a comprehensive view of the universe in which no
element of reality should be suppressed or mutilated.
And the enormous influence which these two thinkers
have exerted over the whole subsequent course of
speculation shows that they were able to determine
at least the main issues of philosophical enquiry,
and to mark out the main lines upon which philo
sophical discussion must proceed. But it was in
the nature of the case impossible that at that early
period, when human experience was so limited, any
conclusive results should be attained. Difficulties

as to the nature of man or of the world he inhabits must be searched to their deepest root ere they can be solved. Oppositions of thought and life must be worked out to their extreme issues ere they can be reconciled; the different aspects of things must be clearly defined and distinguished from each other ere their true relations can be seen. Hence it was impossible for Plato and Aristotle to realise all that is involved in the questions they raised—questions the difficulty and importance of which has since been brought to light by ages of conflict and controversy—still less to reach a satisfactory solution of them. They were constrained to 'heal the hurt' of philosophy 'slightly' because they could not probe its depth. Just because they did not realise fully the difference and antagonism of the elements which they seek to combine in their philosophies, they were often satisfied with an external subordination of one of them to another, and did not realise how far this falls short of a true reconciliation of them. Hence in spite of the great effort after system which is characteristic of Plato, in spite of the analytic genius of Aristotle, the ultimate result is of the nature of a compromise; and however necessary and useful compromise may be in practical matters, in the world of thought it cannot settle anything. Rather it is sure in the long run to lead to a revolt of the fettered intelligence, and even to a violent recoil or reaction, in

which the elements artificially combined are again
torn away from the connexion into which they have
been brought and set in abstract opposition to each
other.

This statement will become clearer, if we recall
the nature of the philosophical presuppositions from
which Plato and Aristotle started, and the consequent defectiveness of the results they reached.   Both
the Platonic and Aristotelian philosophies were
attempts to explain the world on the principle of
Anaxagoras that " all things were in chaos till reason
came to arrange them."   In other words, they
started from a dualism of form and matter which
they sought to overcome by subjecting the latter
to the former.   The ultimate tendency of such a
mode of thought is shown in the Aristotelian conception of the relations of God and the universe.   It is
the conception, on the one hand, of a pure intelligence
which is eternally one with itself, a νόησις νοήσεως,
or divine self-consciousness, in which the difference
of subject and object at once yields to their transparent unity, and their duality is at once expressed
and transcended in one perfect act of intuition ; and
it is the conception, on the other hand, of a world of
conflict and change, which is made up of parts that
are indifferent and external to each other, and which
in its endless revolution is ever seeking, yet ever
failing, to attain to unity with itself and with the

divine centre of its being. Thus the self-centred intelligence of God, whose self-consciousness is at the same time the consciousness of the ideal world, is sharply contrasted with the division and antagonism of the material world, which is never at one with itself but exhibits rather an endless vicissitude of things that can never be rounded into a complete whole. For in the finite world the ideal principles are manifested under conditions which prevent them from ever attaining to perfect realisation, and therefore, in place of one individual reality completely corresponding to its idea, we have an endless series of imperfect existences, each of which is, so to speak, an effort of nature to reach the archetype of which it inevitably falls short. In so speaking we are only using the half-metaphorical language of Aristotle, who tells us that nature, being unable to reach eternity in the individual, seeks immortality in the species:[1] in other words, that the specific form survives, though the individuals in which it is manifested continually pass away and give place to other individuals. Thus all finite things are ever realising, yet never once for all realise the ideal principle which yet constitutes their inmost nature. Even man, as a finite subject, fails to attain to perfect unity with that active reason which yet makes him what he is, as a conscious and self-conscious being.

[1] See Vol. I, p. 289.

The outlines of this dualistic view of things were already drawn by Plato, but it is Aristotle who fills up the sketch and gives definiteness and precision to its details, and who thereby at the same time reveals the fatal flaw that runs through it. Aristotle, indeed, differs from Plato, in so far as he regards the ideal form not as a universalising but as an individualising principle; not as uniting the different elements in each existence into a whole, but rather as distinguishing each individual being from all the others. But this difference only enables them to find opposite ways of expression for the same error. With both the ideal form or principle is viewed as complete in itself and as having no necessary relation to its matter.[1] And this, as we have seen, inevitably carries with it not only the division of God from the world, but also the division of the reason in man from the other elements of his nature. It even implies the division of the intuitive reason in him, which is regarded as eternal, from the discursive reason by which he takes account of the relations of finite things, as well as from all the feelings of desire and aversion, love and hate, which affect his finite life. Thus also the argument for immortality, which in Plato seems to refer to the individual soul, becomes in Aristotle confined to the

---

[1] This, however, must be modified in the case of Aristotle by what is said in Vol. I, p. 277 *seq.*

universal reason, which is ever realising itself in the series of finite subjects, but is never finally realised in any one of them.

Now this dualistic severance of the higher from the lower, of the spiritual from the material, was in the future to be taken up and carried to still further consequences by the Neo-Platonists. But the immediate result was rather to throw discredit on the philosophy which had endeavoured to combine such inconsistent elements, and to provoke a strong reaction towards the simpler ways of earlier philosophy. The theories of Plato and Aristotle, as I have shown, were systematic efforts to comprehend all things as parts of one whole, to understand man as a member of society and a part of the universe, and all the elements of human nature in their due relation to each other. They did not set up one simple principle and try to deduce everything from it, but rather regarded the world as a complex unity in which every part is supported, and, in a sense, proved by all the other parts. This is manifest as regards Plato, for though he tells us that the Idea of Good is the principle upon which all things rest, he does not mean by this that there is one truth from which all other truths are derived. For the Idea of Good is simply the idea that all things are united with each other and with the mind that knows them, the idea that all being and all thought, all subjective and all objective reality, are to be regarded as elements in one whole, in which each part implies and is implied by all the others. The test of truth, therefore, lies for Plato not in the conformity of all things to some one standard, but in the systematic coherence in which each truth becomes the standard for all the rest. There is no tortoise supporting the elephant which supports the universe; for the universe is a rounded and self-contained whole, whose parts are reciprocally reasons and consequents of each other. This is Plato's way of looking at things, and, in spite of Aristotle's tendency to lay emphasis on difference rather than on unity, on distinction rather than on connexion, we may fairly say that it is his also; for he also bids us think of the world as an ordered drama in which there are no episodes. Still, in both philosophers, as we have just seen, there is a presupposition which tends continually to counteract their effort after organic connexion, and to reduce their philosophy to an external combination of irreconcileable elements. Beginning with an unexplained difference, they are never able to overcome it. Thus they fail to realise the conception of system after which they are striving; in other words, they fail to bring the particular elements of their philosophy into harmony with the general idea of it, and this failure in the long run tends to compromise the idea itself.

As, however, philosophy cannot but strive after systematic unity, the post-Aristotelian schools find themselves obliged to endeavour to realise it in another way, not by comprehension but by abstraction, not by binding all the different elements and aspects of the universe into one whole, but by isolating one of these elements, treating it alone as absolutely real, and explaining away everything that is different from or opposed to it. The effect of this method is two-fold. On the one hand, it brings out into startling relief and prominence one of the sides or aspects of the truth, and logically follows it out apart from the others without shrinking from any of the incon-venient consequences of its isolation. On the other hand, this complete and consequent development of what, after all, is only an abstraction, a constituent of truth torn away from its place in the whole, necessarily brings with it a nemesis, in dwarfing or throwing into the shade, if not entirely obliterating, all the other elements of it, and ultimately in depriving even the favoured element itself of all its meaning. Moreover, such a method of abstraction tends to force all the questions of philosophy into the form of a choice between exclusive alternatives; and it is forgotten that there can be no opposition which does not imply relation, and that, if they were absolutely isolated from each other, the ex-tremes would cease even to be exclusive. Hence

Post-Aristotelian philosophy presents the spectacle of two opposite dogmatisms dividing the field of thought; though each of them really has its *raison d'être* in the other, and would lose all its meaning if it were successful in destroying its opponent. Lastly, when it dawns upon the mind that the choice between two such alternatives is arbitrary, and that equal reasons can be given both for and against both, nothing seems to be left for the philosopher but a scepticism, which acknowledges the equipoise and refuses to adopt either alternative. Thus we have the Stoics on the one side, and the Epicureans on the other, engaged in an endless polemic against each other, and the Sceptics coming to draw the conclusion that truth is unattainable, though in doing so they only add another dogmatism to those which they oppose.

From every formal point of view these philosophers show a great falling off from Plato and Aristotle. The crude theories of Epicurus and Zeno as to the criterion of truth, and as to the ultimate nature of reality, are in a distinctly lower key of speculation than the Platonic and Aristotelian metaphysic and dialectic. Still lower from a scientific, if not from a literary point of view, are the epigrammatic moralisings of Seneca, the aphoristic meditations of Marcus Aurelius, and the practical sermons of Epictetus, in all of which the theoretic basis of ethics is rather pre-supposed than explained. But, notwithstanding this inferiority of speculative power, we cannot admit that this new movement of thought is to be regarded as a retrograde one, still less that it shows a failure of the human intelligence in the face of the problem of the universe. It is quite possible that a system of philosophy may be less rich and comprehensive, as well as less stringent in its method, and yet that it may indicate a relative advance in human thought. There may be a dialectical value in the absence of dialectic; and a narrowing outlook upon the whole sphere of knowledge may be the necessary condition of a growing clearness of perception in one direction. When a principle is isolated, it becomes possible to see its full meaning and all its consequences, apart from the confusion and uncertainty which is thrown upon it, when it is combined with other principles in any, even the best, system of compromise. For example, Aristotle's doctrine of virtue, as a mean state of passion which is determined by reason, no doubt combines into a kind of whole all the elements of the moral life; but it suggests rather the idea of a compromise, or of the external subjection of one element by another, than of any true unity of the two sides of man's nature. Aristotle does not show anything like an adequate comprehension of the violence and extent of the conflict between the flesh and the spirit; and therefore he is only able, so to

speak, to patch up a kind of truce between them.   He
has no glimpse of such a fierce inward struggle
between the law of the mind and the law of the
members as is pictured to us by St. Paul, and,
just because of this, he cannot see his way to a
complete reconciliation of man with himself.   Hence
it was a great step in advance when the truce,
which Aristotle had established between the different
sides or elements of human nature, was broken, and
when the effort was made by the Epicureans and the
Stoics to treat each element as complete in itself and
to follow out all the consequences of doing so.   It was
necessary that the fire of a conflict between the
opposing dogmatisms should be kindled, ere it could
be seen that their opposition was merely that of
complementary factors of truth, and ere the true way
of reconciling them in a more comprehensive theory
could be discerned.

Each of the post-Aristotelian philosophies, then, is
one-sided and abstract.   It aims at unity by taking
some one of the elements which Plato and Aristotle
had tried to combine, and explaining away the other
elements.   With this tendency to abstraction there
comes also a tendency of philosophy to concentrate
all its efforts on the practical problem, and that in
its narrowest form, as the problem of the guidance
of the individual life.   This was not, indeed, quite
a new tendency in Greek philosophy ; for, from the

time of Pythagoras at least, philosophy had been
regarded as involving a special kind of life as well
as a system of doctrine. And Socrates, attempting
as he did to base morality on a clear consciousness
of the meaning and end of living, had seemed to
make philosophy not only useful but indispensable
for virtuous conduct. It was, however, only in
the Minor Socratic schools that this tendency was
followed out to its consequences, while both Plato
and Aristotle recognise that the reflective consciousness of philosophy cannot be the sole nor even the
primary guide of human life. Man, they maintain,
must learn the first lessons of morality in the form of
rules and habits of conduct which are supported by
the social influences of the community in which he
lives, and not in the form of ethical theory. And
Aristotle even contends that he who would understand
ethical teaching must, in the first instance, have had
a good moral training and have acquired right habits.
On this view ethical theory may improve practical
morality by bringing to light the principles that
underlie it, and so turning a morality of habit into a
morality of principle, but it cannot, as Socrates had
supposed, be the first teacher of it. At best, it can
only be a guide to the philosophical statesman in
framing or altering the constitution of the State, and
so improving the ethical environment of the individual; but it cannot be the ground on which the

morality of the ordinary citizen should be consciously based. The individual must first be disciplined and moulded by unconscious influences into conformity with the society of which he is a member; and the State institutions, the State service, the State religion, the habits and rules recognised in his particular community, must be the main influences under which he becomes moralised. Hence Plato and Aristotle sought to improve the individual by improving the State, and to improve the State by supplying the philosophical statesman with a better theory to guide him in the work of legislation. But they made no direct appeal to the private citizen, nor did they believe that his morality could be directly based on philosophical teaching. And the value of their speculations on ethics and politics was almost entirely theoretical—in that they analysed the social phenomena of Greek life and discovered the principles which underlay it.

On the other hand, it was, as I have said above,[1] the Minor Socratic schools which from this point of view served themselves heirs to Socrates, setting the State aside and substituting the teaching of philosophy for its social training. It was their doctrine that moral life must be based on the conscious reason and reflexion of the individual, and that therefore each individual must determine for himself the end of his existence and how to seek it.

[1] Vol. I, p. 77.

Thus philosophy had with them to supply the very basis of social training. It had to become practical; and, indeed, it treated the practical guidance of life as its primary, if not its exclusive aim. We must, however, hasten to add that this attitude of the Minor Socratics was not of great practical importance; for in their days the idea of the State was still powerful, and Plato and Aristotle were following the main tendency of the time in making it the centre of their ethical theories. The Minor Socratics were rather in the position of Dissenters, who were in open protest against the general modes of belief accepted by their fellow-countrymen, but who bore in their breasts the promise of the future. They, and especially the Cynic school, were regarded as a peculiar class of men who withdrew from the common life, defied public opinion, and even broke away from the forms and restraints of what in their day was considered a respectable civic existence. Hence their views of morality could have no great influence upon their own time.

But it was entirely different in the post-Aristotelian era. Even in the time of Aristotle a great change was passing over the public life of Greece, by which all its ethical traditions were discredited, and a new importance was given to philosophical theories of morality. By the victories of Philip and Alexander the civic states of Greece were reduced to the rank of subordinate municipalities in a great

military empire; and, under the dynasties founded
by Alexander's generals, they became the plaything
and the prize of a conflict between greater
powers, which they could not substantially influence.
Finally, all their feeble attempts to reassert their
independence were crushed by the organised force of
Rome. Now every step in this direction tended to
take something away from the City-State, and to
widen the gulf between its actual life and the ideal
community which Plato and Aristotle still sought to
find in it or to produce from it. The fundamental
idea of their political writings as of the politics of
their country—that the municipal State was the πέρας
τῆς αὐταρκείας, the exact form of social union in
which the powers of man can best be educated, and
in which they can find the most suitable field of
exercise—this narrowly Greek idea had become anti-
quated and meaningless by the diffusion of Greek
culture over the civilised world, and by the concentration of political authority in the Roman Emperor.
Hence that withdrawal into private life, which to
the Minor Socratics was a voluntary act, had now
become a necessity. Indeed, we may fairly say
that it was at this period that the division between
public and private life, which is so familiar to us but
was so unfamiliar to the Greeks, was first decisively
established as a fact. A private non-political life
became now, not the exception, but the rule; not

the abnormal choice of a few recalcitrant spirits, like Diogenes or Aristippus, but the inevitable lot of the great mass of mankind. The individual, no longer finding his happiness or misery closely associated with that of a community, whose law and custom was his supreme authority and whose service was his highest end, was thrown back upon his own resources, and had to ask himself how he could live and die for himself. Thus, on the one hand, all the traditions of Greek political ethics seemed to be rendered obsolete; and, on the other hand, the need for some new rule of individualistic morality was felt by ever growing classes of the community.

Nor could the ancient religions satisfy any such demand: for they were essentially national, and even political religions, bound up with the life of some society, and unable to contemplate the individual except as a member of it. Hence they lost a great part of their meaning, and tended to become an empty routine of ritual and observance, when they ceased to be the consecration of civic and national life. They could not meet the wants of the new time, or, in attempting to meet them, they became degraded into superstitions. Rome, in fact, when it conquered the nations, conquered their gods as well; but while it dissolved the religious bonds of national or municipal states, it was unable to substitute any new spiritual bond in their place. It was ready, indeed, with politic tolerance to open a Pantheon, into which it admitted all the gods of the conquered peoples, but a new religion could not be made out of a jumble of all the cults of the past. And the worship of the Emperor was too materialistic, too obviously a worship of force, to satisfy any spiritual want; it was a kind of earthly religion based upon a despair of heaven. What Rome did was practically to pulverise the old societies, reducing them to a collection of individuals, and then to hold them together by an external organisation, military and legal. It bestowed on its subjects a greater measure of outward security, justice and peace than any nation had previously enjoyed: but it did little to promote inward unity. The *immensa pacis Romanae majestas* covered with its protection the greater part of the civilised world, but its effect was rather to level and disintegrate than to draw men together.

Now in modern times such a state of things would not have left men without spiritual guidance; or rather, we should say, it did not so leave them. For the modern world also has passed through a period in which the main tendency of thought was subjective and individualistic, in which the rights of the individual, the intellectual independence and moral self-sufficiency of the individual, were strongly asserted against all religious as well as against all social authority. Yet the effect was not to produce that estrangement of all educated men from religion which was associated with the individualism of the ancient world. A similar scepticism did, indeed, find very powerful representatives, but though it greatly weakened the authority of churches and of the fixed dogmatic creeds which they taught, it did not destroy the power of Christianity over the minds of men. And the reason was that the Christian religion, in one aspect of it, is itself profoundly individualistic : in other words, it treats the individual as having an infinite worth in himself, and appeals strongly to the spiritual hopes and fears, to the inner experiences and aspirations of the individual soul. Hence it was able to clothe itself in new forms adapted to the consciousness of the time. In many of the Protestant sects it developed itself in a distinctly subjective form ; in some it even severed the connexion between the inner and the outer life. This over-emphasis laid upon the subjective aspect of Christianity, no doubt, produced as one-sided and inadequate a view of that religion as the over-emphasis of the Latin Church upon its objective aspect. Still it showed that Christianity could speak to the time in its own language and could give it just the kind of spiritual support it required. But in the ancient religions there was hardly anything which could supply such a want. They were essentially objective, and even externally objective; they were essentially social, national, and even political religions, and they decayed and died with the destruction of the independence of the communities into which they had breathed a spiritual energy. Hence philosophy had to step into the vacant place and to supply, at least for the educated classes, the kind of spiritual nutriment which they required. There is thus a measure of truth in Bacon's saying that for the ancients moral philosophy supplied the place of theology—at least if we read religion for theology, and confine the assertion to the Post-Aristotelian period of ancient history. The Stoic or Epicurean philosopher might without much exaggeration be said to have taken upon himself the office, which was afterwards filled by the Christian priest. The hortatory discourses of Epictetus are an anticipation of the sermon, and in his letters to many correspondents, consoling, encouraging, reproving and advising, Seneca seems almost to stand in the relation of a Christian pastor to his flock.

The Post-Aristotelian period, then, was one which had special need of some philosophical theory that could fortify the individual man in his isolation against the world, and could give unity, strength and direction to his life. It was, in a spiritual sense, a period of retrenchment, when the great moral and intellectual movement which had attended the development of the Greek municipal state, had come

to an end in the collapse of all such states before the
overpowering military force of Macedon and Rome.
The individual, living under a political system over
which he had no control, had to abandon the main
interests of his former life for the privilege of living
in peace and security, and to bring his aims within
the compass of a merely private existence.   It was
an age when, if we may so express it, men were
forced to save the ship by throwing overboard the
greater part of the cargo, and the saying of Perseus
had become the motto of life: *Tecum habita et nôris
quam sit tibi curta supellex*.   The great venture of
speculative thought in its effort to understand the
universe, of which the philosophies of Plato and
Aristotle were the principal products, seemed to have
shared the same fate as the effort of Greece to realise
political liberty, and to have ended in disappointment.
In seeking to gain the world man appeared only to
have been losing his own life.   There was, therefore,
a drawing back, a concentration, a gathering in of
the forces of the human soul from their dispersion in
objective interests, such as naturally follows on the
failure or exhaustion of a great movement of expansion.   Happiness, if it lay, as Aristotle thought, in
a successful manifestation of all man's intellectual
and moral energies, which should turn both nature
and society into organs for his self-realisation—such
happiness seemed no longer attainable.   It remained

to be seen whether another kind of satisfaction could be secured which did not involve so great outward efforts and risks, in the ἀταραξία—the peace of one who retires into the secret chamber of the inner life and shuts to the door upon all that can disturb or harass him. It is this kind of happiness which is the common aim of the Stoic, Epicurean and Sceptic schools of philosophy.

Now the subjective and individualistic character of these schools might seem to preclude their having anything important to contribute to theology, even if it did not set them against religion in all its forms. But this is not entirely the case, and least of all with Stoicism. For though the Stoic draws back upon the inner life, what he finds there, as I shall have to show, is a perfectly universal principle—a principle which lifts the individual above all that is limited and particular in his own being, and subjects him to the divine reason, or even, in a sense, identifies him with it. Hence for the individual so conceived, the idea of liberty at once turns into that of determination by a universal reason, and individualism at a stroke converts itself into a kind of pantheism. We shall find that this dialectical movement breathes a religious spirit into even the earliest, but still more into the latest records of Stoicism, making it one of the philosophies which has most profoundly influenced the course of religious thought, especially in the early development of Christian doctrine. With Epicureanism, though it too has a kind of theological bearing, thought begins to turn away from religion, and with the Sceptics philosophy is distinctly anti-theological. For our present enquiry, therefore, the main interest lies in Stoicism. The two other philosophies may be regarded as having hardly any bearing upon the progress of theology except so far as the sceptical collapse of their individualism helped by way of recoil the development of Neo-Platonism—a philosophy which might be described as essentially and entirely a theology or philosophy of religion.

There is one accidental advantage of the stage of philosophical development which we have now to examine, as compared with that which we have had to consider in previous lectures. This advantage lies in the more modern character of the problems we have to deal with. In studying Plato and Aristotle we are, so to speak, travelling in a foreign land, and learning to speak a philosophical language which is not our own. The problems with which they deal do not seem to be our problems, and we require much study and interpretation ere we can bring them into relation with our own modes of thought. In particular, we are embarrassed in the study of these philosophies by the contrast between the naïve assumption of the unity of the individual with society which seems to pervade them, and the equally naïve assumption of the opposition between the soul and the world, the inner and the outer life, which is characteristic of many phases of modern thought. It might be said, with as much truth as can belong to any epigrammatic statement, that the modern mind begins where the ancients ended, and ends where they began. Our fathers have eaten the sour grapes of individualism and our teeth are set on edge. We may, indeed, get beyond the merely subjective tendencies of the modern consciousness, and perhaps the greatest achievement of modern philosophers lies in the way in which they have corrected and transcended these tendencies : but we find it difficult to go back to the position of those who were hardly conscious of such tendencies at all, or who regarded the opposition of subject and object as quite subordinate to the opposition of universal and particular.

But with the Stoics and Epicureans we have a feeling of kindred. Their individualism is so clearly akin to the familiar individualism of the eighteenth century that we have little difficulty in understanding its problems or criticising its attempts to solve them. And even when we come to Neo-Platonism, though there is much which repels us in the abstract theological spirit which it breathes, yet it, like the philosophy of the nineteenth century, is born out of the struggle with individualism. It might, indeed, be described as an attempt to limit individualism so that it may be consistent with the belief in a unity which transcends all the differences of individuals; and, in this point of view, its merits and defects are equally instructive to us. For the highest aim of modern thought is just to combine a deep religious sense of the unity and universality of the divine principle, which reveals itself in the whole system of things, with that firm grasp of particular experience and that developed consciousness of the manifold secular relations of life, which have been given to the modern world.

LECTURE SIXTEENTH.

THE ORIGIN AND PRINCIPLE OF THE STOIC PHILOSOPHY.

I HAVE explained in the last lecture that after the speculative failure of Plato and Aristotle—in spite of their great philosophic genius—to attain to complete systematic unity, and after their practical failure to revive the social life of the Greek State, philosophy tended to become individualistic and subjective, to turn its attention from theories of the universe and the State to the inner life of the individual. As a consequence, greater importance began to be attached to the ideas of the Minor Socratic schools—the Cynics, Cyrenaics and Megarians, who had developed the doctrine of Socrates in an individualistic direction. These ideas, indeed, could not make much way in their original form; but in the philosophies of the Stoics and Epicureans they were freed from the narrowness and one-sidedness of their first expression, and so fitted to gain a

dominating influence over the minds of men. It is,
however, necessary to go back to the earlier
philosophies in order to understand the later, which
were manifestly developed from them. In particular,
it is hardly possible to understand Stoicism without
reverting to the theories of the Cynics and Megarians;
for it was the union of the ideas derived from these
two schools that gave its distinctive character to
the philosophy of Zeno, the founder of the Stoic
School.

Now, the Cynic philosophy was one of those
beginnings of progress which take the appearance of
reaction. When some aspect of thought or life has
been for a long time unduly subordinated, or has
not yet been admitted to its rightful place, it not
seldom finds expression in a representative individuality, who embodies it in his person, and
works it out in its most exclusive and one-sided form,
with an almost fanatical disregard of all other considerations—compensating for the general neglect of
it by treating it as the one thing needful. Such
individuals produce their effect by the very disgust
they create among the ordinary respectable members
of the community ; they have the ' success of scandal.'
Their criticism of the society to which they belong,
and of all its institutions and modes of action and
thought, attracts attention by the very violence and
extravagance of the form in which they present it.

And the neglected truth or half-truth, which they thrust into exclusive prominence, gradually begins by their means to gain a hold of the minds of others, forces them to reconsider their cherished prejudices, and so leads to a real advance of thought. In this fashion the Cynic seems to have acted upon the ancient, as Rousseau did upon the modern world, as a disturbing, irritating challenge to it to vindicate itself—a challenge which was violently resented, but which awakened thought and in time produced a modification, and even a transformation of prevailing opinions. It might be likened to a ferment, which sets agoing a process of disintegration and reintegration, which ends in the destruction of an old, and the creation of a new form of human thought. Such one-sidedness may be weakness, and in the long run may be seen to be so; but for a time it gives an invasive strength which, especially when it is directed against an institution or mode of thinking that has begun to lose its vitality, is almost irresistible.

Antisthenes, the founder of the Cynic school, was a narrow, passionate soul, who took fire at the words of Socrates, words which were for him not so much a call to self-reflexion as a proclamation of revolt against the social and ethical standards of the time. The calm independence of the master, his hardy, temperate and almost ascetic life, his disregard for

opinion and his refusal to be turned from the course
dictated by inward conviction, either by bribes or
threats, by any of the rewards or penalties which
society could offer or inflict, awakened the enthusiasm
of Antisthenes.   He was a ready recipient of the
doctrine that the ends of the moral life must be
self-determined, and not dictated by an external
authority ; and he understood the lesson in the most
exclusive and individualistic sense, as meaning that
each man must take the care of his own life upon
himself, shape out his course by his own thought,
and regard the State with all its customs and laws
as a mere usurpation.   In this spirit Antisthenes
raised the banner of Nature against Convention, and
met every claim of society upon the individual with
contempt and derision.

But in so doing he really broke away from Socrates,
exaggerating the negative part of his master's doctrine,
that which threw the individual back upon himself,
and neglecting altogether the positive part of it—
that idea of the determination of the individual life
by universal principles which, for Socrates, was the
one thing needful in morality.   Antisthenes was a
thorough-going Nominalist, who maintained that the
individual alone is real, and the universal nothing
but a collective name.   Following out this view, he
held that, as things are quite isolated in their
individuality, the only judgments that are true con-

cerning them must be tautological judgments, in which a thing is predicated of itself; for, if the predicate differs from the subject, then the judgment must be untrue when it asserts that the subject *is* the predicate. Hence in strict logic we can say nothing but 'A is A,' 'a man is a man.' Antisthenes, indeed, seems so far to have modified this doctrine as to admit that, when a thing is complex, you can define it by resolving it into its elements; but he maintained that when you have got down to these elements you can only name them. This, of course, involves that the whole of any complex thing is merely the sum of the parts.

It is easier to see the absurdity of this doctrine than to show why it is wrong; for, if it were true, we could have no significant predication or judgment whatever, a tautological judgment being in reality no judgment at all. It seems plausible enough to say that judgment asserts the identity of the predicate with the subject, and that it cannot be true, if they are in any way different. And, indeed, it is not long since a well-known school of formal logicians, not seeing where such a doctrine would lead them, proclaimed the law of identity in this sense as the essential law of thought, and maintained that all affirmative judgments must conform to the type 'A is A,' that is, to the type of tautology. But the truth is that the whole view of logic of which this is a part rests upon a confusion, which arises from looking at one of the aspects of thought and neglecting the other.   There can be no thought, no judgment or inference, unless there be an identity maintaining itself through the different aspects of things that are brought together in these processes : but, on the other hand, the identity must manifest itself in difference and overcome it, else it will mean nothing.   We cannot say ' A is B,' unless there is an identity between both terms, one principle manifested in both and binding them together ; but, if there were absolutely no difference between them, the judgment would not be worth making and would never be made. In any significant judgment the predicate must amplify the conception of the subject, though not in such a way as to destroy that conception.   Thus every judgment forms a new conception out of the union of the subject and the predicate, with only the necessary change produced by their union.

Now the aim of Antisthenes is to discredit any philosophy that seeks to reach the true determination of the particular by means of the definition of the universal.   In this he was, of course, striking directly at the principles and the method of his master Socrates. He seems, however, to have had specially in view the ideal theory of Plato, who maintained that it is only by rising to the universal that we come in sight of the reality which is hid under the particular appearances of sense.   To Antisthenes this seemed nonsense ;

for, on his view, the sole reality lies in the individual, which he supposes to be given in sense, and thought cannot possibly go beyond what is so given. To account for the particular by the universal was, in his view, as if one should seek to explain things by giving them a collective name, and then by pretending that there was some mysterious entity designated by this name, which was not in the particulars.

Now both Plato and Aristotle are particularly scornful when they come across this crude kind of Nominalism, which sees nothing in the world but a collection of isolated individuals. Thus Plato in the *Sophist* speaks of those who regard it as a feast of reason to be ever showing that the one cannot be many nor the many one. " You have met such people, Theaetetus, old fellows who have taken to philosophy late in life, who from poverty of thought are full of delight in such subtilties, and think that they have found in them the grand secret of philosophy."[1] Aristotle mentions Antisthenes by name as the maintainer of this doctrine, and declares that it showed him to be a man of no culture who did not understand dialectic. Still it is clear that Antisthenes was useful to Plato and Aristotle, at least as an irritant; for he stimulated them to develop their logical principles, and to show that thought moves not by identity alone, but by identity

[1] *Sophist*, 251 c.

in difference.   Aristotle, indeed, lays more stress on the individuality of the real than Plato, but he gives as little countenance as Plato to the abstract nominalism which would reduce the world to a mere aggregation of individual substances.

The Cynics, however, were primarily bent upon practice and not upon theory; and the dialectical defence of individualism was valuable to Antisthenes mainly as a support to his ethical views, and especially to his attempt to isolate the individual and maintain his independence, his natural freedom and self-sufficiency.   Indeed, to Antisthenes, the autonomy of the individual, his independence of everything but himself, seemed of itself to constitute that supreme good which Socrates had taught him to seek.   "Virtue is sufficient for happiness," he declared, "and all that it needs is the Socratic vigour" (ἰσχὺς Σωκρατική). Antisthenes may rightfully claim to be the first of the enthusiasts for 'formal freedom,' that is, for a freedom which is nothing but the negation of bondage—the assertion of the self against everything that is regarded as belonging to the not-self, the demand of the individual to be his own law and his own end.   To such a temper of mind, every claim of society upon the individual, every custom or law or authority that demands the slightest deference from him, seems to be an outrage; and outrage must be met with outrage. The Cynic, therefore, is in a continual attitude of protest against what is conventional or artificial; and to him the whole order of social life, every rule of morals or manners, or even of decency, seems to be conventional and artificial. He proclaims the watchword: 'Return to nature,' with all the dangerous ambiguities that have attached themselves to that phrase. For, while nature is set up as the type to which man is led by reason to conform himself, yet it is apt to be taken, not as meaning the ideal to which his development points as its goal, but that which is earliest and most elementary in its existence, as opposed to that which is later (that which is later being assumed to be imported from without). In this way the Cynic seeks the true man in the child, the savage, or even the animal; and the return to nature means for him the repudiation of all civilisation, of all that is due to education or social discipline. This is the fatal circle which moral speculation has trodden again and again from the time of Antisthenes down to that of Rousseau; and in which the attempt to get rid of what is adventitious and unnecessary, to free life from artificial adjuncts, and to get down to the basal facts of existence, converts itself into an effort to strip man of every veil that hides the nakedness of the animal.[1]

[1] Cf. the words of King Lear about the naked Edgar: "Ha! here's three on's are sophisticated! Thou art the thing itself: unaccommodated man is no more but such a poor, bare, forked animal as thou art. Off, off, you lendings! Come, unbutton here."

But this is not all. The Cynic sets up the standard of revolt against all social pressure, as trenching upon the native liberty of man : but, in the strange weakness of this merely negative attitude, the Cynic is found to have his own *raison d'être* just in that very society against which he protests, and without antagonism to which his own life would be empty and meaningless. His independence is an inverted dependence; his pride and contempt for others are in essence one with the servility that hunts for their suffrages. " I see your vanity," said Socrates to Antisthenes, " through the holes in your coat." The Cynics are a crucial example and illustration of the law that men inspired by a one-sided theory and carrying it out unflinchingly to all its consequences, end in becoming a living demonstration of its absurdity. They supply, as it were, the *corpus vile* on which the experiment is made that exhibits the impossibility of an emancipation that is merely negative. They seek to make men free by breaking the ties that bind them to their fellowmen, to the objects of their desires, and to everything that is not themselves. But with every tie they break, with every relation they repudiate, their own life becomes poorer. In rejecting what seems to them the bondage of the State, they give up all the intellectual and moral discipline, all the culture and refinement of manners, all the opportunity for the exercise of human faculty, which made Plato and Aristotle prize the civic life so highly. Refusing to weaken themselves by luxury, because it enslaves men to outward things, they end in counting everything a luxury which man can exist without, that is to say, everything except the satisfaction of the barest sensuous wants. And, after all, they find that man is bound to the world he would escape as firmly as ever, though now only by the vulgar tie of appetite. They thus discover that there can be no end to what they regard as the servitude of the self to the not-self, except in the extinction of the life they would emancipate. And indeed many of the Cynics, having reduced life to its beggarly elements, were ready to throw it away. Death is the only negative freedom; but bare death is not the emancipation of man from natural forces, rather it is their final triumph over him. There is, however, another aspect of the case. The real interest which fills the life of the Cynic, and in which his happiness consists, lies not, of course, in the necessaries of life to which he confines himself, but in the assertion of himself as against the political and social claims upon him. It is not, therefore, that he really excludes the ordinary interests of life, but that he takes them in a negative way. His very contempt and hatred binds him to that which he despises and hates. But he fails to recognise that such contempt and hatred needs the objects against which it is directed, and that, without such objects, it would have nothing to spend itself upon. Thus, after all, the Cynic is a parasite upon the society he repudiates, and that just because he lives to defy and insult it.

Still, in spite of all this, we must recognise that there was an element of truth wrapped up in Cynicism, and this gave it an undoubted power over a certain class of minds. The negative idea of independence may be false and self-contradictory when it is divorced from any positive idea, but it has a real value as an element in the truth. There is a sense in which the 'return to nature' and the repudiation of luxury constitute the conditions of any healthy morality. And the Cynics, in denouncing the artificiality of the Greek State and the whole framework of society connected therewith, might be regarded as defending the integrity of the moral life. For it is true that, in one aspect of it, the civilisation of Greece was an artificial product, based on the social privilege of a slave-holding aristocracy, and, therefore, upon injustice to human nature in the persons of their slaves. Hence also its morality was partial and one-sided, not the universal law of duty but the code of honour of a class, whose honour stood 'rooted in the dishonour' of others. It was no little thing that, in the face of such a civilisation and such a morality, there should be men who main-

tained the dignity of labour, condemned the false
glories of war, denounced the prejudices of class and
race, and maintained that the only true State is the
πολιτεία τοῦ κόσμου, the community of all men. But
in the Cynic expression of these truths there is often
a crudity and violence which seems to show that they
were not appreciated in their highest meaning, that
they were grasped as weapons to throw at the
enemy rather than as expressions of positive truth.
"Follow philosophy till you regard the generals of
armies as leaders of asses." "I would rather be mad
than feel pleasure." "Why should a man be proud,
like the Athenians, of being sprung from the soil
with the worms and snails." "The most noble of
all things is παρρησία, the power to speak out freely
what we think." Are these sentences expressions of
righteous horror at war, of genuine temperance and
self-control, of a regard for humanity which reaches
beyond patriotism, of a simple resolve to speak the
truth at all hazards? Or are they the utterance of
a bitter wrath against the pleasures and ambitions of
others, of a vulgar hatred and jealousy of superiority
either in birth or culture, and of a desire for the utmost
license of intemperate speech? We can only say that
the good and evil are so inextricably mingled together
that we are bound to take the one with the other
in our estimate. But we are bound also to recognise
that the Cynics in their condemnation of the limited

aristocratic State and of the culture and refinement
that went with it, were truer prophets than Plato
and Aristotle, who spent their great philosophic
genius in trying to regenerate a form of social and
political life which mankind had outgrown.

Now in the Stoic philosophy all these ambiguities
are cleared up. Stoicism is Cynicism enlarged,
deepened, idealised, freed from the violence and
exaggeration of men who were outlaws and rebels
against the social system under which they lived,
and transformed into the calm strength of a rational
faith. This may partly be explained by the history
of the founder of the Stoic school. Zeno got his
first initiation into philosophy from Crates the
Cynic, and his whole system bore such distinct traces
of the Cynic teaching that he was said to have
written his works on the dog's tail (an untranslatable
pun). But while he absorbed the lesson of the
Cynic, we are told that he was repelled by the
Cynic's outrages upon taste and decency : repelled
also, we may fairly add, by his narrowness and
hostility to culture. To this, however, Zeno found
a corrective in the teaching of another of the
Socratic schools ; for we hear that he studied not
only under Crates, but also under Stilpo, the
Megarian. Now the peculiarity of the Megarian
school was that it had developed the principles of
Socrates in a diametrically opposite direction to that

in which they were developed by the Cynics. To use the terms of later philosophy, the Megarians were extreme Realists as the Cynics were extreme Nominalists. Socrates had laid great stress on the importance of general notions, and had maintained that it is only when we grasp and define the universal that we can rightly judge of the particular. Thus he might seem to have given countenance to that tendency to exalt the universal at the expense of the particular, which is supposed to have led Plato to attribute absolute reality to the former and to treat the latter as an illusive appearance. But Plato, as we have seen, soon became aware of the danger of this exaggeration, the danger of losing difference in unity and treating abstractions as the only realities; and, at least in his later writings, he insisted on the equal importance of analysis and synthesis. The founder of the Megarian school, on the other hand, being a man of subtle rather than comprehensive intelligence, possessed with the Platonic desire for unity without the Platonic desire for systematic completeness, fell early into the trap of abstraction from which Plato escaped. He set the one against the many, the universal against the particular; and he even went so far in this direction as to revive the abstract doctrine of the Eleatics,—though the influence of Socrates led him to call the absolute unity in which all

difference is lost by the name of the Good, and also,
we may add, to think of it not as a material but as
an ideal principle.   Moreover, like the later Eleatics,
the Megarians devoted all their dialectical skill to
the task of showing that multiplicity and change
are essentially contradictory, and must, therefore, be
mere illusive appearances.

But their doctrine became in this way the opposite
counterpart of that of the Cynics.   They maintained
the exclusive reality of the abstract universal, as
the Cynics maintained the exclusive reality of the
abstract individual ;   and while the Cynics set up
the independence of the individual as the end of
all action, the Megarians taught that the end was
to be found in a pantheistic absorption in the
Absolute, an extinction of all personal feeling in
the contemplation of the One.   But 'extremes meet,'
—in the sense that when we entirely isolate them
from each other and annul all positive relation
between them, their negative relation also disappears,
and they reach the same end by opposite roads.
Thus the Cynic and the Megarian agree in denying
the truth of any judgment which is not tautological ;
because to admit that the universal can be truly
predicated of the individual would be to the
Cynic inconsistent with the self-identity and independence of the individual, and to the Megarian
inconsistent with the absolute unity and reality of

the universal. And, if we consider their respective views of ethics, we can see that the self-centred freedom of the Cynic, to whom any desire or affection that went beyond himself would be slavery, has in it something closely akin to the apathy of the Megarian. It is a curious fact that this community of the two doctrines was already recognised by Stilpo, the Megarian teacher of Zeno, who, therefore, is sometimes called a Cynic, and who may possibly have suggested to Zeno the idea that a higher result might be reached by a combination of the doctrines of the two schools, in which he had received his philosophical education.

Be that as it may, it is the fact that Zeno, looking at the Cynic philosophy with the eyes of a Megarian, and at the Megarian philosophy with the eyes of a Cynic, rose to the conception of a system in which these two theories, which appeared to be diametrical opposites of each other, were united and reconciled. The originality of Zeno consisted mainly in this one illuminating thought—that the individualism of the Cynics and the pantheism of the Megarians, the sensationalism of the Cynics and the idealism of the Megarians, the materialism of the Cynics and the intellectualism of the Megarians, were not really contradictory, but were rather complementary aspects of one truth. The possibility of this union of opposites and the self-consistency of the philosophy founded upon it, we shall have to consider hereafter. But, in the first place, I wish to point out how by this change the spirit, tone, and temper of Stoicism became entirely different from that of Cynicism, and even sharply contrasted with it.   For the Cynic school was, as we have seen, almost exclusively occupied with the negative side of its philosophic creed.   Its activity was absorbed in the manifestation of its scorn and hatred for the institutions and principles of a society which seemed to it to stand in the way of the free development of the individuality of man ; and by the inevitable recoil, it became imprisoned in its own negations, and the half-truth which it grasped was almost turned into a falsehood by the exaggeration of its expression.   For the Stoic, on the other hand, the doctrine of independence ceased to be a doctrine of revolt, and became a positive consciousness of the dignity of man as a rational being.   The self-concentration—the consciousness of being a law to himself and subjected to no external authority, of being an end to himself and not a means to the ends of any other being or society without him—remained to the Stoic as his inheritance from the Cynic.   But he had learned from the Megarian that the reason which made him a true individual, an independent self, was at the same time a universal principle, the principle of a life common to him with all other rational beings and uniting him to them all. Withdrawing into himself from all the entanglements of life, from all the special connexions of society, and realising to the full his individual selfhood and his separation from every other thing or being, he found that, when most alone, he was least alone, and that just in the inmost secret of his soul, he was at one with all mankind.

But in this way the Stoic had discovered that the deepest, and, in a sense, the most individual experiences of humanity are also the most universal. It is what is particular, the special characteristics of the individual and the race, the special traditions of each family and nation, the special disposition and tendencies of each man, that hold us apart and make us incomprehensible to each other; but when we get down to the root of humanity, to the self-consciousness that makes us men, we find that our differences have been left behind or have become transparent, and that the language spoken by each individual is intelligible to all. The inmost secret of each man's heart is the secret of the whole world, and if we only go deep enough, we can evoke an echo in every breast. Hence it is just the greatest poets, those whose range of thought and feeling is widest, who are secure of a welcome everywhere; while those who express the special sentiments of any nation or class cannot be understood beyond their country and time, except by elaborate study and preparation. It is this apparent paradox that the most individual is the most universal, which the Stoics brought to light, and by means of which they, as I have said, changed the whole tone and temper of earlier individualism. While, therefore, the strengthening power of the Cynic doctrine, the ' Socratic vigour,' was not lost, while the Stoics were able to show on many occasions that they found in their philosophy a spring of energy which could lift them above fear and desire, and which could be corrupted or intimidated neither by public opinion nor by the earthly omnipotence of the Roman Imperial power; yet they were not, in the first instance, occupied with resistance or revolt against outward authority or influence, but with the effort to rule their own spirits, to live a life of moral freedom, and to die without doing dishonour to humanity in their own persons. And, in spite of their condemnation of the general tendencies of the society around them, and their resolution to live in independence of it as of everything merely external, their attitude to the world was not primarily antagonistic. On the contrary, they held that the very principle which gives the individual an absolute claim against other men, also obliges him to recognise the same claims in them; and that the same reason which makes him an individual, self-determining being, unites him to all beings like himself—or, at least, would unite him to them, if he and they were to become what, as rational, they potentially are. Hence it is to the philosophy of the Stoics that we owe the watchword of humanity : *Homo sum ; humani nihil a me alienum puto ;* and, indeed, it is also to them we owe it that the word humanity has the double sense of the adjectives 'human' and 'humane.' Thus the Cynic's self-assertion against society is turned into a consciousness of membership in the great *civitas communis deorum et hominum.* And if this universal community remain with the Stoics only an aspiration and does not become a reality, if it be at best a dream of the distant future rather than a consciousness of any actual or possible object of present endeavour, yet even the idea of it did much to break down the barriers between mankind. In short, in passing from Cynicism to Stoicism, we are passing from a self-sufficiency which is all-exclusive to one that, in idea at least, is all-inclusive ; and the Stoic philanthropy, if it had not the invasive energy of Christian charity, yet carried with it a comprehensive sympathy, which softened the bitterness of national and personal prejudice and prepared the way for the religion of humanity.

And this leads me to speak of another point which is of special interest to anyone who seeks to trace the evolution of theology. The Cynic philosophy, as it broke off the community of man with

man and of man with the world, was, at least in
its most prominent aspect, the very negation of
religion. In arming man against his fellows, it also
armed him against heaven. Its self-sufficiency was
the contradictory of all obedience or loyalty to any
power above the individual. But for the Stoic it
is quite otherwise. Freedom from the law without
is at once recognised as binding the individual
to obedience to the law within ; and as the Stoic
thinks of this inner law as absolute, he cannot but
believe that the whole world is subjected to it.
Hence in obeying his own nature, he is conscious
that he is in harmony with the law of the universe,
—a law which all things obey, but which it is
the privilege only of rational beings to know,
and to make into the conscious rule of their
own lives. They alone can see that the world
is the manifestation of the same reason that
speaks within them, and they are therefore able
to identify their own freedom with submission to
a divine law and service to a divine purpose.
Deo parere libertas est.

From the first, Stoicism was a religious philosophy, as is shown by the great hymn of Cleanthes,
the successor of Zeno as head of the school—a
hymn which is inspired by the consciousness that
it is one spiritual power which penetrates and
controls the universe and is the source· of every

work done under the sun, "except what evil
men endeavour in their folly." Man alone is of
pure divine race,[1] and he alone is able to accept
or to resist the divine will—though, after all, his
resistance is naught, being in contradiction with
his own nature, as well as with the nature of the
universe and of God. "Lead me, O Zeus, and thou,
O Destiny, in the work to which I am divinely
chosen, and I shall follow, not unwilling; but even
if I refuse and become evil, no less must I follow
thee." Thus the moral independence of the Stoic
converts itself into a consciousness of unity with
God, in which all caprice and wilfulness are lost; and
the individual becomes strong in himself simply as
he becomes conscious that he is the organ of the
divine will. Stoicism may not be successful in
dealing with all the difficulties of the question of
man's freedom, or in solving the antinomy which
arises when we consider his position as, on the one
hand, a self-conscious, self-determining *ego*, and
on the other, a finite individual who is only
a part of an infinite whole, and whose self-determination cannot be conceived as breaking up its
unity. But it is fair to say that Stoicism first
brought the two terms of the problem face to face
with each other and indicated the line in which

[1] τοῦ γὰρ καὶ γένος ἐσμέν—the words quoted by St. Paul in his
address to the Athenians (Acts xvii. 28).

alone a solution can be sought. How can morality
and religion, free self-determination and absolute
self-surrender to God be united with each other?
This henceforward becomes one of the fundamental
questions of the philosophy of religion. And the
answer to it can only be found, if it be found at
all, in the conception of the fundamental unity of
man's nature with the divine. Thus the Stoics both
set the problem of freedom, and showed in what
direction the solution of it was to be sought.

LECTURE SEVENTEENTH.

THE STOIC SYNTHESIS OF PANTHEISM AND INDIVIDUALISM.

In the last lecture I have shown how Zeno, just because he grasped the essential relation between the two opposed philosophies of the Cynics and Megarians, became the founder of a new philosophy. He was a man of much less speculative power than Plato or Aristotle; yet by this synthesis he rose to an idea which neither of them had attained, the idea of the unity of the consciousness of self—that consciousness which makes a man an individual in a sense in which no other animal is individual—with the universal principle which binds all things and beings together as parts of one world. We cannot, indeed, say that Zeno realised this idea in all its bearings; but it took possession of him, and gave inspiration and direction to his own philosophy and that of all his school. In this principle lay at once the strength and the weakness of Stoicism: its strength, in so far as it overcame the dualistic tendencies which had affected Greek thought from the time of Anaxagoras; and its weakness, in so far as it achieved this result rather by intuition than by explicit reason. Hence it was not able fully to master and reconcile the different elements which it brought together: what it did was simply to identify them and to ignore their antagonism.

Stoicism was essentially what is called a *Monism*: and in so far as it was this, it had a kind of rationality which no dualistic system can ever possess. For any system that, directly or indirectly, denies the unity of the world, may be shown ultimately to lead to the denial that it is an intelligible world at all. How, indeed, can the universe be a κόσμος, or intelligible system, if all the existences included in it be not essentially related to each other, if they be not constituent parts of one whole? To understand anything is to see its distinction from other things; but distinction always implies relation, and relation presupposes a unity within which the related elements are contained. Hence if we try to isolate anything— to conceive it apart from all distinction and relation we make it unintelligible. To understand a thing is to give it a place in the one world of experience which exists for the one self; and to suppose that unity to be broken up and divided, is equivalent to the negation at once of the intelligence and its object.

Hence it has been said with good reason that it is the beginning of true philosophy to realise that all differences and oppositions of thought and reality are relative differences—differences within a unity, and that the very idea of an absolute difference is suicidal: for it is only as its terms are held together within a whole and so related to each other, that their difference has any meaning. This, indeed, was just the lesson to be learnt from the treatment of judgment by the Cynic and Megarian schools; for what they had really shown was that the judgment reduces itself to a tautology, if it does not express the relation of the universal to the particular. And this again implies that both the universal and the particular lose their meaning, if they are taken out of relation to each other. The truth of either can only be discovered, in so far as it is recognised that in their distinction they do not cease to be elements in one whole. In this way, again, we are led to recognise the systematic or organic unity of reality as the first principle or presupposition of all knowledge.

Now Zeno clearly perceived the negative side of this truth, and by his perception of it he was enabled to make a great advance beyond his predecessors, and to free himself from the dualistic presuppositions which had embarrassed their theories. Unfortunately, as I have already indicated, he could not discover a logical way of bridging the gulf between the opposites, or of admitting a relative difference where he denied an absolute one. Hence his monism means only that he identifies the extremes, or treats the distinction between them as simply a distinction of different points of view from which we look at the same thing—points of view which we may take up and dismiss according to the convenience of the moment. Thus Stoicism, on a superficial view of it, seems to be the most confused of all the philosophies : a philosophy which clings to the idea of the unity of all things, but which in its exposition of that unity passes abruptly from materialism to spiritualism, from individualism to pantheism, from sensationalism to idealism, as the occasion may require, and without any consciousness of the difficulty of the transition so made. From this point of view, Stoicism might be regarded as a jumble of all the philosophies or, to use Kant's expression, as a "nest of contradictions," in which every way of conceiving things is represented, and none is carried out to its ultimate consequences.

Yet there is another point of view from which Stoicism might be described as the most logical of all theories, in so far as it persistently keeps hold of one definite principle and purpose, and makes everything else bend to it. For the one object upon which it concentrates all its efforts is to give unity to man's life, a unity which nothing can come from without to disturb. Further, it realises that this unity cannot

be attained by the way of exclusion, or by shutting
out from the individual life everything that is not
a part of it, but only by widening it so that it may
embrace all things.   To give unity to the life of man,
it is necessary to conceive the world of which he is a
part as itself a unity.   Stoicism, therefore, insists
that no difference in the mind, or in its objects, or
between the two, shall be taken as absolute; and as,
after all, it is unable either to resolve the differences
or to explain them away, it tramples them under foot.
It is thus speculatively feeble, and its particular
explanations of difficulties are too often superficial and
sometimes even inconsistent with each other.   But its
general philosophical doctrine does not rest on these,
but on its unswerving conviction, its intense certitude,
that there is a unity and an ideal meaning in things,
which answers to the demands of our reason.   This
truth the Stoic grasps with resolute faith, even when
he cannot logically apply it to the solution of particular difficulties, and it makes him easily satisfied
with any ratiocination, however external, that seems to
remove them.   Stoicism, from this point of view, may be
regarded as a bold stroke for a monistic and optimistic
view of the universe, made at a time when everything
external seemed to point to dualism and pessimism,
and when, we may add, the speculative power to deal
with such a problem was altogether wanting.   In the
Critique of Pure Reason Kant maintains that the

understanding of man is quite incapable of realising the ideal which is set up for him by his reason; and whatever exception may be taken to such a view, as an account of the powers of the human mind, it very well describes the position of the Stoic philosophers. They had grasped very firmly the ideal after which philosophy strives, but they were able to do little towards its realisation. Their contribution to the solution of the problems of philosophy is not great, but throughout the whole history of the school they held to one central principle. It must, indeed, be admitted that under the severe criticism to which the Stoic doctrine was subjected by the Academic school, some of the Stoics of the middle period, the contemporaries of Cicero, made inconsistent modifications in their system, and even fell back on something like the dualism of Plato. But Epictetus, one of the latest and greatest of the Stoics, is in his general attitude of thought quite faithful to the teachings of the original heads of the school, and especially to its monistic principle.[1] In truth, Stoicism could not renounce this principle without losing a great part of its moral strength and efficiency. The enormous influence which it exerted over the mind of the ancient world, its power to strengthen the souls of the noblest men for action and endurance, lay in its firm grasp of this central idea, that there is a

[1] See especially Bonhöffer, *Epictet und die Stoa.*

rational principle in the world, which is one in nature with the self-conscious intelligence within us, and that, through all apparent disorder, this principle is inevitably realising itself. And this also explains how Stoic ideas became so easily blended with the nascent reflexion of the early church, and exercised so powerful an influence on the development of Christian doctrine.

The physical philosophy of the Stoics consists mainly in the development of the monistic view of existence, in opposition to the dualism that separated form and matter. It is often stated that the Stoics were materialists; but the truth which underlies this charge is, that they altogether rejected the dualism which had maintained itself in Greek philosophy from the time of Anaxagoras. The Stoics could not be content with any philosophy which divided heaven from earth, the spiritual from the material, which, in short, divided the ideal reality which we grasp in thought from the things which we touch and see. There is in them something of the same impulse which makes St. John insist upon the actual presence of the divine Lord in human form, in opposition to the Docetism which reduced his humanity to a semblance—" that which our eyes have seen and our hands have handled of the Word of life." Or, to take a more exact parallel, they rebelled against the idea of a transcendent God and a transcendent ideal world as

modern thought has rebelled against the supernatural-
ism of medieval religion and philosophy. The ideas of
Plato and the forms of Aristotle seemed to them far
off and unreal, and they declared against them in the
same spirit in which Goethe repudiated the idea of a
God who worked upon the universe from without
(*ein Gott der nur von aussen stiesse*), and was not
immanently present in nature and in the soul of
man. Just as Spinoza spoke of God and nature
as two words for the same thing, and maintained
the identity of the one divine substance which is
presented to us under the two disparate attributes
of thought and extension, so the Stoics refused to
divorce, or even to distinguish, mind and matter,
or to exalt the soul by opposing it to the body.
Hence they asserted that nothing exists which is not
corporeal or material, though they immediately quali-
fied this statement by maintaining that there is
nothing corporeal which is passive or inert, and that
all activity implies a *Logos* or spiritual principle.
The absolute antagonism of a purely active form and
a purely passive matter, which is the crux of the
Aristotelian philosophy, is thus set aside; and in its
place we have the relative opposition of two elements,
both of which are regarded as having ultimately the
same nature and origin, and both of which are viewed
as in one aspect material and in another spiritual.
When, therefore, the Stoics are called materialists, we

have to remember that they can be so regarded only from the point of view of a dualistic philosophy, which holds that in order to be spiritual, reality must be absolutely dissociated from that which is corporeal or material. On the same ground, we might as legitimately apply the term materialist to Spinoza or Goethe: for Spinoza maintained that extension and thought are only different attributes under which the same principle is revealed to us, and Goethe refused to think of God except as realising himself under the forms of sense, or of the material world except as the ' living garment of Deity.'   In fact, the Pantheism of these later writers is closely akin to that of the Stoics, who assert, from one point of view, that the universe is a product or manifestation of divine reason, and, from another, that all things flow from and return to the fiery breath, the πνεῦμα διάπυρον, which is the quintessence of all matter.

And this enables us to understand why, in seeking a metaphysical basis for their philosophy, the Stoics should go back not to Plato and Aristotle, but to Heraclitus, a philosopher who lived before the opposition of idealism and materialism had been formulated, and who therefore easily passed from one form of expression to the other without any consciousness of transition.   Thus Heraclitus could speak of the secular process of the universe as the evolution of all things out of an ever-living fire and their return to it again, without being hindered from also regarding it as the manifestation of the supreme thought or reason, the γνώμη or λόγος that 'steers all things through all things.' He could even say without any sense of violence that the fiery heaven which embraces all things is full of mind and reason (λογικὸν καὶ φρενῆρες). At the same time, we must recognise the essential difference between the position of those who lived before the two elements had been distinguished, and the position of those who lived after this distinction had been so much insisted on by Plato and Aristotle. For those who, in this later time, refused to accept the dualistic theory there were only two logical alternatives: either to explain away one of the two principles, or to show that their opposition is merely relative, an opposition within a unity. But the Stoics could not adopt either of these alternatives. They were too anxious to grasp the whole truth to be content with abstract materialism or abstract spiritualism; yet, though they saw the weakness of such partial explanations, and had an intuitive perception of a unity beyond them, they could not bring them together as correlated factors of one complete system. Being thus unable either to admit that the opposition was absolute or to transcend it, they were driven to the alternative of simply denying it, except as an opposition of different aspects of the same thing, and falling back on the ideas of a philosopher who had lived before it was recognised.   Matter and mind, therefore, appear in the Stoic as in the Spinozistic philosophy, as two parallel aspects or attributes of one substance. And though the Stoics are not so careful as Spinoza in marking off from each other the two lines of specula- tion which are thus opened up, according as we look at reality under the one or the other attribute, yet it is possible in their writings to trace out each line almost without relation to the other.

On the material side then, the world, according to the Stoic view of it, may be thus described.   In the first place, the idea of a purely passive matter is rejected, and we have in its place a corporeal nature whose ultimate and most active form is a fiery breath πνεῦμα διάπυρον, or, as Cicero translates it, *anima inflammata*, a kind of quintessence of matter, which unites the activity of fire with the diffusiveness of air.   This fiery breath, again, evolves from itself the opposition of two relatively active and two relatively passive principles—fire and air on the one side, earth and water on the other—which stand to each other as do form and matter in the Aris- totelian system, though the Stoics conceive the opposition as a relative and not an absolute one.   Out of these elements all the particular existences in the world are produced.   In every existence there is a fiery principle of unity, which holds it together and keeps it in tension against the other existences that might invade or destroy it. But this tension, this power of self-assertion and self-maintenance in all finite things, is limited, and only capable of holding out for a certain time. The Stoic, therefore, maintains that there is a kind of circular process of existence, in which all things that emerge from the central fire ultimately return to it again. The movement of expansion and differentiation is followed by a movement of contraction or integration, in which all things are drawn back into the 'fiery breath' or spirit from which they were originally derived. The central fire at last reclaims all that it has given out, even that purest portion of itself which constitutes the soul of man.

Again, all this material process has to be translated into idealistic or spiritualistic terms; for the fiery breath is also conceived by the Stoics as a 'germinative reason' which produces and penetrates the whole world by its thought. And from it are derived the 'germinative reasons' which are the principles of unity in all the different forms of finite existence. Thus in inorganic things the germinative reason takes the form of a dominating quality ($\xi\xi\iota s$); in plants it appears as a 'nature' or principle of organisation; in animals as a 'soul' or principle of sensation and appetite; and in man it rises to its highest form as a 'rational soul,' which is a pure reflex of the divine reason. While, therefore, we are able to say that all

things are derived from the germinative reason of
the world, we can say this in a special sense of
the soul of man, which immediately partakes of the
nature of God, and may even be described as a part of
Him, directly communicated to one privileged creature
(*divinae particula aurae*).   And this is shown by the
fact that it not only is a principle of unity in human
life, but is directly conscious of itself as such.   Thus,
just as God is the ruling principle in the universe,
sustaining, penetrating, and subduing all things to
himself, so the inner self or ruling principle in man
binds his whole existence into one, and subordinates
all his other powers to itself.   Yet we must not, in
either case, make too much of the opposition between
that which rules and that which is ruled; for the
Stoic always remembers that this distinction is relative.
God is not to be regarded as really separate from the
world; and the particular existences on which he
is said to act are all modifications, or, we might even
say, parts of himself.   And in like manner, in man
also, the senses and desires, over which the ruling
power or inner self has command, are, after all, only
emanations of the ruling power itself, and not really
external to it.   As God realises himself and only himself in the world, so it is the *ego* and the *ego* alone
that realises itself in all the powers of sensation and
desire.   And we may add that, just as, in the secular
process of the universe, all existences spring from God,

and are again resolved into His pure essence; so with man, life is a process of expansion, which is followed by a process of contraction, ending in the disappearance of all the other powers of the soul in the ruling part, and the separation of the soul from the body. And even this is only a preparation for the final consummation, in which the soul returns to the divine unity from which it came.

Now we need not farther dwell on the physical or materialistic side of this process, the evolution of the world out of the central fire and its resolution into it again. The general theory is borrowed from Heraclitus, and the Stoics added to it nothing of importance; or rather, we should say, that they sacrificed whatever meaning it had as a physical theory in the effort to carry out the parallelism of matter and mind. Thus, while they maintained that all things are corporeal, they found themselves obliged to assert that matter is essentially active, and even to admit the possibility of a complete inter-penetration of material bodies by each other, and of all matter by the etherial fire. In other words, in order to be the counterpart of mind, matter had to give up its essential nature as extended and solid, as consisting of *partes extra partes* which repel each other. Hence the physical theories of the Stoics may be at once set aside as having no scientific value; as, indeed, for them the material world had no real interest except as a part of man's life. Or perhaps we should rather say, that their interest was confined to the general doctrine that matter and mind are distinguished only as different aspects of the same thing, and that, this being granted, they cared nothing about the nature of special physical processes. And as time went on, they gradually ceased to concern themselves with physical subjects, except as supplying certain postulates which were necessary for their ethics. Thus the only important part of their physical philosophy came to be that which should rather be called metaphysics or theology, the part which has to do, not with the relations of physical phenomena to each other, but only with the relations of the material universe to God, who is at once the central fire and the spiritual principle to which all things are referred.

When we have got thus far, it becomes easy to see that the kernel or central meaning of the Stoic system lies in the combination of two ideas, which appear at once to be essentially opposed, and yet necessarily related to each other. The *first* is the idea of the self-centred individuality of the particular things and beings that make up the universe, and above all of man as a self-conscious being. The *second* is the idea of the unity of the universe as a whole, as the realisation of the one divine principle which makes the individuality of all particular things and beings, and even the individuality of man himself, into its expressions and instruments. In the antithesis and the synthesis of these two ideas lies the whole interest of Stoicism.

As to the first of these ideas, I have already said that the world is to the Stoic an aggregate of individual things and beings, each of which is an efflux from the principle of the whole, and in a sense a whole in itself; in other words, each of them has in it a principle of unity with itself, which renders it an individual, separate from and opposed to all other individuals. And with this individuality goes in each case the natural impulse of self-preservation—what Spinoza calls the *conatus in suo esse perseverandi*, the effort to maintain and augment its own being. This individuality appears in more intensive forms as we rise in the scale of being, but only in man does it reach self-consciousness. And this, indeed, makes so marked a distinction between men and other animals that we might fairly say that he alone has a self in him. The ruling power of reason so dominates over his nature that he cannot be described as anything but a self-conscious *ego*; and, just because of this, all his impulses become concentrated in one great effort after self-realisation, in which he shows a high-strung energy wherewith nothing else in nature can be brought into comparison. In him the *conatus in suo esse perseverandi* swells into an absolute demand for happiness, for a perfect completion and manifestation of his rational being, in which nothing shall be left to be wished or hoped for.

Only—and here the Stoic decisively parts company with the Cynic—the self-seeking impulse, as it becomes self-conscious, must recognise its own universal character. The impulse of a rational being, as such, is not to seek the gratification of its particular impulses; it is to seek to satisfy the self. Nor is it even to seek to satisfy the self as one particular being, in opposition to other particular beings. To think so would be to forget the universal nature of the self, which lifts man above his own individuality, and enables him to identify himself with the whole and with its divine principle. The Stoic, therefore, in seeking his true self or its good, must detach himself from his immediate life and all its special interests. He must look upon the fate of his own particular being with the same calmness and freedom from disturbance, with which he contemplates the fates of other beings altogether unconnected with himself. For what he must desire is to realise himself as reason, and reason is equally related to all objects, but not bound up with any one of them except in so far as it is a manifestation of rational principles.

This doctrine gives us the means of reconciling the self-seeking of man with that to which it seems

directly opposed, the realisation of the divine principle which binds the universe into one whole.
Every thing and every being springs from this principle, and nothing can be taken as capable of
opposing it.   There is no 'matter' in the Aristotelian
sense, to limit its realisation of itself; and the idea
that any particular finite creature should interfere
with its self-determined course is essentially absurd
and self-contradictory.   As the original unity is the
source of all and immanent in all, it dominates with
irresistible energy over all, and turns their efforts to
realise *themselves* into a means of realising *itself*.
Man alone, in virtue of his self-consciousness, can conceive the idea of separation from it or resistance to it.
But this means only that he has the choice whether
he will be a willing or an unwilling servant of it:
unwilling, if he makes it his aim to satisfy his particular self—an aim which he can attain only so far
as the general system of things allows him; willing,
if he identifies himself with the divine reason which
is manifested in that system.   His only prerogative,
therefore, is that he can freely accept the service of
the whole, which he must serve whether he will or
not.   *Fata volentem ducunt, nolentem trahunt.*   The
world is one world, and the idea of escaping from the
unity on which its existence rests is futile.   The wish
to escape, indeed, could only arise in the mind of a
rational being through ignorance of what he, as well

as of what it, is. For if he understood these two things, he could not but see that his own good can lie in nothing but the realisation of reason, and that the world-process is nothing but this realisation.

Now to appreciate the strength and the weakness of this view, we must recall the way in which it was attained. It was attained, as we saw, through an immediate perception of the truth that the same reason which makes man individual—because it makes him conscious of a self—at the same time lifts him above the point of view of his own individuality. The *ego* that is conscious of all things in relation to itself is, as such, impartial; it separates itself from all objects alike, even from its own particular being, and looks at them all with equal eyes. It takes up a central point of view in reference to the whole world it knows, and is thus capable of estimating all things according to their place in the whole, without reference to the special feelings, sensations, prejudices, impulses which belong to it as this individual This point of view is essential to man as a rational and therefore also as a moral being; for knowledge and moral action are possible only if, and so far as, we can discount the speciality of our own feelings and desires. The ὁρμή, the essential *nisus* or impulse of rational beings, as such, is to see all things in their proper relation to the whole, and in all their actions to make themselves the organs and instruments of the principle of that whole.

Now, to this view it is naturally objected that reason in man does not show itself to be such a universal and impartial power of judgment as the Stoic describes. Rather we seem to find the views and aims of men always subjected to distortion and limitation by their national and individual character and circumstances. In their thought they are influenced by illusions and prejudices due to racial or individual bias, or to the peculiar experiences of their lives; not even in their highest intellectual efforts do we find them rising to a quite impartial and objective view of things. And in their practical conduct also they are continually misled by interests and desires, which prevent them from devoting themselves to any object independent of their individuality, and still more from acting with a single eye to the highest and most universal good. All this is obvious enough, but it is not inconsistent with the general truth of the Stoic doctrine—the doctrine that it is the essential characteristic of a rational being to look beyond himself, and both in theory and in practice to rise above his own individuality. For it is clear that if any man were utterly incapable of taking up a general point of view, or of looking at himself as an object just as he looks at other persons and things; if he were absolutely imprisoned in his own sensations, and were not able to make any allowance for their individual character or to regard them as he regards the sensations of others: if, in short, the world were centred for him in his own particular self, he would be literally insane. Similarly, if in action, he were quite unable to regard anything but his own impulses, and could not direct his will to any objective ends whatsoever or submit it to any general laws or social obligations, he would be a moral idiot; and we should be obliged to treat him as an irresponsible animal. Hence, in spite of all that is irrational and immoral in man's life, we must regard the reason that makes him man as essentially universal, that is, as a consciousness of self in relation to other beings and things as parts of one whole—a consciousness which, even while it constitutes his individuality, takes him beyond it. For to be a self, in spite of the apparent paradox, is to go beyond the self; and a human being cannot find a centre in himself, except so far as he recognises himself as part of a wider whole in which he is centred.

At the same time—and this is what the Stoics in their abstract way of looking at things altogether fail to observe—the existence of this potential universality of reason in every rational being is one thing, and the conscious realisation of it in all the extent of its meaning is another. If we appeal to experience

what we find is, that every individual has some
elementary consciousness of a world in which all
the objects he knows are brought into relation with
each other, and some elementary consciousness of a
society in which he regards himself as a member.
But it is only through a long process of evolution
that, out of such beginnings, there could arise the
idea of the world as an ordered system, and the
idea of a universal law which binds all rational
creatures into one society. And when in the Stoic
philosophy these ideas did arise, they at first
took an abstract and therefore an imperfect form—
a form in which the general conviction of the
rationality of the system of things failed to lead
to any consciousness of the excellence of the special
parts of it, and in which the universal good of
man, as determined by reason, appeared to be the
negation of every particular end. The Stoic gets
so far as to see that there is a unity beyond the
differences of the particulars; but he is not able to
use the conception of this unity as a principle by
means of which each particular may be put in its
right place in the whole. And a very long process
of evolution was needed ere men could conceive
the idea of a rational and organic order of the
universe or of human life, in which each particular
element, though rejected as an end in itself, might
be reinstated as a necessary element of the whole,

and all mankind, with justice done to their special characteristics, might be united in one πολιτεία τοῦ κόσμου. The idea of such a process of development, by which man gradually comes to the realisation of himself and of all that is involved in his rational nature, is entirely hidden from the Stoics. Recognising no distinction between what is actual and what is potential in man, they, as it were, stereotype the moral consciousness in the form that was given to it by their own philosophy; and they fail to see that that form is itself a stage in a long process reaching back to the beginning of human history and containing in it the germs of the still higher ethical spirit of the future.

Hence they state the rationality of man's nature in a way that seems paradoxical and inconsistent with facts; and they are unable to find a logical place in their theory for anything but absolute knowledge or absolute ignorance, absolute virtue or absolute vice. The value and importance of their moral idealism as an expression of one aspect of the truth, is easily seen, but, in putting it forward as the whole truth, they deprive it of all verisimilitude. We cannot do justice to the nature of man without recognising that he is essentially rational, rational even in his utmost aberrations and follies; but it becomes utterly impossible to maintain this truth in the face of the most ordinary experience of life, unless we also recognise that he is a being who always *is more than he knows himself to be*, and whose consciousness of himself is not a fixed and definite conception, but an idea that lives and grows and is never completely at one with itself. When, therefore, we attempt to say what he is, we have to remember that we are expressing not what has already realised itself in him, but what is ever in process of being realised, and what cannot be realised except through a long conflict with nature and with himself. The abstract, unreal, and almost Utopian character of Stoicism lies in this, that it ignores the characteristics of man as a developing being, and treats his good and his evil as fixed entities between which he stands to make an arbitrary choice. And it remains an insoluble problem how, on such a view, there should be any possibility of his making a wrong choice at all.

In order, however, that we may appreciate thoroughly the moral attitude of the Stoics, it is necessary that we should look a little more closely into their psychology.

LECTURE EIGHTEENTH.

THE STOIC CONCEPTION OF THE CHIEF GOOD.

I HAVE already spoken of the way in which the Stoic psychology emphasises the unity of the soul, both in its intellectual and in its moral life, in opposition to the dualistic views of Plato and Aristotle. According to the Stoics the conscious self occupies the place in man's nature which the divine reason holds in the universe. It is represented as a central power which, from one point of view, may be distinguished from the senses, but which, when so distinguished, must be taken as absolutely dominating over them. In fact, the distinction is for the Stoics only a relative one, nor is there any real separation between the principle that dominates and the powers and tendencies that are controlled by it. They belong to the same self, and are described as emanations from the ruling power, or as only that power itself under a special modification. Nor, again, do the Stoics admit any separation between the reason and the will, except as different aspects of the same faculty. The will is, as with Kant, simply the reason in its practical exercise. We may ideally distinguish the reason that seeks to discover the nature of the objective world from the reason that seeks to realise itself in that world; but, as the world can be nothing but the realisation of reason, there is no real separation between the two. The first truth of psychology for the Stoic is, therefore, this: that it is the same soul or self that thinks and wills, perceives and desires; and that, though for some purposes it may be convenient to distinguish these different powers, though indeed the difference of the organs of sense to a certain extent forces this distinction upon us, yet it must never be supposed that they are like different beings which are, so to speak, enclosed in one skin, and which act and react externally upon each other.

Now, in our ordinary descriptions of the inner life, we are too apt to assume or suggest such externality of its elements to each other, and to forget the unity of the soul in the diversity of its manifestations. We are apt to think of the mind as a kind of arena in which intellect and will, sense and passion, and all the other faculties which we personify, play out their game, now conflicting and now co-operating with each other, without interference from any power that lies beyond their divided life. And in the philosophy of Plato and Aristotle, as we have seen, there is something that favours this misconception. The opposition of form and matter introduces itself into the conception of the relations of reason and passion, and the intuitive intelligence seems in its pure nature to be regarded as independent of that connexion with the other elements of man's being, into which it is brought in our experience. This division especially troubles the psychology of the will, and its supreme act of choice is described by Aristotle as a combination of the two elements of desire and deliberation, without any clear indication of a principle of unity beyond their difference.[1] But the Stoic at once sets aside all such dualistic ways of describing the life of the soul. To him the dominating self is at once reason and will. And though, as we shall see, he lays great stress upon the division and conflict of the moral life, yet he will not for a moment allow that desire and passion are other than forms of the life of the one self, or expressions of its self-determined activity. This point is apt to be misconceived, because we frequently find Stoics speaking of the passions as unnatural or irrational. Such language might seem to involve a similar point of view to that of Plato, when he distinguishes the rational and the irrational elements in our being, or to that of Aristotle when he says that the desires are partly irrational, though so far participating in reason as to be capable

[1] Vol. I, p. 316 *seq.*

of submitting to its law.   Now the Stoics allow, as of course everyone must allow, that man does not always act in accordance with the dictates of reason, which yet they regard as constituting his nature.   Nay, they conceive that the passions are irrational in an even deeper sense than is admitted by Plato and Aristotle, as being not only indifferent to reason, but directly opposed to it.   But they do not conceive of this as due to the existence in men of any separate element which is indifferent or recalcitrant to reason.   No Stoic who was faithful to the fundamental ideas of his philosophy could admit that any feeling or desire is irrational in the sense of being independent of reason, or as, even in its utmost perversion, capable of exhibiting the characteristics which would exist in a creature altogether devoid of reason.   The passions, irrational as they are in one sense, as perversions of our rational nature, are yet quite rational as being the determinations of a rational self and the manifestations of its characteristic power of judging and choosing.   The folly, or, as the Stoics often designated it, the madness of man, in which he rebels against the rational principle of his being, is still in another sense quite rational.   It is not the corruption or perversion of his nature by a foreign principle, but the division of that nature against itself.   Hence we can never explain away intellectual error or moral guilt by attributing it to the influence of an irrational part of our being upon that which is rational. We must explain it as a failure of man to be faithful to his true self, as a revolt of the rational being, as such, against reason. If man be said to be misled by sense, this only means that he has not properly tested the images through which he apprehends the objects without him; if he be said to be carried away by passion, this only means that he has failed to make clear to himself the conception of the supreme good which is bound up with his rational nature.[1]

Now I think that from one point of view this doctrine marks a distinct advance upon the psychology of Plato and Aristotle. It is true, as I have already indicated, that it leaves out of account the process of development by which the implicit unity of man's nature becomes explicit; in other words, it forgets that, though reason makes man what he is, he is ever becoming, and has never become completely rational and self-conscious. But it forces us to realise that the germinal reason is in him from the first, that it is the distinctive principle which constitutes his selfhood, and that, if there were not, even in his most undeveloped stage such an expression of the unity of the self, there would be in him no self, and, strictly speaking, no humanity at all. Even in the consciousness of an animal there is such a universal unity, that it would be absurd to treat its different appetites as isolated or standing in merely external relations to each other. The animal at least feels *itself* in all it feels, and this gives an individual unity to its life through all its changes. Yet as this unity in the animal is not self-conscious, the animal might still be said to live wholly in the present, and to pass from one impression or impulse to another, not relating or connecting them, but identifying itself wholly with each in turn.

But a self-conscious being cannot live thus, just because it is self-conscious, or, in other words, because it refers all its action and passion to one *ego*. To forget, in considering him, this essential reference, is to leave out the unity which gives its distinctive character to his life, and then to treat the whole as if it were the sum of the parts, or the result of their action and reaction upon each other. On the other hand, if we do take account of this unity at all, we must realise its presence in all forms and changes of the soul's life. Perhaps we may put the truth more exactly by saying that the life that is self-conscious has in it both a new kind of unity and a new kind of division; for in such a life the self is necessarily set against the not-self— at once distinguished from it and essentially related to it—and this division, as well as this unity, is carried out in all its conscious states. But this means that in it sensation becomes perception, and appetite desire.

Hence, if in one sense we may be said to start with the feelings and impulses of animals, yet the very dawn of our rational life carries us beyond them, so that we never are simply sensitive or simply appetitive. In other words, our sensations and appetites are never what they are in the animal; they may be better or worse, higher or lower, but they are never the same thing. Our sensations may often be less keen in themselves than those of some animals; but they are subject from the earliest dawn of consciousness to a new interpretation, being referred to objects which are conceived as standing in definite relations to each other in the one world of experience which exists for one self. And they have become capable, because of the new meaning which is thus put into them, on the one hand, of conveying to us general truths which are beyond the reach of animal capacity, and, on the other hand, of deceiving and misleading us in a way and to a degree in which the comparatively simple nature of the animal can never be deceived or misled.

It is difficult, indeed, to describe the intelligible world as it exists for the inchoate self-consciousness without seeming to attribute too much to it; for in describing it we necessarily analyse it as it cannot analyse itself. Still, even allowing for the way in which, in the slow process of evolution, a change of kind hides itself under the appearance of a mere change of degree, we can see that the dawn of self-consciousness brings with it the transformation of a sensitive continuity of life into the apprehension of a diversity of objects, which, as they are related to one self, form one world of experience. And in this we have already all the elements of a rational consciousness, a consciousness which is guided by general principles, however little the subject of it may as yet be capable of reflecting on such principles. Such a being can scarcely be said to have sensations at all, in the sense in which a being not self-conscious could have them. It is not that something has been externally added to the sensitive consciousness, but that development has brought with it a new differentiation and a new integration which have essentially transformed its whole nature.

And the same is true of the appetites of the animal. We have them in us, yet in another sense we have them not. For in us, as I have said, they become better or worse than animal impulses, just because they are referred to definite objects and ends, and because these objects and ends are not isolated from each other, but form elements in the life of one self, and so constitute parts of the good or happiness which it necessarily seeks. The self-conscious being, as I have said in a previous lecture, cannot seek merely to satisfy its desires; it must seek to satisfy itself, that is, it must seek

the particular end or object as part of a general good.
And, though it is possible that for the moment these
two things may seem to be identical, and the soul
may throw itself with all the energy of passion into
one pursuit, such a concentration must in the long
run lead to a recoil. For it is impossible that a
rational being should permanently identify the good
with one element in it, or that he should live wholly,
like the animal, in each impulse as it arises. There
may be an approximation to this in a low stage of
humanity ; but, even then, there is a restlessness
and dissatisfaction which indicates that the universal
good, the end which a self-conscious being as such
must seek, is separating itself from the particular
objects in which it has been sought. A self-conscious
being, as such, necessarily has the consciousness of
itself in relation to a world, and its complete satisfaction cannot be less than to have its world for itself.
This limitless self-seeking is the background of all
the desires of a self, and it infuses into them all an
element which may either exalt or degrade them, but
which in any case cannot let them be like the simple
and direct impulses which come with a definite
physical need and pass away immediately with its
satisfaction. The appetites of man, if we may call
them so, are capable of being overstrained and perverted in a way that is not possible in the animal life,
just because in them he seeks the satisfaction of a

self, and tries, as it were, to expand a finite into an infinite good. And, on the other hand, they are capable of being purified and idealised by being made the natural basis of a higher spiritual satisfaction, elements in that comprehensive good which alone can be regarded as adequate to the self.

It was, therefore, a very imperfect psychology which led Hume, as it has led many, to speak of the passions as if they had an independent nature of their own, which reason could not alter. On the contrary, we have to realise that, from the beginning, reason enters into the constitution of the desires, giving even to the simplest of our appetites a character which they could not have except in a rational being, and continuously transforming them by the idea of the good as the realisation and satisfaction of the self. For, as Plato declares, man necessarily seeks the good, "having an anticipative consciousness of its nature," which gradually becomes clearer and more comprehensive with every step in the widening of his experience and the development of his powers. Hence, whatever may be the explanation of that division in man's life which we ordinarily speak of as the conflict of reason and passion, we must recognise that it is a conflict within our rational nature, between different expressions of reason, and not between reason and something else. In insisting upon this point, therefore, the Stoics hit upon a truth which was obscured or neglected in the Platonic and Aristotelian philosophies. For it is the essential problem of human life that we can thus be divided against ourselves, in spite of the identity of the self of which we are conscious. The division and conflict of the soul, indeed, would not be so deep and deadly, if it could be explained by the opposition of matter to form, of sensuous passion to an ideal principle, and if it were not that the ideal principle in us is turned against itself. That the passions of men mislead them is the superficial aspect of the fact, but the deeper aspect of it is that we mislead ourselves; for the passion that misleads us is a manifestation of the same *ego*, the same self-conscious reason which is misled by it : and thus, as Burns puts it, it is the very " light from heaven " that leads us astray.

The great question, therefore, is how such self-contradiction is possible, or, in other words, how a being whose nature is reason, can act irrationally. This question is one to which the Stoics directed much attention ; and their answer to it is well worth consideration, though it is made incomplete and unsatisfactory by the fact that, like Socrates, they are unable to think of reason except as conscious and reflective, so that for them unconscious reason is no reason at all. Hence they always treat conduct as the result of definite acts of judgment and reasoning. Their view may be summarised thus.

We always seek the good, but frequently we mistake something else for it, and, when this happens, we commonly say that our passions mislead us. But such passions are really the result of false judgments, in which we subsume under the idea of good actions or objects that are not good. And this again implies one of two things; either we make a mistake as to the idea of good itself, or we make a mistake as to the nature of the things which we subsume under it. In other words, either we do not clearly realise what we mean when we call a thing good, or we do not clearly perceive what the particular thing in question is, and, therefore, we suppose it to have a character which it has not.

But both kinds of knowledge are, in the opinion of the Stoics, within our reach. The idea of good is within our reach, for it is bound up with our rational nature; and if we do not attain to a definite under-standing of it, it is because we do not undergo the labour of reflexion which is necessary to make it clear and distinct. And the knowledge of particular things, at least so far as is necessary to determine their value, is also within our reach, if we rightly use and carefully interpret the images which we receive from sense. To use an Aristotelian mode of expression, the rightness of our conduct depends upon the way in which we develop the practical syllogism, whose major premise is the definition of the good, and whose minor premise brings under that definition the distinct image of the object we have to choose or reject. And both premises may be made definite and certain by anyone who rightly uses the faculties he has and the opportunities which experience brings him. We have, therefore, to examine the way in which the Stoics carry out this view in both cases, as regards the idea of good and as regards the objects brought under it.

The idea of good, according to the Stoics, is derived from within, from certain presuppositions or presumptions which are bound up with our rational nature, and which experience only calls into activity. They are called by the Stoics ἔμφυτοι προλήψεις, ἔννοιαι φυσικαὶ τοῦ καθόλου, and they are entirely confined—this at least seems to be the general view of the Stoics—to the sphere of morals and religion. There is some controversy, indeed, as to the force of these expressions; and some accounts would suggest that these so-called 'innate ideas' are regarded as the results of the natural and inevitable action of the mind upon the data supplied by sense, while other accounts make them to be pure *a priori* principles directly involved in the nature of reason and independent of experience. It is this last view which seems to be supported by the most authentic expressions of Stoic doctrine.[1] At the same time we

[1] Bonhöffer, p 188 *seq.*

are not to think of them as innate ideas in the sense which Locke attached to the name, that is, as fully developed conceptions which the mind has before it from the first, and which from the first it is clearly conscious of possessing. On the contrary, the Stoics frequently speak of the mind as only gradually coming to the knowledge of its own contents, and they even try to define the exact age at which it attains to a realisation of its innate ideas. They are innate, therefore, only in the sense that they are bound up with self-consciousness, so that no man can have reason developed in him without the apprehension of them. All men who are sane and who have come to maturity in the development of their faculties, have an idea of good and evil: an idea of good as that which is useful to the self and helps it to self-realisation, and of evil as that which prevents or obstructs such self-realisation. And the ultimate spring of all our activity is just the effort to attain the former and avoid the latter. In fact, every creature, as we have already seen, has in it the *conatus in suo esse perseverandi*, the effort to maintain and realise itself, as the fundamental impulse of its being. And man only differs from the rest in so far as he is self-conscious, and therefore conscious of the good he seeks as distinct from the particular objects in which he seeks it. And this he shows even in his use of such words as good and evil, right and wrong, in his judgments as to particular objects and acts.

At the same time, the mere use of such terms, as Socrates showed, is far from implying a clear consciousness of what they mean, and is therefore consistent with the most erroneous use of them in our practical judgments. Hence the Stoic insists, almost as earnestly as Socrates or Plato, on the shallowness of mere opinion, and on the necessity of defining our general terms, and so rising to a clear consciousness of ourselves. Thus Epictetus speaks of a rhetorician, who attacked Plato because he sought to define such terms as goodness and justice, the meaning of which everybody knows.[1] Epictetus answers that Plato cannot be supposed to deny that we have by nature ideas or preconceptions of such virtues, but only that it is impossible to make an accurate use of them till we have analysed and defined them. How, for instance, can we know whether anything, say, pleasure or wealth, is really a good, if we have not realised exactly what we mean by good ? We know generally that the good is that which alone is useful to us, and we go on at once to apply the term to any object that produces a pleasing impression. But the one thing necessary, before any such vaguely apprehended idea can help us, is a reflective analysis which shall sift out

[1] Epict. *Dissert.*, II, 17.

all other ideas that have got confused with the idea
of good, and shall clearly distinguish all the elements
contained in it.   In like manner Cicero,[1] speaking
for the Stoics, frequently insists upon the idea that
it is the business of philosophy to disentangle and
explicate the obscure and complex notions of virtue
that nature has given us.   It is only such a process
which can enable us to rise above popular opinion,
and can deliver us from the vague associations of the
common consciousness, which attaches the predicate
'good' to many things that are evil or indifferent,
just because it has never asked itself what it means
by that predicate.

If, however, we ask how the Stoics carried out
this process of analysing our innate notions of good,
we find that the result is rather negative than
positive.   In other words, the process of analysis is
for them mainly a process of elimination, in which the
universal good of reason is emptied of all particular
content.   As rational beings, they tell us, we transcend
in consciousness our own particular existence, as
well as the particular existence of all the objects
we know.   We are, in Plato's language, "spectators
of all time and existence," and therefore not limited
in our knowledge to any particular object or class
of objects.   And, in like manner, in our practical
life we are not confined to any special end; for the

---

[1] Cic. *De Officiis*, III, 81: cf. Bonhöffer, p. 208 *seq.*

good is the realisation of the self and not of any
special tendency or desire. The good has thus to
be distinguished from all particular objects of desire.
So far we may admit the force of the Stoic reasoning.
But if this be all that we can say, shall we not
end by opposing the general idea of good to every
particular form which that good can take? To this
the Stoic's answer is, that there is a motive or end
derived from our nature as rational beings: for it
is the characteristic of reason to look at all things
from a general point of view, from the point of
view of the whole; and this originates in us a love
of law or order for its own sake. Further, as this
motive springs from our inmost self, so it may
become supreme over all other motives and even
take the place of them all. Nay, they contend, it
must do so, in every one who is fully conscious of
himself.

This conception is well illustrated by the Stoic
account of the development of man's moral consciousness, which is reproduced by Cicero in the treatise
De Finibus.[1] According to the view there stated,
the primitive consciousness of man is a consciousness
of himself, and his primitive motive is to realise
himself. But what self? Cicero's Stoic answers
that man begins with the consciousness of his
particular self, and his desire is therefore for objects

[1] *De Finibus*, III, 5 *seq.*

that are useful towards its preservation and well-being. These objects are therefore called the first aims of nature (τὰ πρῶτα κατὰ φύσιν, *prima naturae*). They are objects such as health, wealth, honour, and the like, which are primarily sought for themselves, and not for the pleasure which is the result of their attainment. For we do not seek them because they give us pleasure, but they give us pleasure because we seek them; and it is a great error of the Epicureans to suppose that pleasure is the primary object of desire. Still at this stage we seek only such particular ends, vaguely recognising them as good. But reason as it awakes within us, carries us beyond the particular to the universal, and makes us think of life as a whole. We become conscious that as rational beings we carry within us a principle of order and unity, or, as it may otherwise be expressed, a principle of ὁμολογία or self-consistency, and that it is just this principle which makes us selves. As, therefore, we become conscious of what we are, we recognise that we can realise ourselves only as we maintain order and self-consistency in our lives. The *conatus in suo esse perseverandi*, which at first took the form of desires for particular objects or for the furtherance of the individual life, now takes the form of an exclusive impulse to realise the law of reason, and all the special ends of desire are regarded as indifferent.

Only he who thus acts with a single eye to the
general end can be regarded as performing a moral
action in the highest sense of the word, or, as the
Stoics call it, a κατόρθωμα.   In Kantian phrase, duty
must be done for duty's sake alone, and not for the
sake of the particular ends to be attained by it; and
if any other consideration enters into our action, it
drags it down to a lower, and so to speak, a non-
moral level, even if it does not make it positively
immoral.

Now there may be elements in the view set
before us by Cicero which did not belong to the
original form of Stoicism.   But the conception of
morality as resting upon the idea of ὁμολογία, or
self-consistency, seems to be derived from the
founder of the school.   Stobaeus [1] tells us that Zeno
declared the end to be simply to live consistently
(τὸ ὁμολογουμένως ζῆν), i.e. to live according to a
law of reason which agrees with itself in all its
applications (καθ' ἕνα λόγον καὶ σύμφωνον).   But the
Stoics who followed him introduced a further qualification of this idea, and declared the end to be living
in consistency with nature.   Cleanthes, who succeeded
Zeno as head of the school, was the first who made
this addition; and we are told that he specially
referred to the nature of the universe as that with
which the virtuous man must be in harmony; while

[1] *Ecl.*, II, 134.

Chrysippus, who was *his* successor, though not rejecting the conception of Cleanthes, yet dwelt more upon the harmony of man with his own nature.

Now, if we take the account of Stobaeus as authentic, the first statement of the Stoic principle of morals coincides in a remarkable way with the ideas of Kant. Zeno said: " Act consistently on one principle ": Kant said, " Act so that you can will that the maxim of your action should become a universal law." Both views go upon the idea that the reason which makes us men is an impartial faculty, a faculty in us that abstracts from our own individual case, and, indeed, from every individual case; and both views imply that we cannot act consistently on one law or principle and yet act wrongly. Immoral action is simply a case of using double weights and measures, and it is impossible to do evil consistently. Just as error and untruth are always partial, and a lie must break down somewhere by its own self-contradiction, if worked out logically to all its consequences; so an evil act is always an act which implies the very principle which it denies, and we cannot turn it into a universal law without bringing it into conflict with itself.

And this shows how easy was the transition by which the idea of self-consistency was translated by Zeno's followers into the idea of consistency with nature. Kant also translated his principle into the form: "Act as if by your action the maxim of it were to be turned into a law of nature." It is easily shown, and has often been shown by critics of Kant, that nothing can be made of the idea of formal self-consistency. Any idea, if we keep it in its abstraction, may seem to be consistent with itself: it is only when we work it out in the concrete, and bring it into relation with other elements of experience, that it can be shown to be inconsistent. Or, to put it more exactly, an idea can be shown to be inconsistent only so far as it is shown to imply other ideas and yet to be at variance with them. To universalise the maxim of an act, therefore, must mean, if it means anything, to conceive it as an element in the system of things, which can be realised consistently with the realisation of all the other elements that make up that system. Thus the idea of self-consistency, the moment we try to give it a definite meaning, turns into the idea of consistency with the whole system of the universe: and this in the Stoic idea is the same thing as consistency with our own nature; for the nature of man corresponds to the nature of the universe as the microcosm to the macrocosm. Indeed, we have to remember that the demand for consistency comes *ex hypothesi* from our own nature which, as rational, is compelled to think and act on universal principles. "The end," says Diogenes Laertius,

speaking of the Stoic doctrine, " is to act in conformity with nature, that is, at once with the nature
which is in us, and with the nature of the universe,
doing nothing which is forbidden by that common
law which is the right reason that pervades all
things, and which is, indeed, one with the Divine
Being who administers the universal system of
things. Thus the life according to nature is that
virtuous and blessed flow of existence, which is
enjoyed only by one who always acts so as to maintain the harmony between the God within and the
will of the power that orders the universe." [1]

There is, however, in all this a certain ambiguity,
which we meet with also in the philosophy of Kant,
and which neither the Stoics nor Kant ever cleared
up. All the different formulae in which the moral idea
is expressed—self-consistency, consistency with nature,
consistency with the nature of man—are abstract
phrases. If they carry us away from the particular
to the universal, from the part to the whole, from the
ideas of special objects and ends to the general
principle which realises itself in the whole system of
things within and without us, yet they do not tell us
anything definite about that principle except that it is
not realised in any particular object or end. It is
realised, according to the Stoics, in the system of the
whole, and it is realised in the individual man, so far

[1] Diog. Laert, VII., 1, 53.

as he can repeat that system in himself: and they are ready to maintain that that system is organic, that all nature is but the environment of a world-community of spirits, and that we are all members one of another in so far as we are organs of it. But when we ask what is behind these brave words, their meaning seems to melt away from us, and that, whether we look to the universe or to the individual soul. As regards the latter, acting by reason seems to be opposed to acting by any particular passion, by any passion that points to a special end or attaches us to an individual person; but if, in order that reason may rule, all such impulses have to be driven out, reason will rule in an empty house. Hence it is not easy to answer the charge brought against the Stoics that, after all, they were merely ascetics; in other words, that their morality not only begins with the mortification of the passions, but ends there. They may not, and do not, intend this result; for they are possessed with the idea of a systematic ordering of the whole nature of man, which is to be attained by this negation of the passions; but in excluding under that name all particular desires and affections as such, they have deprived themselves of all the elements out of which such a system of life might be constructed, and put the bare idea of system in place of its actuality. It might, indeed, be answered that they only break the links that bind man to particular beings and things without him in order to bind him closer to the whole of which he and they are parts; that they withdraw him from the special affections of kindred and race, only in order to unite him as man to all mankind. But this, again, raises the question as to the possibility of realising such a union, a union of men that takes no account of time or circumstance, or of individual or national character. What is meant by a φιλανθρωπία that is not fertile in special affections to individual human beings, affections which adapt themselves to their special character and the special relations into which they are brought? And what is meant by an organic unity of mankind in a πολιτεία τοῦ κόσμου, if the reason that is to bind them together be taken merely as a common element in the nature of each, which connects them in spite of their differences in other respects? A real community cannot be constituted except between those whose common nature shows itself just in their differences, and makes these very differences the means of binding them together, by fitting each for a special office in the common life. But the logic of the Stoics will not carry them to this farther step. Hence the idea of the organic unity of mankind remains abstract, or turns into a mere ideal which never can be realised. For, as a mere ideal, it remains something purely subjective, something which exists only in the soul of the individual, and cannot be found or produced in the world without. As subjective, however, it loses all its content, or finds its content merely in the negation of the particular passions. Thus the wise man of the Stoics becomes a mere bundle of negations; for when we have said that he is free from all particular influences, whether from within or from without, we have left nothing but the formal self-consistency of a will of which nothing can be said, except that it is ever at one with itself.

If, again, we look to the Stoic theory of the nature of the universe we arrive at a similar result. The Stoic is prepared to say that all things are the manifestation of reason, and that even by their defects, as particular things, they must contribute to the realisation of reason; but he is not able to take a single step towards the recognition of any particular thing as so contributing. Still less is he prepared to show how any special interest of human life may become an embodiment of the good, or how any endeavour of man will help to realise it.

Now it may be admitted that it is just here that we find the crucial difficulty of any idealistic view of the world such as the Stoics profess—a difficulty which Mr. Bradley puts vividly and epigrammatically when he says that "The world is the best of all possible worlds, and everything in it is a necessary evil." In other words, it is hard to combine a consciousness of the evil or imperfection of each part of the world with a perception of its value as an element in a perfect whole. Yet it is obvious that just this is the task which must be undertaken by any philosophical system that bases itself, as Stoicism based itself, upon the idea that the world is a rational or intelligible system. Otherwise, the doctrine that 'the real is the rational' will remain a bare presupposition, an assertion in regard to the whole which is not in any way proved in relation to the parts. Now this seems just the position reached by the Stoics; nor would it be unfair to say that Mr. Bradley's epigram, taken literally, represents their view of the universe. For if Stoicism be an optimism in one aspect of it, it is a pessimism in another. It is pessimistic and hopeless, when it looks at the particular things in the world, at the particular phases of its history, at the particular interests of human life: but when it turns to the universe and its law, it is optimistic even to the extent of an absolute disbelief in the reality of evil. And it leaves these two aspects of things in unrelieved antagonism, sometimes even putting them side by side in startling paradox. This is true of all the Stoics; but it is specially characteristic of the noble, but sad-hearted Marcus Aurelius, who is constantly declaring to us his faith in the perfection of a universe, in which nevertheless he can hardly find anything but disappointment.

He has no doubt of the existence of the world-community of spirits, yet he is continually exhorting himself to expect nothing but misunderstanding and malevolence in those with whom he has to do. He presents to us the pathetic figure of a great Roman Emperor, struggling to maintain the order of the imperial system against the disintegrating forces that are attacking it from without and from within, and supporting himself by a conviction of the eternal reality of an ideal which everything outward seems to contradict, and which he can find nowhere realised except in his own soul. The Stoic could not get beyond this noble hopelessness: he could not see how by losing his life he might save it, or how the idea of the rationality of the world-system could blossom into a personal hope for himself or for any of his fellows, in whom reason for the time had found its embodiment. He was essentially a soldier left to hold a fort surrounded by overpowering hosts of the enemy. He could not conquer or drive them away, but he could hold out to the last and die at his post.

LECTURE NINETEENTH.

THE STOIC VIEW OF PRACTICAL ETHICS.

In the last lecture I said that the Stoic treats conduct as the result of a practical syllogism, in which
a particular act or object is subsumed under the idea
of the good. But in order that such a practical
syllogism may be possible, we must be able to obtain
a clear definition of the good in general, and we
must also be able to understand the particular case
to which it is to be applied. The former is possible,
because the idea of good is bound up with our self-
consciousness, and only needs to be brought to light
by reflexion and analysis. And I attempted in the
last lecture to show how this task was performed
by the Stoic and criticised the result to which he
was led. In doing so, I partly anticipated the
second question as to the minor premise in the
practical syllogism—the question how, on Stoic
principles, we are able to determine the nature of
the particular things which have to be subsumed

under the idea of the good. But we cannot do full justice to their theories until we have directly examined their answer to this question, and especially their thoughts as to the absolute or relative indifference of all outward things.

First of all, then, let us ask how, according to the Stoics, we get knowledge of particular things. To this the answer is that our knowledge of such things is not, like our knowledge of the good, innate, but must be derived from sense. This, however, does not mean that the truth of such objects is immediately given to us through sensation. It is true that the metaphor of 'impression' is taken literally by the Stoics, and that the outward object is conceived as stamping its image on the soul as a seal impresses itself on wax. At the same time this idea of the passivity of the soul in receiving impressions is partly corrected by the thought that the mind, in receiving the impression, is in tension against the object that impresses it, and grasps that object with more or less energy in the moment of perception. Now, knowledge depends just upon the firmness of this grasp. We are not to take all impressions as equally true or equally representative of reality. The impressions which we receive when the mind is feeble in its action and takes things just as they come, are vague and uncertain. But we are able, by directing the attention steadily and persistently to

the object, to get images whose outlines are clearly
defined, and which bear with them the evidence of
their objectivity in the vividness and distinctness with
which they present themselves.   In Cicero's language,
such images carry with them a peculiar and con-
vincing testimony to the things they represent
(*propriam quandam habent declarationem earum quae
videntur*).[1]   Such a well-attested image is called a
φαντασία καταληπτική, a phrase which has been
interpreted in various ways.   Zeller and others have
taken it as meaning an image which can lay hold of
the mind or is borne in upon it ; but more probably it means a presentation or idea which grasps, or
enables the mind to grasp the object as it really is.[2]
The sanity or strength of the mind, according to this
view, is shown in its refusal to commit itself or give
its assent to any belief as to the object, until it has
got a clearly defined and persistent image of it.
Till we have compassed such an image, we ought
to withhold our judgment ; but when we have
attained it, we have a right to take it as representing reality.   The φαντασία καταληπτική is therefore declared to be the criterion of truth ; in other
words, it is declared to bear with it its own evidence, and to be in its turn a touchstone for other
ideas which are less distinct.

[1] Cic., *Acad.*, 1, 41.
[2] Zeller, III, 1, p. 72 (2nd ed.) : Bonhöffer, p. 160.

It is easy to see that we have here a very naïve and elementary consciousness of the difficulties which stand in the way of scientific knowledge. Accordingly the Stoics were greatly harassed by the objections of the Academics, who pointed out, on the one hand, that it is impossible for images of sense to be so clear and complete as to make deception impossible; and, on the other hand, that very clear and complete images often impress themselves on our minds, which yet cannot be supposed to correspond to any objective reality. Further, they pointed out that there is a great risk of misinterpretation entering into the process whereby we form a definite image of any object out of the data of sense—a risk which the simple theory of the Stoics hardly recognises at all.

And there is a more vital objection behind. For the Stoic explanation of the act of perception presupposes a materialistic conception of the relation of the mind to its object, and involves that they are external to each other in the same way that one piece of matter is external to another. But if this were a true view of the relation, the mind could directly know only itself; and it could know other objects, if at all, only indirectly and by inference. What is present to the mind must, *ex hypothesi*, be only its own states and the impressions it has received; but how then can it get assurance that any such state or impression represents the object correctly, or indeed that it represents any external object at all ? If we begin by presupposing a division of subject and object —and on the materialistic theory of the Stoics we must so begin—the mind can be conscious in the first instance only of itself and its own ideas; and it is impossible that it should go beyond itself, so as to assert absolutely the reality of anything else. Thus materialism cuts away the ground from under itself by the externality of the relation which it establishes between the mind and its object. Obviously also, if we put the problem in this way, if we ask how we can know that the states or impressions of the mind correspond to a reality which is outside of the mind, we can solve it only by an assumption ; for there is no *tertium quid* beyond the subject and the object, which can decide whether the one corresponds to the other, and the only tests which can be applied to distinguish true from false images— such as, for instance, their distinctness, their per- manence, or their self-consistency—are themselves subjective, and cannot authorise us to bridge the supposed gulf between subject and object. Obviously, on this basis, the game is in the hands of the Sceptic, who maintains that we cannot know any- thing whatsoever about objective reality. This difficulty can be escaped only by giving up the presupposition with which the Stoic starts, that the relation between the mind and the object involves the physical externality of the one to the other. We then see that the real question is how the division of subject and object actually arises in our experience. For it must arise in our experience, if it is to exist for us at all; and, so arising, it cannot be an absolute division, or a division in which the object is spatially external to the subject. It cannot be a distinction between our experience and something else which, *ex hypothesi*, cannot come into that experience.

These objections to the Stoic theory of knowledge are, however, of less consequence than they might seem, because the Stoic does not attach importance to knowledge for its own sake, but only with a view to practice. What he desires to understand, therefore, is not the specific character of objects, but only their value, or want of value, in relation to the moral end. In his eyes the great danger lies in taking external objects for more than they are, and so exalting them into the place of the real good of life. If, on the other hand, we clearly realise the limited and imperfect nature of such objects, we shall be able to see what they can, and what they cannot, give us. Dispel the magnifying mist that hangs about the things of sense and time, making them seem more desirable or more dangerous than they really are, and we shall cease to love or to fear them. Marcus Aurelius is continually dwelling upon this lesson: " Always define and clearly picture to yourself the object presented to you, so that you may see exactly what kind of thing it is, discriminating it in its totality from all other things and in your own mind assigning to it, and to all the elements of which it is compounded and into which it will be ultimately resolved, the name that properly belongs to each. For nothing is so productive of magnanimity as the power of systematically and truthfully testing every object that comes before us, and so looking into it as to discern the nature of the universe to which it belongs, the special use it subserves, its value in relation to the whole system of things, and, in particular, to man as a citizen of the supreme city, of which all other cities may be regarded as the households." [1]

Now, with the Stoic, this careful looking into the value of outward things ends always in the discovery that they have little or no value. "When we have meat or eatables of any kind before us, let us grasp the images of them firmly, and say to ourselves: This is the carcase of a fish, and this of a fowl or a pig; and again: This Falernian wine is only a little grape-juice, and this purple robe is nothing more than sheep's wool dyed with the blood of a shell-fish; for, when we thus represent things to ourselves, we penetrate to their inmost nature and search through all their relations so as to realise

[1] *Comment.*, III, 11.

exactly what they are. So ought we to deal with our whole life, and whenever imagination presents things to us as specially worthy of admiration, we should strip them bare and discover their cheapness, setting aside all the fine names by which they are exalted to the skies."[1] Again: "Decay is in the material substance of all things; they are but water, dust, bones, and stench. What is marble but knobs of earth; gold and silver but sediment; raiment but tags of hair; purple but the blood of the shellfish? Even the breath of life is no better, ever changing from one to another."[2] "Little value wilt thou set upon the delights of music, if thou wilt but decompose the melodious sound into its component notes, and ask thyself as to each of them: Is it *this* that overpowers thee? Thou wilt be ashamed to confess it. The same result will follow the analysis of dancing or athletic exercises into the movements and postures which constitute them. In short, setting aside virtue and virtuous acts, thou hast but to carry out this method of dissection of things into their elements, and the result will be contempt for them all."[3] Above all the 'bubble reputation' is to be reduced to its true value by reflexion on its exact meaning. "He who is greedy for fame perceives not that of those who remember him every one will soon be dead: and so in due course will it be with each of their successors till the last flicker of memory,

[1] *Comment.*, VI, 13.   [2] *Id.*, IX, 36.   [3] *Id.*, XI, 2.

through flutterings and failings, dies altogether out. Nay, suppose that those who will remember thee were immortal and their memory of thee also immortal, what is their good report to thee ? To thee, dead, absolutely nothing. Well, but to thee, living, what value is praise, except indeed for some secondary result ? Why then wilt thou be so foolish as to neglect nature's present gift, and cling to what one or another says hereafter ? " [1]

The object of this close scrutiny is, of course, to reduce all finite and changing things to their proper finitude, that is, not to let them bulk too largely or assume to themselves any absolute value. Wealth, honour, health, sensual and aesthetic pleasure, domestic affections and bonds of friendship, and even life itself, every one of them is to be reduced to what it is in itself, and its limited scope is to be recognised. For thus alone can we be in a position to compare it with the good, and see what is its relation thereto. And the ultimate result at which the Stoic aims is to dis-illusionise us, and make us reject the idea that anything external is essential to the good of a rational being, or can have more than a relative value for him, if it has even that.

With this is connected another thought, which points in the same direction, namely, that things external are mainly gifts of fortune, and that no effort

[1] *Comment.*, IV, 19.

of the individual can make them secure. To place our happiness in them is, therefore, to fill our mind with disturbance and anxiety, which he alone can avoid who fixes his interest and desire upon the things he can control, that is, upon the thoughts of his own mind and the acts of his own will. This thought is specially emphasised by Epictetus, who puts it in the forefront of his *Manual of Ethics*, as the lesson which of all others is most important for the guidance of life. " Of things that exist, some are in our own power, some are not in our own power. In our own power are opinion, will, desire, aversion, in a word, whatever are our own acts; not in our own power are the body, property, reputation, political authority, in a word, whatever are not our own acts. And the things that are in our own power are naturally free, not subject to restraint or hindrance; while the things that are not in our own power are weak, slavish, subject to restraint, alien to ourselves. Remember, then, that if you think the things that are by nature slavish to be free, and the things alien to yourself to be your own, you will be obstructed in your efforts, you will ever be in sorrow and disturbance, ever blaming gods and men; but if you think that only to be your own which is really your own, and that which is alien to be alien, no one will ever be able to constrain or hinder you. You will blame no one, you will accuse no one, you will do nothing against your

own will; no one will be able to harm you, and you
will have no one for your enemy. If, however, you
do aim at such high objects, remember that you cannot
hope to attain them with a divided will, but only if you
dismiss all other aims, abandoning some of them once
for all, and setting aside the rest of them at least for
a time. For, if you attempt to attain both kinds
of goods, both those higher ends and such objects
as wealth and power, you may probably lose the
latter because you seek also the former, and in
seeking the latter, you will certainly lose the former,
which are the most real sources of freedom and happiness. Practise yourself, therefore, in saying to every
threatening appearance: 'You are but an appearance,
and not the reality you pretend to be.' Then weigh
well each appearance by the rules of reason, and,
above all, consider whether it relates to things in your
own power, or to things not in your own power; and
if it relates to anything not in your own power, be
ready to say: 'Then it is nothing to me.'"

In connexion with this we have to remember the
religious point of view from which the Stoic starts
in considering the events of life. The divine power
which rules the universe, has, he believes, put into
each one's hands everything that is necessary for his
own welfare. Whatever, therefore, it is not in our
power to secure, must be regarded as unnecessary
or indifferent. The things that are really mine, or

important to me, are simply what I choose to think of and what I resolve to do—the inner movement of my mind, the inner determination of my will. In these alone lie good and evil for me. My will may be defeated in the effort to attain any objective end, and if I place my good or happiness in such ends, I am the slave of fortune. But no one can hinder me from thinking and willing what I please: no one can prevent me from determining myself in a right or a wrong way, however they may thwart the outward realisation of my will, or even fetter me so as to prevent any outward activity at all. But everything outside of the act of my will is to be regarded as indifferent, even the particular objects to which the will may be directed: for the essential good is simply the state of the will itself.

For the Stoics, therefore, as for Kant, the "one thing in the world or out of it that can be called unconditionally good is a good will," and that altogether irrespective of its effect. *In magnis voluisse sat est.* The good will is the one treasure that no one can take from us, the bad will is the only evil for which we are responsible or which we need to fear. And the will is always master of itself, if it is content with its own act and does not look to external results. Hence the Stoic commendation of apathy, which does not mean the absence of all feeling and desire, but the quenching of all such feeling and desire as is produced by an undue estimate of external things. The whole intensity of emotion and impulse, the whole energy of our being, is to be concentrated upon the one thing needful, the inner state of the mind and will.   For it is not external things that are dangerous to us, but our own false opinions about them.   Now, in the Stoic's view, we have the power so to regulate our opinions and control our thoughts, that we shall see nothing but the truth; and if we use this power so as to realise the goodness of what is really good and the indifference of everything else, we can direct our whole love and desire to the former.   If, therefore, we do not come between ourselves and the good, no one else can prevent our attaining it.   "You can be invincible," says Epictetus, "if you refuse to enter into any conflict in which it is not in your power to conquer."[1]

We are apt to see something like folly and presumption in the Stoic pictures of the wise man, of his irresistible clearness of insight, and his impregnable strength of will: and, indeed, we cannot avoid doing so, if we suppose that the Stoics meant them as descriptions of themselves.   Horace's jests on this subject are well known.   But we might almost as reasonably take Kant's "I can because I ought" as an assertion of his own impeccability.   The Stoics believed that the ideal was realisable, and even that it

[1] Epict., *Man.*, § 19 : *Dissert.*, III, 6.

had been realised in one or more of the sages of the past, such as Socrates. But it would be impossible to find a Stoic claiming himself to be the wise man, and Epictetus and Seneca and Marcus Aurelius tell us plainly that they have not attained. We are to regard such descriptions rather as exhortations, addressed by the Stoic to himself as well as to others—efforts of strong men to raise themselves above the chances and changes of mortal life to a consciousness of the better part that could not be taken from them. "What should we have in readiness in such circumstances?" says Epictetus, speaking of the dangers to which good men were exposed under a tyranny like that of Nero, "What but this, to keep clear in our minds the distinction between what is our own and what is not our own, what is committed and what is not committed to us? Suppose that I have to die! Am I then obliged to die lamenting? Suppose that I am to be imprisoned! Need I weep over my chains? Suppose that I am to be banished! Can any man hinder me from going into exile with smiles and cheerfulness?"[1] Such language seems somewhat overstrained, and would become absurd, if we took it as a profession of absolute indifference to the greatest calamities; but if we take it as the voice of a man, calling upon his fellows in the hour of danger to bear themselves nobly, or rebuking his own

[1] Epict., *Dissert.*, I, 1.

fainting heart like a Homeric hero, and challenging
himself to regard every outward evil and death itself
as nothing in comparison with the loss of the integrity
of his moral life, it takes quite a different aspect.
We do not consider Luther ostentatious, when in his
well-known hymn, he says:

> "And if they take our life,
> Goods, honour, children, wife,
> Yet is their profit small,
> These things shall perish all":

and the Stoic also, in his own sense, could say
with Luther that even if they all perish, "The city
of God remaineth."

But, it will be said—though the Stoic may be
right in treating most outward goods as infinitely
less important than the maintenance of truth and
inner integrity—is it not absurd for him to say that
they are indifferent, if that means that they are of
no importance at all; and this especially when under
outward things are included, not only wealth, honour,
and life, but also the fortunes and life of family and
friends and all who are dear to him? To this it
is at least a partial answer to say, that the Stoic,
when he asserts that outward things are indifferent,
does not mean that they are indifferent in every
point of view, but only that they are indifferent as
compared with the inward goodness of the will; for
that which has a price, however great, becomes

indifferent, when set against that which is priceless. The good will alone is an absolute good, and nothing can be measured in the same scales with it. You cannot weigh death against a bad action, or wealth and honour against a good one. In other words, you cannot by the summing up of finites reach an amount which you can set in the balance against the infinite; for, so measured, the greatest possible collection of finites is the same as nothing at all.

This thought throws light upon another doctrine of the Stoics, which is often misunderstood or treated as an inconsequence. It has often been said that their doctrine of the indifference of outward things was so absurd, that they were obliged in the long run to get out of the *impasse* by making a distinction to which they had no right, between various kinds of indifferent things. They are accused, in short, of hedging before the difficulties caused by their own uncompromising statements. Unfortunately for this view, the doctrine that there is distinction of value between indifferent things, is not a qualification subsequently introduced into the Stoic system, but belongs to the earliest form of it. And I think we can see, on consideration, that it is a necessary part of that system.

The doctrine is that, among things indifferent, there are some which are naturally to be preferred, and others which are naturally to be rejected, while there are only a very few things that are absolutely and from every point of view indifferent. The things that are naturally to be preferred are those that make for welfare in the ordinary sense—health rather than sickness, wealth rather than poverty, honour rather than dishonour, the love of friends and kindred rather than loneliness and bereavement. All these things the Stoic grants to be naturally eligible from the point of view of our finite individuality : nay, he admits that, other things being equal, it is or may be, our duty to choose them. But, in regard of them all, he insists on three points : first, that they are finite and transitory ; secondly, that they are not in our own power ; and, lastly, that, because of both characters, they are capable of turning into the greatest evils, if we attach ourselves to them as if they were absolute goods.

In reference to the first point I have already shown how the Stoic is constantly arguing against the tendency to idealise finite things and treat them as if they were infinite. " Always remember," says Epictetus, " exactly to realise what each thing that attracts you is. If it is a piece of pottery you are fond of, say to yourself ' this is but a piece of pottery,' and you will not be greatly moved, when it is broken." [1] This mode of estimating things as they really are is to be practised in regard to all our

[1] *Man.*, § 3.

possessions, and we are constantly to recognise that even the highest of them, even the love of friends and kindred, is a finite and not an infinite good. We must love it, therefore, as finite and as transitory; for, as finite, it cannot fill the soul, and, as transitory, it cannot afford a support on which the soul may safely lean. And if we treat such things as absolute goods, the really absolute goods which alone are in our power—the unclouded vision of truth, the pure energy of righteous will—must escape us. The Stoic, therefore, while admitting that these things are in themselves eligible, counsels us to be continually realising to ourselves their limited value and our uncertain tenure of them; and sometimes, for discipline's sake, or as a counsel of perfection, he would have us turn from them altogether.

This is well expressed in two paragraphs of the *Manual* of Epictetus. In one of these[1] he says, "Remember that you ought in life to behave as if you were at a banquet. Suppose some dish is carried round and is placed before you; stretch out your hand and take a portion with decency. Suppose that it is carried past you; do not detain it. Suppose that it has not yet reached you; do not send your desire forward to it, but wait quietly till it comes. Do so with respect to children; do so with respect to a wife; do so with respect to the honours of office;

[1] *Man.*, § 15.

do so with respect to wealth: and so you shall one
day be a worthy partner at the banquet of the gods.
But if you take none of the things set before you,
and even despise them, then you will be not only a
fellow-banqueter with the gods, but a sharer of their
dignity; for by so acting Diogenes and Heraclitus
deserved to be called, and to be, divine." Or, take
another passage,[1] where he says: "As on a voyage
when the vessel has reached a port, and you go out
of the ship to get water, it is an amusement by the
way to pick up a shell or a flower. But your
thoughts all the while ought to be directed to the
ship, constantly watching for the call of the captain:
and when he does call you, you must throw away all
these things and hasten, that you may not have to be
bound and thrown into the ship by others. So in life
also if, instead of a flower or a shell, there be given
to you a wife or a child, there is nothing to hinder
you from taking them for your own. But if the
captain should call, run to the ship and leave all
such things behind you." "Especially," the old Epictetus adds with a touch of pathos, "if you are an
old man, do not go very far from the ship, lest
you should lose your passage."

Epictetus, indeed, regards the life of absolute
renunciation as an ideal, much in the same way that
the medieval Church regarded the life of a monk

[1] *Man.*, § 7.

or a nun ; but he did not expect, any more than that Church did, or than the Roman Catholic Church does now, that every one should adopt such a life. He even earnestly warns off from it every one who has not a special vocation for such a life and who has not counted the cost. For all who have not this special vocation, he is content if, without renouncing relative goods, they should constantly remember that such goods are relative, and that the absolute good must never be sacrificed to them. Finally he bids them always remember that all outward things are in the hand of God, and therefore must be rightly disposed. In this respect the attitude of the Stoic is essentially religious ; and what gives him strength to meet misfortune and bereavement, is not so much indifference as confidence in the divine power that gives and takes away.

But there is still another aspect in which the Stoic modifies his conception of the indifference of all outward things. He is obliged to recognise that action is particular, or that in each action we have to deal with a particular object. Our motive may be to realise the general idea of law or order, but in every special action we have to apply that idea to some specific end. Hence, though the inner attitude of the will be everything, yet it always is an attitude toward something external. This the Stoic is obliged to admit ; and hence, while he

maintains that virtue is entirely concerned with the
general idea of law, and that a good act in the full
sense of the word (a κατόρθωμα) must be done
entirely for the sake of the law, yet he has to allow
that in each case there is a certain propriety (καθῆκον)
to be observed, though the observance of this propriety could not of itself make the act moral. From
this point of view, the Stoic is fond of speaking of
particular objects, in the treatment of which the
good will has to be realised, as the materials of
morality; and he calls upon us to have faith that
the right materials are always provided for us by
divine providence. But what he most insists upon
is that the important thing is not the materials, but
the way in which we use them. Hence he regards
all human lots, whether fortunate or unfortunate in
the ordinary sense, as nothing more than opportunities
for the exercise of those moral qualities which in
his view constitute the highest, and indeed the only
absolute values in life. "What," says Epictetus,
"are outward things? They are materials for the
will, in dealing with which it shall attain its own
good or ill. But how is it to attain to such good?
By not being dazzled by the materials it works
with, or confusing them with the good itself. For
our opinions on this subject, when right, will make
the will right, and when wrong will make it wrong.
This law hath God established and declared: 'If

thou wouldest have aught of good, receive it from thyself.'"[1] Or, again, take this passage from the *Manual*:[2] "Whatever happens to you, turn to yourself and ask what power you have to make use of it. If you see beauty, regard it as an opportunity to exercise self-restraint: if what comes to you be labour, you will find in it the material for your powers of endurance: if what comes be reproach, you will find in it the material for patience."

This quotation illustrates another point, namely, that, while the Stoics do not deny that good fortune is 'eligible,' they are disposed to dwell upon misfortune as the best opportunity or material for virtue, and to regard good fortune rather as a temptation. On the whole, however, the main lesson they press is that men should take what comes, and attach as little importance as possible to it, and as great importance as possible to the way in which it is used. Thus their last thought is expressed in the following aphorism, in which, as frequently, Epictetus compares the world to a stage. "Remember that you are an actor in a play, and that the character of the play is fixed by the author and the stage-manager. If he wills that you should play the part of a poor man, see that you do it to the life: if of a lame man, if of a magistrate, if of a private person, it is all one. For it is your business to

---

[1] Epict., *Dissert.*, I, 29.   [2] *Man.*, § 10.

act well the character given you to represent, but to select what it shall be, belongs to another." [1]

We may bring out the strength and the weakness of this view by contrasting it with that which Aristotle expresses in the *Ethics*. Aristotle also insists that outward goods are merely the materials or instruments of the moral life, but that they do not constitute its real good, and may even be adverse to that good. Still, on the whole, he holds to the view that, in order to attain the moral ideal, we must be well provided with such instrumental goods. Happiness depends upon the exercise of the virtues, or, in more modern language, upon activities in which the highest powers of man as a rational being are developed and manifested. But, in Aristotle's view, it is only in the position of a citizen of a free state that these activities are possible, and such a position implies many advantages of fortune. Aristotle, indeed, is not without a perception that nobility of character may 'shine through' misfortune and suffering; but as a rule he regards them not as opportunities, but as obstructions which may even, in extreme cases, be fatal to all exercise of high moral or intellectual qualities, seeing that they take away from the moral artist the proper materials with which he has to work. Hence the idea of moral excellence in a

[1] *Man.*, § 17.

slave or artizan does not come within Aristotle's
scope; and he would certainly not have understood
what Bacon meant when he said that "prosperity
was the blessing of the Old Testament, but adver-
sity the blessing of the New."

Now the Stoics stand above Aristotle in one
respect, namely, that as they break away from the
limited ideal of the Greek State, and hold that the
highest good of man is not dependent on the special
environment of the citizen in such a State, or on the
special forms of social life that were developed by
it. But they go much farther than this when they
maintain that all outward interests, even the interests
of the social life in all its forms, are, from the
highest point of view, indifferent, and that, indeed,
from every point of view, such interests are to be
regarded as unessential. For thus they are driven
back upon the isolated inner life of the individual,
and have to confine the absolute good to the bare
state and direction of the will. Now the mistake of
this negative attitude may easily escape notice, so
long as it shows itself merely in treating wealth, or
fame, or pleasure as indifferent; but when it leads
the Stoics to deal in the same way with the ties of
kindred and friendship, of family or nation, and to
place virtue in obedience to an abstract law which
is independent of all these, we begin to suspect
some mistake or overstatement. And the mistake

seems to be that, in spite of their identification of
the reason that constitutes the nature of man with
the divine reason which manifests itself in the
universe, they do not realise that the consciousness
of self as a moral being, and the consciousness of
other selves as members of one society, are two
factors that cannot be separated.   In other words,
they fail to recognise that the inner and the outer
life are not two spheres of activity, but only different
aspects of the same thing; and that if we fall back
on the former to the exclusion of the latter, we
deprive it of all its meaning.   The whole contents of
my thought, the whole interest of my feelings, the
whole material of my desires, have reference to
things and beings other than myself.   Man, as
Aristotle says, is " a social and political animal "; and
to treat him as having an inner life of his own,
which is complete in itself, or only stands in accidental relations to the things and beings without
him, is to empty life of all its interests, and then
to claim for the bare self—the blank form of self-
consciousness—all the rights to which it is entitled
just because its interests are as wide and comprehensive as the universe itself.

And here, I think, we find at once the truth that
underlies the Stoic theory, and the point where it
is deficient.   The greatness of a self-conscious being,
that which makes him an end in himself in a sense

in which no other being is such an end, is his universal potentiality.   His knowing faculty, as Aristotle
saw, is not limited to any one kind of objects, but
carries with it the idea of the universe as an
all-embracing whole.   Hence it cannot be entirely
absorbed by any one impression or interest, or lose
the power of bringing it into relation with other impressions and interests.   Men may be limited and pre-
judiced, but, so long as sanity is maintained, their
minds cannot be so occupied by any special objects or
aspect of objects as to blind them to everything else,
or absolutely to shut their eyes to the teachings of
new experience.   And the whole progress of culture
and science is just the continual effort of man,
prompted by his essential nature, to rise above
partial views and impressions, and to see the world
as a whole, without unduly emphasising any special
aspect of it.   In like manner, our moral life also is a
continual effort after universality.   For, in the first
place, if we consider the manifold interests of the
individual—all his activities of sense and intelligence,
of appetite and desire—we cannot but recognise that
each of them has only a relative value, and that that
is an imperfect and lop-sided life, in which one of
these interests is allowed to swallow up all the rest.
Hence, if, at any special stage of our development
one element seems all-important, yet, as life goes
on, we are carried past it, or checked in our pursuit

of it, by the necessity of attending to other elements, or by the discovery that the satisfaction of the ruling passion still leaves us unsatisfied. Thus the lesson of experience is that the life which will satisfy the self must be complex and full: nay, that it must find a place for all interests in due proportion. Nor, again, can we avoid looking beyond the individual life to the wider whole of which it is a part. No one can entirely escape the necessity of seeing his own life from the point of view of the society to which he belongs; of recognising the claims of its other members upon himself, and feeling that he has done wrong, if he has treated these claims in a quite different way from his own. The individual has, of course, a bias in his own favour; but he recognises the wrongfulness of unsocial action in the case of others, even when he tries to excuse it in himself. It is this potential universality of interest which makes man capable of a social life that goes beyond the herding of animals, and which in the progress of history gradually widens and deepens the conception of his social duties and relations. All moral progress, indeed, is bound up with this widening of the claims of man upon each other and the deepening of their ideas as to the character of these claims, as claims for each individual, not only to life and its elementary blessings, but to all the share he is capable of taking in the great heritage of humanity, in all the interests, lower and higher, of its manifold existence.

Now, in a sense, the Stoics did recognise the potential universality of man's life, and the acknowledgment of it was, indeed, the very centre of their philosophy. Their mistake lay in opposing this universality to the particular interests in and through which alone it can be realised. As to the former point, take the following passage from Marcus Aurelius.[1]   "What are the capacities of the rational soul?   It sees itself, analyses itself, makes itself what it wills.   The fruits which it bears, it itself plucks and enjoys—unlike the fruits of plants and the produce of animals which are enjoyed by others.   At whatever point the limit of its life may be fixed, it attains its own proper end.   Thus it is not as in a dance or play where the whole action is incomplete if anything cuts it short, but wherever and whenever it may be interrupted, it makes the life which has been given to it full and complete, so that the individual can say, ' I have what is my own.'   Moreover, it traverses the whole universe, and the void beyond, and reaches forth into eternity, and embraces and comprehends the periodic regeneration of the universe; and it per- ceives that our fathers had no other vision, nor will our children see anything new.   And thus, in virtue of the uniformity of things, a man of forty

[1] *Comment.*, XI, 1.

years of age, if he has any understanding, has in a manner seen all that has been and all that is to be, Another property of the rational soul is the love of neighbours, coupled with truth and modesty and that supreme self-reverence which is likewise an attribute of universal law, the law or reason which is one with the law of justice."

In such a passage we see a recognition of that universality of man's mind and will, of which I have spoken, his capacity for embracing the whole in his thought, and of identifying his will in action with the principle that is realising itself in that whole. But we see also that Marcus Aurelius takes that principle abstractly, as a principle manifested, indeed, in everything, but not as a principle that binds all things into a system, and connects all the successive stages of their history as parts or phases in one evolution. The Stoic sees that man's knowledge cannot be confined to any one object or class of objects, nor his desire and will to any one particular interest. He sees, also, that there is no one interest which he may not be called upon to sacrifice to the good of the whole, or to the realisation of that principle on which the whole rests. But, admitting the truth of all this, it does not carry with it the consequence which he seems to draw from it—that these interests in their totality are indifferent, and that the inner life is all in all. For the very ends or goods which the individual is required to sacrifice in view of the whole are all elements in that whole ; and if, one after another, we reject and renounce each and all of them, the whole must disappear.

We might put this in the conversational manner by which Epictetus often tries to give point to his lessons. We might suppose the Stoic to ask the question, 'Is not every finite object capable of coming into collision with the universal law, and so of standing between us and our duty ?' To this we are forced to answer, 'Yes.' 'Is not, then, each such object indifferent, in the sense that its attainment cannot be weighed against the necessity of doing our duty ?' To this again we should have to answer, 'Yes.' But the Stoic goes on, 'Is it not, then, true that all outward objects, that is, everything but the good will must be regarded as a mere material of life, which has no good in itself but only in the way it is handled ?' Here we should be obliged to answer with a distinction. If it be meant that the good of life lies in the good will as a mere internal state of the subject, and not as the realisation of man's moral capacity in the family, in the State, and in all the various social relations into which human beings enter with each other, then we must answer, 'No.' To talk of a πολιτεία τοῦ κόσμου, a union of all rational beings with each other, is to utter a mere wish or dream of good, if this idea of universal community is not to be worked out in detail, and to lead to a reconstitution of all the particular relations of society. And to say that the latter is indifferent and the former essential, is like speaking of an 'Invisible Church,' in which all religious men are united, while remaining content that all the branches of the visible Church should be at war with each other. At the same time, it was something that even the idea of such a universal community should be set forth as truth. It was something to direct the thoughts of men to a great idea, although the form it took was unpractical, and even impracticable. If it did nothing else, it at least set aside all lower aims as unsatisfactory, and prepared the language in which the universal conceptions of Christianity could be expressed.

And this leads me to say, in conclusion, that the Stoic philosophy was in its very essence a movement of transition, a connecting link between two stages of moral progress. It was primarily the negation of a past phase of life; and it would have been barren, if it had not pointed forwards to something more positive than itself. What it really showed was, not that men could realise a moral life in themselves without any effective social bonds to unite them to each other, but that the old bonds of society, the bonds of race and nation, had ceased to be effective, and that the only possibility of their renewal lay in the realisation of the deeper principle of humanity. We may, therefore, fairly regard Stoicism as a recoil of man upon himself, which showed that his institutions had become inadequate to his growing life, and at the same time indicated that the only basis upon which they could be reconstituted was the unity and equality of mankind. Nor must we forget that it directly connected its consciousness of the unity of humanity with the idea that the same reason, which makes the individual man a self, is also the absolute principle revealed in the whole system of the universe.

LECTURE TWENTIETH.

THE TRANSITION FROM STOICISM
TO NEO-PLATONISM.

In the preceding lectures I have tried to indicate the general scope of the ideas of the Stoics—ideas which are very important for the history of theology both in themselves and because of their influence upon Christian thought. Let me gather up the main points in a few words.

In the first place, the Stoic philosophy did a great work negatively, in so far as it lifted moral and religious ideas out of the national or racial setting to which they had hitherto been confined. It completed the work of Socrates in emancipating the individual from tradition and throwing him back upon himself—teaching him at the same time to regard this emancipation as one in which every human being has an equal share. The fact that the two greatest of the later Stoics were a slave and an emperor is itself a kind of illustration of the levelling tendency of their doctrine. Everyone from the highest to the lowest was taught by them to regard himself as a law and an end to himself, and to recognise the same universal right and the same universal duty as belonging to all men in virtue of their common humanity. It was this idea, under the name of the 'law of nature,' which inspired and guided generations of Roman lawyers, and which gradually transformed the narrow legal system of a Latin town into the great code of Justinian, that body of legislation upon which the jurisprudence of all civilised peoples is based. At the same time, the levelling and universalising influence of Stoic ideas was felt in all the literature of the later Empire, and did much to complete the humanising work which was begun by the spread of Greek culture, and to prepare a universal language of thought in which East and West could freely communicate to each other their philosophical and religious conceptions. The idea of God as a λόγος σπερματικός— a germinative principle of reason which manifests itself in the universe, and, above all, in the spirits of men as the actual or possible members of a world community—was in itself somewhat vague and abstract; but it needed only to be vitalised by some more direct and concrete vision of truth to produce a reorganisation of the whole spiritual life of man. It could not supply the place of a universal religion, but it prepared the soil upon which a universal religion could grow. Above all, it is to be noted that by the Stoic philosophy the individual was brought into direct and immediate relation with the divine, in a way that could only find its parallel in the later prophetic teaching of Israel.

This last statement suggests an interesting comparison. The religion of Israel, after the captivity, had ceased to be a national religion in any exclusive sense. At least the special claim put forward by the later prophets was only that the Jews were to be the divinely commissioned interpreters of Monotheism to all other nations, that "through them all the families of the earth should be blessed." And though the Jewish people generally never gave up their exclusive national aspirations, yet actually they were dispersed through the Empire, and even in their own land they did not constitute an independent State. Their unity was rather like the unity of a Church. The highest utterances of their devotional spirit were individualistic in character, expressing the sorrows and joys, the aspirations and experiences, of the individual soul in its relation to God : and as the sacrificial ritual was confined to Jerusalem, the worship of the synagogue was almost completely dissociated from it, and had become a purely spiritual service—a service of teaching, prayer, and praise, and not of ceremonial observance. In this way the religious ideas of the Jews, like those of the Greeks, had become universalised and liberated from that which was national and peculiar; and the time had come when it was possible for them to be amalgamated, if not yet organically united, with each other.

Of this amalgamation I shall speak presently. But in the first instance I should like to refer to the way in which the two systems came to approximate so closely to one another. You will remember how the Stoics repudiated the philosophy of Plato and Aristotle because of its dualism, and asserted in the most emphatic way that there is no division of principles in the universe. Their so-called materialism sprang out of a deep conviction of the unity of the world, expressing itself in a denial of the distinction between matter and mind, which they treated as different aspects of the same thing. Yet they were quite unable to work out the consequences of such a unity, or to show how the one principle could manifest itself under such different forms. The result was, therefore, either a confusion of the two aspects or an alternation between them. The Stoics could not show how matter involves mind or mind matter. Hence in their theory of knowledge they were driven to explain the relation of mind to its object by the metaphor involved in the word 'impression'; and they were quite unable to meet the sceptic objection that, if this analogy be taken strictly, the mind can know nothing but its own states.   Again, on the same hypothesis, the individual must be conceived as confined to his own inner life, and incapable of direct communion with any one else.   It was, therefore, only as each individual was identified with the universal principle of all intelligence, that he could be conceived as entering into any but external relations with other individuals.   And this meant that each of them was alone in his inner life, and could escape from himself only as he found God within him.   The result was that despair of the world without, and that certitude of meeting the absolute Being in their own souls, which is so characteristic especially of the later Stoics. Thus the deep principle of subjective religion, which was to find its highest expression in the *Confessions* of St. Augustine, is already present in the *Meditations* of the Stoic Emperor, who in almost every page declares his hopelessness in regard to everything that presents itself in outward experience, and then turns away to find everything restored in those convictions that are for him bound up with his inmost consciousness of self.   Yet this restoration remains, like Plato's city in heaven, purely ideal.   That in which Marcus Aurelius finds support and consolation, is just the *idea* of a rational order realised in that world in which empirically he finds nothing but disorder, and the *idea* of a perfect communion of those very human spirits who, except in very rare instances, seem to be hopelessly divided from each other.

Now the later Judaism passes through a process of thought which is the same in essence, though the outward form of it shows all the difference between the intuitive and unspeculative mind of the Jew and the discursive and philosophical genius of the Greek. In Judaea as in Greece, the ethical and religious consciousness was at first closely united with the idea of nationality; and in Judaea as in Greece, the time came when the extinction of the political life of the nation made it necessary for that consciousness, if it were to survive at all, to attach itself to something more general. As the ruin of the City-State was the beginning of a cosmopolitan philosophy, so the subjection of the Jewish nation made it necessary for the prophets to seek for the realisation of the hopes of Israel in something wider than the Davidic kingdom—in a Messianic empire of a higher kind, which should embrace not only the Jews but all the races of mankind. But, as no such empire was in the way of being realised around them, the consciousness of it had to remain, like the Stoic ideal of a ' world-city,' a faith which found no support in experience, but maintained itself simply by its agreement with the higher self-consciousness of the time. What, however, the Greek sought in an ideal, which he believed to be one with the ultimate reality of things, the Jew sought in the picture of a future, in which the whole state of the world would be changed. The insight of the Jews expressed itself as foresight; their intuitive apprehension of truth took the form of a prophecy of a reign of the Messiah, in which all evils should be redressed and all sorrows healed. But the result was very similar in both cases. The difference was only that the practical Jewish mind could not reconcile itself to a world in which the ideal was not realised, but dwelt persistently on the hope of better things in the future. If the world were for the present given over to the control of the power of evil—and it was the general belief that it was so—yet this could be only for a time, and only to try the spirits of men. Nevertheless, as the blessing was still in prospect, and not in fruition, religion had to take the form of an inner spirit of devotion which had no outward manifestation, or which was manifested, not in the setting up of the kingdom of God on earth, but only in the private union of a number of individuals who sympathised with each other in longing for it and " waiting for the consolation of Israel." The whole life of religion was thus driven inward, and became, not a worship of God as the bond of union in an actual society, but the immediate relation of the isolated soul to him. Thus the era of ritual and sacrifice, of symbol and ceremony, by which, not as separate individuals but as members of a community, men were lifted above themselves to a sense of the principle of their common life, had come to an end; and the era of subjective religion, of the lonely struggles of the soul as it seeks for its good, and of its lonely joys as it finds that good, had begun. " What do you wish to know ? " says St. Augustine to himself in his *Soliloquies*, and the answer is: " God and the soul." " Nothing more than this ? " " This and this only." But this kind of subjective religion was initiated long before St. Augustine's time, and even before the advent of Christianity. It was independently originated both among the Jews and among the Greeks, and it was its existence which made the rapid success of Christianity possible. It ' came to its own ' and ' its own received it.' It came to men who had turned in disappointment from the world and had fallen back upon themselves and upon God; and it quickened to life their vague certitude that in spite of all, the ideal must somehow and somewhere be realised.

We have thus, as the general result in both cases, a religious consciousness which is subjective, but which, as it is universal, cannot be content to remain subjective. We have a religion which brings the individual into direct relations with God, and

withdraws him from all special connexion with the
world and with his fellow-men.   The keen interest in
knowledge for its own sake which was characteristic
of the age of Plato and Aristotle is lost, and even the
practical interest of realising a society corresponding
to man's moral requirements has all but disappeared.
The old conception of the political life has been forgotten, and the State is now regarded, not as the
highest organ of man's ethical life, but rather as a
purely legal and administrative institution for the
preservation of the rights of person and property.
And though the Jew still looks forward with obstinate
hopefulness to a Messianic kingdom, and the Stoic
strives to believe that the world, though it seems in
the concrete to be full of folly and wickedness, is yet
in some ideal way capable of being regarded as an
ordered system in which reason is the only ruler; yet
in both cases this ideal remains an aspiration, a faith
or hope which derives no support from experience.
The Jew did not believe that the Messianic kingdom
could come by any natural development out of the
actual state of things, but only by a sudden and
miraculous interference from above; and the Stoic
could scarcely be said to hope for anything, but rather
to be content, as Plato in the *Republic* tried to make
himself content, to treat the bare idea in the soul as
if it were its own realisation.   The wise man lives by
the laws of a city in the heavens which is not and

cannot be realised anywhere on earth—a city which,
in Tennyson's language,

> " is built
> To music, therefore never built at all,
> And therefore built for ever. "

We have now to trace the connexion between
the attitude of thought we have been describing,
and that to which it gave place in the last age of
Greek philosophy.   Stoicism contained a principle
of dissolution in itself.   It rested on the immediate
identification of the individual subject with universal
reason.   The individual, in other words, was conceived
to be strong in himself, just because, as rational,
he was lifted above his own existence as this
individual.   He had a proud consciousness of his own
liberty, just because he refused to identify himself
with anything finite or transitory in himself or in
the world.   This, in the main, is the point of view
of the earlier Stoics, and it is that which must be
most prominent in our minds when we try to
characterise the moral attitude of Stoicism.   But
there is another aspect of the Stoic doctrine which,
if it were emphasised, would turn the strength of
the Stoic into weakness and his pride into humility.
The individual subject cannot be identified with
divine reason, except by a process in which he is
stript of all that belongs to him as this particular
individual.   He can only live to God as he dies

to himself. This point of view could never completely prevail in the Stoic school, but we find traces of it in the later Stoics, especially in Seneca and Marcus Aurelius. In these writers we find the beginnings of a tendency which was to find expression in subsequent philosophy and, in particular, in the philosophy of the Neo-Platonists—a tendency to substitute self-despair for self-confidence, and through self-despair to rise to the religious spirit that loses to find itself in God. This change, which seemed to lead to an attitude of spirit the very reverse of that of the Stoics, was yet, as I have said, the natural development of Stoicism. But the transition was mediated by the attack upon the doctrines of the Stoics, and indeed upon all positive philosophical doctrines, which was made by that school of philosophers called, *par excellence*, the Sceptics.

To understand this, we need to remember that not only the Stoics but the Epicureans and, indeed, all the philosophers of the time were individualistic. Their main effort was to make the individual strong in himself and independent of the world; but they all committed the inconsistency—as it seemed to the Sceptics—of basing this strength upon some belief as to the nature of that world as it is in itself apart from our thoughts about it. The Sceptic, on the other hand, maintained that no such external support is necessary. We cannot know anything about the

real nature of things, for, as is admitted by all
these schools of philosophy, we know them only
through our own sensations and ideas, and these
sensations and ideas are only states of our own
subjectivity. We thus know nothing but ourselves.
But neither is it necessary to our peace that we
should know anything else; on the contrary, he
who rests on anything external to himself is resting
on something of the truth or reality of which he can
never be sure. We cannot know things in themselves, but only how they appear to us. The only
secure course is, therefore, to refrain from all
judgment as to the objective reality of things, and
content ourselves with what is within our own
consciousness. And it is just in doing so, the Sceptic
maintains, that the individual can find the peace he
seeks. For, if we rest in ourselves without commit-
ting ourselves to any affirmation as to objective
reality, we hold an impregnable position, a position
which cannot be invaded by any doubt or fear; and
in the negation of all theory we find that very
security and unity with ourselves which the dogmatic
philosophies sought in vain. The man who has
thus, as it were, retired into himself, is beyond the
reach of disturbance. The whole Sceptic philosophy
is just an attempt to prove the exclusive rationality of
this attitude of mind by a systematic attack on all
forms of dogmatism. The Sceptic endeavours to show

that every positive doctrine as to the nature of things is embarrassed by the ἰσοσθένεια τῶν λόγων, by the fact that there is an equal weight of reason for and against it. Reason, to put the matter in a more modern way, is essentially antinomical, and its exercise on any question invariably leads to the rise of two opposite dogmatisms, each of which is strong in its attack upon the other, but weak to defend itself. The only safe course, therefore, is to renounce all dogmas whatsoever, and to fall back upon the bare subjective consciousness as all-sufficient for itself.

At first the position of the Sceptic might seem to be a very strong one, and, indeed, some have thought it to be impregnable. But it really shows itself to be the weakest of all dogmatisms whenever it turns from the task of attacking others to that of defending itself. This may be seen whether we look at its positive result, or at the basis of certitude on which it is supposed to rest. From the former point of view, it is obvious that the Sceptic does not get rid of the objective consciousness by asserting that it is only a consciousness of shows or appearances. These shows or appearances, on the contrary, supply for him as for others the whole content and interest of life. The Sceptic, indeed, makes that content almost worthless, and weakens the interest in it by treating it as a mere appearance; but he has nothing else to put in its place. He has to play the game of life like others, though he is convinced that it is an illusory game, and, that the prizes in it are worth nothing; and therefore he is not in earnest in playing it. But a life that is occupied with nothing but vanity must itself be vain. We cannot say that such a consciousness is at rest in itself. We must rather say that it is given over to endless unrest, in so far as it is continually denying the reality and value of the objects, with which nevertheless it has continually to occupy itself.

But it will be contended that the soul of the Sceptic finds its rest *just in* the assertion of itself which accompanies its negation of the reality of everything else; and that in this point of view the Sceptics anticipate Descartes, who sought for the basis of all truth in the *Cogito ergo sum* of an immediate self-consciousness—a consciousness which, as he contends, is untouched by any of the doubts which may be cast on other things. We have, however, to consider, what Descartes and the Sceptics equally forget, that this consciousness of self is real-ised only with, and in relation to, the consciousness of the not-self to which it is opposed, and that, if we could altogether cancel the latter, the former would disappear with it. Hence it is impossible without con-tradiction to fall back on the consciousness of self to the exclusion of everything else. This objection was brought home to the Sceptics by an argument based upon their own doctrine, which they vainly endeavoured to repel. It was pointed out that, in asserting the incomprehensibility of things and the impossibility of knowledge, they were setting up a dogma which could be turned against itself as easily as against other dogmas. They were, as Bacon said, making a dogma of the unknowableness of things; and this dogma was, indeed, essential to that which they conceived as the practical end of philosophy, the attainment of peace in themselves. If, therefore, their doctrine were true, the practical end was impossible of attainment. This attack the Sceptics could meet only by the strange assertion that the doctrine of the impossibility of attaining truth included itself, and that, as they express it, it was like a medicine which purged itself out as well as the disease. But this is an obvious subterfuge; for a negation that includes itself contradicts itself; and, indeed, it is impossible to realise it at all, except by a *progressus in infinitum* in which each step is the negation of the previous step. We deny, and deny our denial, and deny that again, because we cannot separate any denial from a positive assertion which, *ex hypothesi*, must in its turn be got rid of. This process of thought, therefore, is a continual attempt to leap off one's own shadow, or, in other words, to deny without any affirmative basis for our denial.

The philosophy of the Sceptics, then, may be

said, in a sense which they did not intend, to purge itself out along with the disease; it is the *reductio ad absurdum* of itself. It is the attempt to get beyond the intelligible world by an act of the intelligence itself. But, as I have said elsewhere,[1] any attack upon the possibility of knowledge is foiled by the impossibility of finding a ground on which to fix its batteries: for if we try to fix them on anything *within* the intelligible world, we assert the knowableness of that world in the very act of denying it, and there is no place *without* the intelligible world where they can be fixed. We can direct our doubts or our denials against any particular assertion or doctrine, only in so far as we can fall back upon some more general consciousness of the real, which we assume as true, and with which we show it to be inconsistent; but an attempt to attack the very idea of truth and reality only leads to a reassertion of it in another form. On the other hand, to assert that the subject of knowledge is complete in itself without the object, is to rend the seamless garment of truth by setting up one element of consciousness against the whole to which it essentially belongs. But the only result that can come of such an attempt, is to show that, apart from the whole, every such element becomes meaningless and self-contradictory.

[1] *The Critical Philosophy of Kant*, I. 5 ; II. 42.

Now, in this result we see at once what is the mistake of a purely subjective philosophy and how it can be corrected. For what it forces us to realise is that the consciousness of the subject, like that of the object, presupposes a unity in which both are contained as elements. Or, to put the same thought in a more direct way, the consciousness of God, as the unity in all things and beyond all things, is the presupposition of both, and neither has any reality apart from it. Thus the logical result of Scepticism is to reveal the ultimate basis of all truth. This is not, of course, seen by the Sceptics themselves; but it underlies the general movement of thought by which the era of subjective and individualistic philosophy was brought to an end and the era of religious philosophy initiated. In this we have a remarkable illustration of the natural course of the development of thought. Philosophy in Greece, as elsewhere, begins with the objective, the not-self; then it turns from the outward world to the self; finally, it ends with the effort to grasp the principle of unity which is beyond this and all other oppositions. Unfortunately in Greece the movement from one idea to the other was mainly by a process of abstraction, in which thought as it advanced altogether set aside its previous points of view. The result, therefore, was a theology which vindicates the reality of the Divine Being at the expense of all his creatures, and represents the Absolute and Infinite as excluding rather than as including all that is relative and finite.   The failure of Stoicism to work out successfully its idea that there is an immanent principle of unity under all the differences of things and of our knowledge of them, leads subsequent philosophy to conceive God as essentially transcendent.   But in this way it becomes impossible to suppose that there is any rational connexion between him and the world, or any rational apprehension of him by the human mind.   If under such a view there is to be any relation established between God and man, the activity that produces it must be entirely on God's side, and on man's side there can be only passivity.   And if any human consciousness of God remains possible, it must be in an ecstatic condition in which man is rapt beyond himself so that all self-consciousness is absorbed and lost. Hence we have an apparently paradoxical result, the rise of a philosophy which might from one point of view be called Agnosticism, and which yet does not mean disbelief or doubt, but rather the profoundest certitude of the reality of the Absolute Being, whom man's thought cannot measure nor his words express.

Now in this aspect of it also there is a parallel movement of Jewish with Greek thought.   Even within the books of the Old Testament, we can trace

how the universalising process to which the religion
of Israel was subjected, produced an increasing
unwillingness to attribute the definite characteristics
of human individuality to God, or even to admit his
direct agency in relation to men. Such agency is
rather referred to some special power or attribute of
God, to his Wisdom or his Word, or to some angel who
has a mission from him to man. Moreover, though
there is no thought of denying God's omnipotence, yet
anything that seems to have the nature of evil is
rather attributed, directly at least, to some evil spirit.
And we know that before the Christian era this
tendency had hardened into a doctrine of demoniac
influence, and this world was even supposed to be
subjected to the rule of Satan, up to the time when
the Messiah should come to dethrone him. The
loyal allegiance of the race of Israel to the God of
Abraham, Isaac, and Jacob, whose worship was bound
up with the national life, was changed into an awful
reverence for a Being who, just because he was
conceived as the God of the whole universe, seemed to
be too high to be comprehended or even approached
by the reason of man. The idea that "no one could
see God and live," the idea that man cannot measure
or understand God, the idea of the absolute passivity
and powerlessness of man in relation to God,—these
ideas take complete possession of the religious mind.
God is so far from his worshippers that he cannot be

apprehended by them, yet so near that no room is left for any consciousness of freedom, or for the special interests of politics or science, of literature or art. A form of piety has arisen which begins and ends in religion, and which can hardly be said to supply any principle to idealise and elevate the secular life of man.

But along with this tendency to reduce the idea of God to an abstraction, till it becomes hardly possible to say anything of him except negatively, we have the appearance, both in Jewish and in Gentile literature, of another idea to which I have already alluded—the idea of mediation. The extremes which cannot be brought together directly, have to be linked with each other by means of intermediate terms. This tendency shows itself in Greek philosophy mainly in the adoption of the Stoic idea of the *Logos*, which, however, is now treated not as a name or attribute of the Supreme Being, but as the equivalent of the world-soul of Plato, that is, as the organ of the manifestation of the Supreme Being in the finite universe. Among the Jews, again, it shows itself in the tendency which I have already mentioned, to personify some attribute of God, especially his wisdom, or to bring in the ministry of angels between him and his creatures. If God be secluded in his heaven where no one can see him, yet a ladder is let down to the earth, by which divine influences may descend upon the worshipper, and by which he may be drawn up towards the source of his, and of all existence. Yet, after all, the final contact of human and divine is regarded as inexplicable, except as a trance or ecstasy in which the finite drops away from man and, in some incomprehensible way, he loses and finds himself again in God.

We have now seen what were the general features of the movement of thought towards the end of the pre-Christian era. We should need, of course, to introduce many special qualifications, if we attempted to apply the description to any particular writer. Still, enough has been done to show that, at this epoch, Jew and Gentile were tending in the same direction. Even apart from any direct influence upon each other, their thoughts were prepared to blend; and, when they did blend, it was natural that the common tendencies should be strengthened. Yet I think it essential to a comprehension of the facts that we should clearly realise that it was not the case, as is sometimes represented, that Western was overpowered by Eastern thought. Each found something in the other to help its progress in the direction in which it was naturally developing, but we cannot say that either was warped from its natural tendencies by a foreign influence. Hence each may be explained from its own history. Thus the tendency to separate God from man, and to thrust in mediators between them, and the tendency to take an almost pessimistic view of the world in its actual state, were the natural consequences of the universalising process which had begun to transform religion as early as the first prophets. And, on the other hand, when we come to Plotinus, who is the highest product of Neo-Platonism, we shall find him referring back all his doctrines to the previous philosophy of Greece; and, what is more, we shall find that he can point to sources in Plato and Aristotle, or even earlier philosophers, from which every element in it could be derived. And, though we cannot say that he simply reproduces his authorities, we are obliged to recognise that his doctrines are legitimate and even necessary developments of theirs.

Before, however, we can deal with Plotinus, it seems necessary to say something of a remarkable writer in whom the two lines of development of Jewish and Greek thought meet together, illustrating and explaining each other—a writer, who did not, indeed, succeed in reconciling these different elements, but who by his syncretism did much to bring to light their essential identity. For it was Philo who, more than any other single writer, prepared the way for that marriage of Greek thought with Christianity which was the main agency in the development of theology in the early church.

LECTURE TWENTY-FIRST.

THE PHILOSOPHY AND THEOLOGY OF PHILO.

IN the last lecture I said that Philo occupies a peculiar position in the history of theology, because he, more than any other writer, exhibits to us the process by which the two great streams of thought, from Greece and from Judaea, came to unite in one. Just at the time when Christ was teaching in Galilee, Philo in Alexandria was using the lessons of Greek philosophy to guide him in his interpretation of the Old Testament. And in one sense he was quite justified in doing so; for the development of Jewish religion had brought it to a point of view closely analogous to that which had been reached by the independent movement of Greek thought; and in the later books of the Old Testament we can discern the elements of that spiritual and universal conception of religion, which is found in Philo. Philo, therefore, it might be said, was only reading backwards into the earliest expressions of the religious ideas of Israel what was implicitly contained or involved therein. He was only looking for the oak in the acorn, for the man in the child, when in the books of the Law and the Prophets he sought for the source of his own conceptions of God and of his relations to the world.

But, even allowing that there is a measure of truth in this view of the case, we have to observe that what Philo tries to prove is not that his own doctrine is contained potentially, or in germ, in the Hebrew Scriptures. He has no conception of a historical process of evolution, nor does he make any distinction between what is implicitly contained in the Old Testament and what is explicitly expressed there. To him the Old Testament as it stands, especially the teaching of the books of the Law, is the absolute revelation of divine truth, the verbally inspired word of God, which contains once for all the declaration of God's nature and will. And as there is much in Philo's view of that nature which is not found in the letter of the Scriptures, nay even much that seems to contradict it, he is forced to maintain that that letter was intended to convey a higher truth than its immediate and obvious meaning, and that the facts narrated and the expressions used are to be understood as an allegory. So far does Philo carry this view that he contends that some things, which in their direct sense are irrational and even immoral, have been put into the text to warn the reader to look deeper for the real meaning. By a process which is sometimes called 'spiritualising,'—a process similar to that which St. Paul applies to the story of Hagar and Ishmael,— Philo gets out of the Old Testament all the conclusions to which he is led by the philosophical and religious consciousness of his own time; and he never seems to be aware that he brings with him the greater part of what he seems to find. We cannot discover in his writings any attempt to gather up the general meaning of the books of the Old Testament, or to view the parts in relation to the whole, or the earlier in relation to the later revelation of divine truth. He simply takes each chapter, verse by verse, and interprets it by certain arbitrary rules of symbolism—taking, for instance, the earth in the narrative of the creation to mean sensibility and the heavens to mean intelligence, and arguing that, when it is said that the heavens were created before the earth, it means that intelligence is prior to sense. On such a method it is not difficult for him to find, even in the first chapters of Genesis, all the main principles of his own theology.

Now this method of allegorical interpretation, which was afterwards extensively used by the Christian Fathers, and which is not altogether disused in the present day, had one recommendation. It enabled those who employed it to find a basis for their religious life in the sacred books, without being limited by the immediate meaning of those parts of the Bible which expressed the moral and religious ideas of an earlier time. It served, in fact, the same purpose, which in more modern times has been served by the theory of evolution, enabling men to connect the present with the past without allowing that connexion to become a hindrance to progress. We may realise how great a service this was, if we remember how in modern times, as among our own Puritans and Covenanters, the acceptance of the Old Testament as equally inspired with the New produced a reactionary tendency to confuse Christianity with Judaism. Such misconceptions were to a great degree precluded by the allegorical method of interpretation. Still we must acknowledge that it was, after all, an arbitrary and unscientific method, and that it altogether precluded a true view of the religious history of man, which must neither deny the fundamental identity of man with himself in all ages, nor the difference of the phases through which he has had to pass in his development.

In considering Philo's theology we have to remember the characteristics of the two terms between which he is seeking to mediate. His task is to translate Hebrew conceptions into their Greek

equivalents, and to bring Greek conceptions into a
form suited to the Hebrew mind.   But, in every formal
respect, the Greek and the Hebrew ways of thinking
are antagonistic, even where the matter or content
of their thought is most similar.   The Hebrew mind
is intuitive, imaginative, almost incapable of analysis
or of systematic connexion of ideas.   It does not hold
its object clearly and steadily before it, or endeavour
exactly to measure it;   rather it may be said to
give itself up to the influence of that which it contemplates, to identify itself with it and to become
possessed by it.   Its perceptions of truth come to
it in a series of vivid flashes of insight, which it
is unable to co-ordinate.   For the most part it
expresses its thought symbolically, and it constantly
confuses the symbol with the thing signified, or
only corrects the deficiencies of one symbol by setting
up another.   In his native language, the Hebrew has
only the scantiest means of expressing the dependence
of one thought upon another or of building up a
connected argument.   If a complex object be por-
trayed by him, it is only in large and indefinite outlines
and never as an ordered system of related parts.
Hence he is almost incapable either of grasping prosaic
fact in its bare simplicity, or of rising to a scientific
consciousness of general laws;   he lives rather in a
consciousness of the unanalysed whole, which presents
itself now in one aspect and now in another, as when

one stands before a scene which is illuminated from moment to moment by gleams of lightning.

The Greek mind, on the other hand, is essentially discursive, analytical, and systematic, governing itself even in its highest flights by the ideas of measure and symmetry, of logical sequence and connexion. Even in poetry it seeks for definite pictures, in which the object represented stands out clearly from other objects and displays distinctly all the relations of its parts. Its epics and dramas have order and organisation, so that their plots work forward logically from the first presentment of the situation to the final catastrophe; and even its lyrics have plan and sequence in the evolution of the idea that inspires them. The Muse of Greece, to use an expression of Goethe, is the companion of the poet and not his guide. The same mental characteristics are shown in the political life of the Greeks, in their historical literature, and above all in their philosophy. They are never satisfied to leave anything obscure or undefined, or to let any element stand by itself without being carefully distinguished from and related to the rest. The Homeric hero who cried for light, even if it were but light to die in, was a genuine representative of the Greek spirit. Hence, in spite of their great aesthetic capacity, their love of the beautiful and their power of creating it, there never was a nation that was less disposed to rest in the contemplation of a beautiful symbol, without trying to analyse it into its elements and discover its exact meaning. The Greek, again, was essentially reflective; he was never content to wield the weapons of thought without examining them; rather he sought to realise the precise value of every category or general term which he found himself using. And it was this that made him the creator of most of the abstract language of thought which philosophy has ever since been employing.

Now in Philo, as I have said, we find the first comprehensive attempt at a synthesis of these two modes of thought; and we need not be surprised that, in spite of the common tendencies to which I have referred in the last lecture, the amalgamation is somewhat external and incomplete. Thus, for instance, in his treatise on the creation of the world, we find him reading almost all the leading ideas of the *Timaeus* into the simple narrative of Genesis. The double account of the creation in the first and second chapters, and the phrase " every herb of the field before it grew," are supposed to express the idea that God first by the pure action of his intelligence created an ideal or intelligible world, and then, using this as his pattern, constructed the visible world out of chaotic matter. Again, the phrase: "Let *us* make man in our image" is interpreted as meaning that God, as in the *Timaeus*, has to call in the aid of angels or subordinate powers, in order to create a being who is not altogether good.[1] Philo, indeed, thinks that in so using Plato's conceptions, he is simply restoring them to their original owner: for, in his view, Plato and the other Greek philosophers had stolen all their good ideas from Moses. But this only means that Philo had become unable to read Moses except in the light of Plato. No doubt, in this process Plato also is forced to make considerable concessions. In accommodation to Jewish notions, God must be supposed to create the matter in which his ideas are realised; and the "created gods" of the *Timaeus* have to be conceived either as angels or as powers like angels, which issue from the divine nature, but which have a certain relative independence bestowed upon them. The result, therefore, is neither distinctively Greek nor distinctively Jewish; nor can we even say that it is any *tertium quid* in which the peculiar characteristics of Greece and Judaea are united. What we have in Philo is rather the imperfect product of a process of fermentation which has not yet been completed, and in which the elements combined still retain a great deal of their original form.

Passing from these general considerations, it will be sufficient for our purpose to examine how Philo deals, first, with the idea of God: secondly, with the

[1] *De Confusione Ling.*, § 33.

mediation whereby God is connected with the world: and, finally, with man's relation to God.

I have already shown how the later development of Jewish religion tended to universalise the idea of God, and to remove those special characteristics which had been at first attributed to him as the national God of the Hebrews. Also I have shown how this process found a parallel in the movement of Greek thought, by which the Stoic conception of immanent reason was set aside and the Neo-Platonic idea of a transcendent unity took its place. Both these movements have great influence on the mind of Philo. He is continually anxious to explain away the anthropomorphic traits with which in the Old Testament God is invested. When the Bible speaks of God's hands or his feet, his eyes or his face, no one supposes that it is speaking literally. As little, argues Philo, can we take it as prosaic truth, when it speaks of God as 'angry' or being 'appeased,' as being 'jealous of other gods,' or 'repenting that he had made man.' All such expressions, we are to regard as used in condescension to the needs of those who could not understand or would not be rightly impressed by any other language. The two most important statements of the law, says Philo,[1] are, first that "God is not as a man" (Numb. xxiii. 19) and second, that "he is as a man" (Deut. i. 31): but the second is introduced for the instruction

[1] Philo, *Quod Deus Immut.*, § 11; *De Somniis*, i., § 40.

of the mass of mankind, and not because God is such in his real nature. In other words, when the Scripture speaks of God as if he were a man, and attributes to him the acts and motives of men, it is by way of accommodation to the wants of those who are intellectually and morally at a low stage of culture; but for those who have got beyond this stage, whose intelligence is not limited by their imagination, and whose will is not governed by selfish fears and hopes, there is another lesson. *They* can rise to the consciousness of God as the absolute Being, to whom none of the attributes of finite things or beings can belong, not even those of humanity. Of this being we know only *that* He is and not *what* He is; and this is what is meant when God is spoken of by the name "I am that I am," which is equivalent to saying that God's true nature is not expressible by any name. We know him only *negatively*, and not *positively*: for all the predicates we can possibly attach to Him are predicates which express the contrast of his pure being with the limited and determined nature of finite creatures. Thus He is represented as *one* in opposition to their division, as *simple* in opposition to their complexity, as *immutable* in opposition to their variableness, as *eternal* and *immeasurable* in opposition to their conditioned existence in time and space. But these attributes are all to be taken as simply repelling from him every qualification by which He might be reduced to the level of his creatures, and not as expressing the infinite fulness and completeness of his own Being, which is incomprehensible to the mind of man. To determine what He is in his essential being would be impossible; for to define is to relate, and He is above relation. Even the words, " I am thy God," are, Philo declares, employed in an inexact and figurative way, and not in their primary sense; for the self-existent Being, regarded simply as self-existent, does not come under the category of relation. " He is full of himself, and sufficient to himself, equally before and after the creation of the universe; for He is un-changeable, requiring nothing else at all, so that all things belong to him, but He, strictly speaking, belongs to nothing."[1] These last words show the true movement of Philo's thought, which carries everything back to the absolute Being, but will not allow us to invert the process, or to see in the nature of that Being any necessity for the existence of any being other than himself; seeing that this would make him dependent on his creatures or responsible for their imperfections. In other words, they are regarded as related and essentially related to him, but not He to them.

Now this is just the logic of mysticism or pantheism, which carries back everything finite to the infinite but cannot think of the infinite as manifested in the

[1] " De Mutatione Nom.," § 4 : quoted by Dr. Drummond, *Philo Judaeus*, II, 48.

finite. But it was impossible for a pious Jew like
Philo to be a mystic or a pantheist, and so to reduce
the God of Abraham, Isaac, and Jacob to an absolute
substance, in whom all the reality of the world is
merged. Philo might be ready to treat as allegorical all
the expressions that seem to attach any physical character or any of the limitations of fallible, finite beings
to God; but he could not part with God's personality
or sacrifice God's moral to his metaphysical attributes.
The phrase 'strictly speaking' in the passage just
quoted partly hides and partly betrays Philo's
consciousness of the necessity of finding *some* way
in which the expression 'my God' might be justified,
and God might be conceived as going out of himself
and relating himself to his creatures. Or, if God in
his pure essence were regarded as above such a
relation, some power emanating from the divine must
be found to mediate the transition. The first naïve
solution of this difficulty—a solution which lay very
close to the Hebrew mind—was to attribute to God's
will what could not be referred to his nature; and to say
that God had chosen " out of his mere good pleasure "
to create a world and to promise certain blessings,
first, to the race of Israel, and then through them to
mankind, on condition of their obedience to his
revealed will. And when objections arose, they could
always be silenced, as they were by St. Paul, with the
question : " Who art thou, O man, that repliest against

God?" But to take this course was to cut the knot instead of untying it; and Philo was too much imbued with the spirit of Greece to rest in the bare idea of will without reason.

The sacred books, however, when interpreted in the light of the conception of the *Logos* supplied him with a better solution of the difficulty. Originally, indeed, the expression 'Word of God' had not carried with it any notion of mediation, or of a mediating being. On the contrary, in such passages as: "By the word of God were the heavens made and all the host of them by the breath of his mouth," what the writer sought to convey was rather the idea of a direct divine action which needed no mediation or instrument whatever. But gradually, as the idea of God became universalised, the same feeling which caused the name of 'Jahveh' or 'Jehovah' to be avoided, and the word 'Lord' substituted for it, gave rise to an inclination to attribute divine acts not to God but to some personification of one of his attributes, generally of his wisdom. This tendency is shown in *Ecclesiastes* and also in a still more decided form in one of the apocryphal books, *The Wisdom of Solomon*. And for Philo, who wrote in Greek and under the influence of Greek philosophical ideas, the Stoic use of the word *Logos* to express the rational principle which is immanent in man and in the universe, seemed to throw a new light on those numerous passages in the Old Testament in which the phrase 'Word of God' is used in a half-personal way. We may thus explain how Philo arrives at the notion of the Word, as a second divine principle, which connects the absolute divine power with the world—a God who reveals, as contrasted with the God who hides himself: a principle through which God creates and governs the universe, through which he binds all the parts of the finite world to each other and unites it as a whole to himself. In fact, we find concentrated in the idea of the *Logos* all that Philo has to say of God's revelation in the world as opposed to his absolute essence; and he is very fertile in forms of expression to convey the relation of this principle of revelation to God and to man respectively. In the former aspect, the Word is declared to be the Son of God, the first-born, the highest archangel, the oldest of the angels: in the latter aspect, he is said to be the man who is the immediate image of God, the ideal or prototype in whose image all other men are created.

If, however, we ask whether the Word is to be taken as an aspect of the divine nature or as a separate individual being, we find that the language of Philo is very ambiguous and uncertain. He seems to fluctuate between modes of expression which point to something like Platonic ideas, and modes which suggest the conception of the angels of the Old Testament. The separation and relative independence of the

Logos is specially emphasised when Philo is speaking of the creation of man. " Why is it," he asks, " that God declares that He made man 'after the image of God,' and not after *his own* image, as if there were another God in question ? This oracle of God is of the highest value, and what it expresses is literally true; for no mortal being could have been formed in the similitude of the Supreme Father of the universe, but only after the pattern of the second Deity, who is the Word. It was necessary that the rational part of the soul should exhibit the type of the divine Word. But while God's Word is higher than the highest rational nature, the God who is higher than the Word holds a place of singular pre-eminence and glory, and no creature can be brought into comparison with him." [1]

This passage seems certainly to suggest personal agency; yet in other places Philo seems rather to speak as if the Word were only a general name for all the attributes of God. I think, however, that two things may be made out clearly: first, that the idea of the *Logos* gains importance for Philo just because his primary conception of God is such as to make it impossible to connect Him directly with the finite: and secondly, that the Logos is viewed as the principle of all the activities that are involved in that connexion. In particular, Philo speaks of

[1] *Quaest. et Solut. in Genesin II.*, § 62.

two attributes or active powers which find their manifestation in the world, the power by which He creates and sustains the world, and the power by which He rules it: powers which roughly correspond to his *goodness* and his *sovereignty*; and he thinks that the two terms 'God' and 'Lord,' *Elohim* and *Adonai*, are used in the Bible to designate and distinguish these two powers. Thus he tells us that, while meditating on the two Cherubim who were stationed with flaming swords at the gates of Paradise, he was suddenly carried away by a divine inspiration which made him speak like a prophet concerning things he did not know. And the revelation then made to him was that in the one God there are two powers, goodness and sovereignty, and that it is by goodness that God made the world and by sovereignty that He rules it; but that there is a third Being uniting the other two, namely, the Logos, "since it is by the Word or reason of God that He is both sovereign and good. . . . For reason, and especially the causal reason, is a thing swift and impetuous, which anticipates and overpowers everything, being thought before all things, and manifesting itself in all things." [1]

In some passages it seems as if this duality of powers, and even the Logos in whom they are united, were regarded merely as an *appearance* which is due

[1] *De Cherub*, § 9.

to the imperfect apprehension of truth by the finite mind: as where it is declared that " God appears in his unity when the soul, being perfectly purified and having transcended all multiplicity, not only the multiplicity of numbers but even the dyad which is nearest to unity, passes on to the idea which is un-mingled, simple and complete in itself." [1] But if this way of thinking were followed out to its utmost consequences, the world itself must disappear in the highest Being, who is above all relation. Hence it was a logical necessity for one who would not reduce the world to an illusive appearance to regard the primal unity as going out of itself and producing a manifestation which was relatively independent of it. And from this point of view the idea of the *Word*, through whom this manifestation takes place, could not be treated as merely an accommodation to an imperfect mode of human thought.

The truth is that Philo brings the dualism, which, as we have seen, was latent both in Hebrew and in Greek thought, to a more definite expression than it had hitherto reached. He holds, on the one hand, to the idea of an absolute God, pure, simple and self-subsistent; yet, on the other hand, he cannot avoid conceiving God as a principle of being and well-being in the universe, who binds all things to each other in binding them to himself. And he

---

[1] *De Abrahamo*, § 24.

puts these two aspects together as 'two Gods,' who
yet must in some way be reduced to unity.[1] But
it was impossible for Philo to explain the nature
of this unity without either giving up the conception
of what God is in himself, or reducing the relative
independence of the principle that manifests itself
in the universe to an illusion. Sometimes, as in
the passage just quoted, he approaches the former
solution of the difficulty : sometimes, as when he is
speaking of the goodness of God as the cause of
the existence and preservation of his creatures, he
approaches the latter solution of it. But he never
definitely brings the two conceptions together, nor does
he realise fully the consequences of either alternative.

We are, therefore, left with the idea of an
absolute substance which, strictly taken, would exclude all difference and relation, even the difference
and relation of subject and object in self-consciousness; and, on the other hand, with the idea of a
self-revealing Word, who manifests himself in and to
his creatures. And Philo employs all the resources
of symbolism, allegorical interpretation, and logical
distinction, to conceal from others, and even from
himself, the fact that he is following out two
separate lines of thought which cannot be reconciled.
All that he can say is that one of these Gods is
subordinate to the other. The *Logos*, he declares,

[1] Cf. Vol. I, p. 252.

is neither uncreated like God, nor created like us;
but he is at equal distance between the extremes,
serving as a keeper of the boundaries and as a means
of communication between the two.[1] The *Logos*,
then, appears as a *second* divine principle, whose
office is to reveal the first God, but who can never
reveal him as He is, seeing that by his very nature
He is incapable of revelation: for to reveal him
would be to bring into relation a Being who, *ex
hypothesi*, is beyond and out of all relation. In strict
logic, therefore, the revelation of God—that is, the
whole universe and the divine Word who creates and
sustains it,—must not only be subordinated to the
Supreme Being, but must be merged and lost in him.
Or, if we follow the other line of thought and
dwell upon the reality of the *Logos*, we must inevitably give up the idea of his subordination: we
must treat God as essentially self-revealing, and
as 'beyond relativity' only in the sense that He
is the source of all the existences to which He
relates himself. But it was impossible for Philo
to adopt either of these alternatives without surren-
dering what for him were the essential principles
and presuppositions of all his religious and philosophical consciousness. The value of his philosophy,
therefore, lies in this, that it constitutes another
step in the evolution of the dualistic tendencies

[1] *Quis rerum*, § 47 : cf. Herriot, *Philon le Juif*, p. 259.

that underlay Greek thought from the time of
Anaxagoras, and which the Stoics vainly endeavoured
to escape. And this step had a higher significance
because it was partly the result of a similar movement in Jewish religion, and showed that the Eastern
was involved in similar difficulties with the Western
mind. For the first time in the history of the world,
these two great streams of thought had run together,
and a beginning was made in that process of fusion of
which the whole development of Christian theology
was the outcome.

The same tendencies receive further illustration
when we turn to Philo's treatment of the nature of
man and his relation to God. Take first the following passage in which the simple Mosaic narrative is
strangely re-interpreted or rather transformed by the
aid of the great myth of the *Phaedrus*: "After all
the other creatures, man, as Moses says, was made in
the image and likeness of God. And he says well;
for nothing born on earth has more resemblance to
God than man. Not, indeed, in the characteristics
of his body, for God has no outward form, but in the
intelligence which has supremacy in his soul. For
the intelligence which exists in each individual, is
made after the pattern of the intelligence of the
universe as its archetype, being in some sort the
God of the body, which carries it about like an
image in a shrine. Thus the intelligence occupies

the same place in man, as the great Governor occupies in the universe—being itself invisible while it sees everything, and having its own essence hidden while it penetrates to the essences of all other things.   Also by its arts and sciences, it makes for itself open roads through all the earth and the seas, and searches out everything that is contained in them.   And then again it rises on wings and looking down upon the air and all its commotions, it is borne upwards to the sky and the revolving heavens, and accompanies the choral dance of the planets and fixed stars according to the laws of music.   And being led by love, the guide of wisdom, it proceeds still onwards, till it transcends all that is capable of being apprehended by the senses and rises to that which is perceptible only by the intellect.   And there, seeing in their surpassing beauty the original ideas and archetypes of all the things which sense finds beautiful, it becomes possessed by a sober intoxication, like the Corybantian revellers, and is filled with a still stronger longing, which bears it up to the highest summit of the intelligible world till it seems to approach to the great King of the intelligible world himself.   And, while it is eagerly seeking to behold him in all his glory, rays of divine light are poured forth upon it, which by their exceeding brilliance dazzle the eyes of the intelligence." [1]

[1] *De Mundi Op.*, § 23.

It is easy to see that there is more of Plato than
of Moses here; and a further consideration of Philo's
psychology shows that the main difference of it from
that of Plato is just that in the former the dualistic
tendency is more fully developed. Plato's idea of
the body as the tomb or prison of the soul, his idea
of the moral life as an effort to dissociate the soul
from the passions which it acquires by its commerce
with the body, his idea that practical life involves a
disturbance of the soul's peace and a darkening of
its inner light, and that its only pure exercise is to be
found in the contemplation of absolute, ideal reality
—all these Platonic conceptions are literally accepted
by Philo. He even gives some countenance to the
extremely un-Hebraic conception that the very entrance of the soul into mortal life involves a certain
tainting of its purity. Man, for Philo, is distinctly
a "compound of dross and deity"; and the proper
object of his life-effort is declared to be the liberation
of his intelligence from its baser companion, the
attainment of that apathy, or freedom from the
passions, in which alone the spirit can energize
freely according to the inmost tendency of its own
being.

Philo, however, could not rest satisfied with this
view; he could not, like a Stoic, fall back on the
inner life, and seek to emancipate it as far as possible
from entanglement with the world; for he had learnt

that man can as little find his good within himself as he can find it without him. Hence he argues that the great source of evil lies not directly in our sensuous nature itself, but rather in the fact that it leads us to rest in ourselves and not in God. Thus, speaking of the passage in Genesis that tells how Adam sought to hide himself from God among the trees of the garden, Philo tells us that the garden means the mind of man as an individual ; and that " he who is escaping from God flees to himself." For there are only two principles which can exercise power over our life, the mind of the universe which is God, and the separate mind of the individual. He, therefore, " who escapes from his own mind flies to the mind of the universe, confessing that all the things of the human mind are vain and unreal, and attributing everything to God ; while he who seeks to escape from God declares by so doing that God is not the cause of anything, and looks upon himself as the cause of all that exists." [1] Hence the soul that would attain to the heritage of God must not only despise the flesh and regard all the objects of outward sense as things which have no real exis-tence, it must not only free itself from all the illusions of speech and opinion, but it must also flee from itself and empty itself of all self-love and all trust in anything which is its own.[2] If, there-

[1] *Leg. Alleg.*, III, § 9.   [2] *Quis rerum*, § 14-16.

fore, self-knowledge be the beginning of wisdom, it is because it involves self-despair; and he only who has despaired of himself can know Him who eternally is.[1]

"Only he who dies to himself can live to God." There is a sense in which this is the highest of all truths, the truth which constitutes the essence of Christianity. But, as it appears in Philo, in connexion with a dualistic view of human nature, it seems to mean, *not* that we find God in so far as our individual nature becomes the organ of a higher spirit, but only that we find God in so far as all individual life is expelled from us or reduced to inactivity. And this appears to be the ultimate thought of Philo, which is expressed in his doctrine of ecstasy. For, according to this doctrine, the highest perfection of man is not the realisation of his nature as man, not the development of all his powers of mind and will, but an absorption of them in the divine vision, which annihilates all consciousness of himself and of the world. Philo is too much of a Jew to accept the ultimate consequences of this view; but it is obviously the conclusion to which his philosophy points, and it is only imperfectly warded off by his doctrine of the *Logos*. For, if God is not in his own essential nature a self-manifesting being, but is withdrawn from all relation to his creatures, it is clear that man can

[1] Drummond, II, p. 288.

become united to God only as he rises above his own existence as a creature.

Here also, therefore, in relation to human nature, we find Philo's ideas as to the transcendence and the immanence of God warring with each other; and, as the former is that to which he gives the precedence, the perfection of man for Philo is that he should rise not only above sense but also above intelligence, till his whole being is lost in the absolute One. Yet, on the other hand, we have to remember that, though subordinated, the ideas of God as self-revealing, and of the universe and especially man as his revelation, are never entirely lost sight of; and that the contradiction between these two views never leads Philo to abandon either aspect of his doctrine, or to seek for a narrow logical consistency at the expense of its comprehensiveness. Hence, if he has not solved the great problem of his time, we may fairly say that he first *stated it in all its fulness*. Or, to put it more directly, he first gave utterance to both of the two great requirements of the religious consciousness, the need for rising from the finite and relative to the Absolute, and the need of seeing the Absolute as manifested in the finite and relative; although he could find no other reconciliation of these two needs except externally to subordinate the latter to the former. It was this problem with which the Neo-Platonic school from its foundation to its close continued persistently to wrestle. But we have hardly a right to say that its efforts were unsuccessful, until we have considered how it was dealt with by a man of far greater philosophical power than Philo, by the greatest of all mystics, *Plotinus.*

LECTURE TWENTY-SECOND.

THE GENERAL CHARACTER OF THE PHILOSOPHY
OF PLOTINUS.

PLOTINUS is one of the greatest names in the history
of philosophy, the classical representative of one of
the main lines of human thought; he is the Mystic
par excellence.   And what makes his Mysticism more
important is that he presents it as the ultimate
result of the whole development of Greek philosophy.
Further, if we look to the development of thought
after Plotinus, we can see that it was mainly through
him, and through St. Augustine as influenced by
him, that Mysticism passed into Christian Theology
and became an important element in the religion
of the middle ages and of the modern world.

What is Mysticism?   It is religion in its most
concentrated and exclusive form; it is that attitude
of the mind in which all other relations are swallowed
up in the relation of the soul to God.   This conception may become more intelligible if we recall

one or two points in the nature and history of religion. The relation of the soul to God—of the individual, conscious of his finitude, to the whole in which he and all other creatures are embraced, and to the principle or Being who gives unity to that whole—is not at first a clearly recognised factor, much less a predominant factor, in the conscious life of man. But it is always implied in that life; it is presupposed in all our consciousness of the world and of ourselves; and reflexion makes us aware that, without the recognition of it, we cannot understand either the intelligible world or the mind that knows it. Further, it is *the* fact from which religion springs; for it is just because this idea underlies all our consciousness that we are unable to rest in any finite object, or even in the whole world of finite objects, as complete in itself or as a perfect satisfaction of all our desires; and, for the same reason, we are equally unable to find such complete reality or such perfect satisfaction in the inner life of the self or in any of its states as such.

This inability to rest in the finite as its own final explanation, or to be satisfied with it as an ultimate good, is the real source of the superstitions that darken and confuse the life of the savage. It is the source, at a more advanced stage, of that imaginative effort to idealise particular objects, and, above all, to idealise man himself, which is the creator of mythology.   Finally, as the reflective tendency, the tendency to turn back upon the self, gains predominance over the tendency to seek reality in external objects, it is the source of a subjective religion, such as appeared in later Israel, a religion that divests its God of every likeness to anything in the heavens above or in the earth beneath or in the waters under the earth, which, in short, removes from him everything but the bare nature of a thinking subject as such.   In this latter religion God, as a spiritual being, seems to come close to the very self of man and to lay his hand directly upon man's inner life, upon " the very pulse of the machine "; yet at the same time to stand apart from him as another self, before whom "his mortal nature doth tremble like a guilty thing surprised."   " Whither shall I go from thy spirit, whither shall I flee from thy presence ?   If I ascend up into heaven, there art thou : if I make my bed in hell, behold thou art there."   The thought of God's holiness, his utter isolation and stainless purity, and at the same time of a nearness to man which is yet complete separation from him, makes the worshipper shrink into himself with an awe of which he can only partly free himself by the most scrupulous obedience to the divine laws.   For to think of the Absolute as spiritual, and yet as standing over against us like another finite subject—between whom and our own subjectivity a great gulf is fixed—is to have religion in its sternest form, a religion which may purify the soul from the base compliances of idolatry, but which at the same time is apt to petrify it in its isolation.   In spite of its moral spirit, however, we have to recognise that this religion also, so long as it remains in its pure type, falls short of the idea of religion ; for the worship of a God who is conceived as an abstract subject, though more elevating, is as one-sided as the worship of a God who is conceived purely as an object.   And we cannot say that the principle of religion has become self-conscious, till God is clearly conceived as the unity presupposed in all being and all thought, the One who is alike beyond mere subjectivity and mere objectivity.

Now the Mysticism which finds its classical expression in Plotinus consists just in the predominant and even exclusive consciousness of this negative unity. God, for the Mystic, is the One who is presupposed in all, God as God, as the unity above the difference of subject and object, to which everything is related and which itself is related to nothing.   The Absolute One is, indeed, necessarily conceived as the source of all that is ; but, for Mysticism, the negative so decisively preponderates over the positive relation, that God and the world cannot be included in one thought.   The religious consciousness thus tends to exclude and substitute itself for all other consciousness, leaving no place, or at least a quite separate and lower place, for any intellectual interest in nature or man as apart from the contemplation of God, or for any practical interest in secular ends, social or individual, apart from the realisation of God's life within us. Something of the same purely religious attitude of mind had been shown, no doubt, in later Judaism; but the Jew was always defended against the extreme of Mysticism by his strong sense of the separate personality of God and man, and, as a consequence, his vivid consciousness of moral obligation as involved in the worship of God. In Plotinus, however, the barrier between the infinite and the finite is thrown down, and the former is brought into immediate contact with the latter, so that every distinction and relation of the finite vanishes away. Religion ceases to be the consecration of life or of any of its secular interests, and becomes itself the whole of life—the gulf into which man throws all his earthly joys and sorrows, the anodyne with which he puts to sleep the energies of will and thought, all the cares of his divided life, and ultimately his divided life itself. For the one supreme desire of the Mystic comes to be this : to merge the consciousness both of the world and of himself in the consciousness of God, or rather, we should say, in God himself.

Now such a view, as I have already indicated,[1]

[1] Vol. I, p. 34.

carries with it a complete inversion of all our ordinary thought. The ordinary consciousness indeed rests on the presupposition of a unity beyond all difference; but it does not directly set that unity before itself as an object, or at least, does not treat it as exclusive of other objects. Here, on the other hand, the unity is no longer presupposed, but made the immediate object of thought; and, in the direct gaze at it, everything, even the thought which makes it an object, seems to be cancelled. The world is not denied a lower kind of reality, but its interests are regarded as external to the higher life; and the soul, emptied of all finite content, can have no desire but to break down the last barrier which separates it from the divine.

At this point, however, there arises a peculiar difficulty of Mysticism, which tends even to confound it with its extreme opposite. For the mystic who finds everything in God seems to speak the same language as the Agnostic who finds nothing in him, or who finds in him only the negation of all that we can perceive or know or think. In the ascent to the divine unity, the mystic loses hold of everything by which he could positively characterise it, and when he arrives at it, it is with empty hands. He begins by separating from it everything that is material, removing from it every attribute which we attach to things conditioned by time and space.

Mysticism Agnosticism

He is thus enabled to determine it as eternal and indivisible " without variableness or shadow of turning," as resting ever in its own pure self-identity. But he cannot stop here; he must go on to deprive it of all, even ideal, activity. Thus, in the first place, he excludes from it all discursive thought, all thought which moves by inference from one point to another; for such discourse of reason, he contends, always involves incompleteness, involves that we pass from one imperfect notion to another, seeking to complete our consciousness of the object or to find an ultimate reason for it. Thus there remains only the possibility of a pure self-consciousness, such as Aristotle attributes to the divine Being, an intuitive consciousness which, in one supreme act of vision, sees the whole as one with itself through all its differences. But Plotinus declares that even such a consciousness as this, even pure self-consciousness with its transparent duality of subject and object, must rest upon a unity which is above itself. To find the absolute One, therefore, we must free ourselves from all the conditions of an intelligence which goes out of itself to any object, even if that object be immediately recognised as identical with itself. The absolute unity, which is the presupposition of all difference, is, as Plato had said, " beyond being " and " beyond knowledge "; for even the 'I am' of self-consciousness breaks away from it.

" Wherefore," says Plotinus,[1] " it is in truth unspeakable; for if you say anything of it, you make it a particular thing. Now that which is beyond everything, even beyond the most venerable of all things, the intelligence, and which is the only truth in all things, cannot be regarded as one of them; nor can we give it a name or predicate anything of it. But we try to indicate it to ourselves as we are able. When, therefore, in our difficulties about it, we say that it neither perceives itself, nor is conscious of itself, nor knows itself, it must be considered that, in using such language, we are getting at it through its opposites. Thus, if we speak of it as knowable and as knowing, we are making it manifold; while if we attribute thought to it, we are treating it as in need of thinking. If, indeed, in any way we suppose thinking to be associated with the One, we must regard such thinking as unessential to it. For what thought does is to gather many elements to a unity and so to become conscious of a whole; and this it does even when it is its own object, as is the case in pure thinking. But such a self-consciousness is one with itself, and has not to search beyond itself for anything; whereas, if thought be directed to an external object, it has need of that object and is not pure thinking. Thus that which is absolutely simple and self-sufficient needs

[1] V, 3, 13.

nothing whatever, while that which is self-sufficient in
the second degree, needs nothing but itself, that is, it
needs only to think itself. And its end being only
in relation to itself, it makes good its own defect and
attains self-sufficiency by the unity which it gives to
all the elements of its consciousness—having communion with itself alone and directing all its thought
to itself. Such consciousness, then, is the perception of
a manifold content, as indeed is indicated by its name
($\sigma\nu\nu\alpha\iota\sigma\theta\eta\sigma\iota\varsigma = conscientia$); and the thinking which is
presupposed in it, when it thus turns upon itself, *ipso
facto* finds its unity broken : for even if it only says,
'I am in being,' it speaks as one who makes a
discovery, and that with good reason, for being is
manifold. Thus when in the very act of apprehending its own simple nature, it declares 'I am in
being' ($\mathring{o}\nu$ $\epsilon\mathring{\iota}\mu\acute{\iota}$), it fails to grasp either being or
itself. . . . It appears, therefore, that, if there is
something which possesses absolute simplicity, it
cannot think itself."

"How, then, are we to speak of it ? " asks Plotinus.
"We speak, indeed, *about* it," he answers, "but itself
we do not express : nor have we any knowledge or
even thought of it. How, then, can we speak of it at
all, when we do not grasp it as itself ? The answer
is that, though it escapes our knowledge, it does
not entirely escape *us*. We have possession of it in
such a way that we can speak of it, but not in such

a way that we can express it; for we can say what it *is not*, but not what it *is*. Hence we speak of it in terms borrowed from things that are posterior to it, but we are not shut out from the possession of it, even if we have no words for it. We are like men inspired and possessed, who know only that they have in themselves something greater than themselves —something they know not what—and who, therefore, have some perception of that which has moved them, and are driven to speak of it, because they are not one with that which moves them. So it is with our relation to the absolute One. When we use pure intelligence, we recognise that it is the mind within the mind, the source of being and of all things that are of the same order with itself; but we see at the same time that the One is not identified with any of them but is greater than all we call being, greater and better than reason and intelligence and sense, though it is that which gives them whatsoever reality they have." [1]

In these words we have a picture of the embarrassment of the mystic when he tries to say what is that divine unity which is above all things. He is obliged to dismiss, one after another, every predicate as inadequate, and to characterise the One as the negation of all things other than itself. Even the names 'Good' and 'One' he finally has to reject as

[1] V, 3, 14.

expressing rather what it is in relation to us than what it is in itself. And to say that this relation is negative, and that, for instance, we call it 'One' simply in opposition to the multiplicity of the finite, does not enable us to escape the difficulty; for a negative relation is still a relation, and must have some positive basis. Nor would there be any meaning even in denying a predicate of a subject with which it had no point of community.

If, therefore, we are to cut off all such community between the Absolute and Infinite and the relative and finite, we cannot even negatively relate the former to the latter. But thus we seem to be landed in the abyss of Agnosticism, and to have lost the last characteristic by which our thought could take hold of the Absolute. We cannot even determine it by negation of the finite, but have to go on to deny even our negative predicates. Such failures in our speech as to the Absolute are for Plotinus explained by the fact that the Absolute is not presented as a definite object but κατὰ παρουσίαν ἐπιστήμης κρείττονα,[1] in an immediate contact which is above knowledge. What we are speaking of is too near to us to become properly an object for our thought, and when we try to make it an object, we fall away from it. And the difficulty seems to be that while in every move-

[1] VI, 9, 4.

ment of our thought we always presuppose it, we are always looking from it to something else, and to look directly at it, and to realise it in itself, is for our consciousness to return, as it were, to the source from which it sprang, and to lose itself therein. It is to still all the movement of the world without and of the soul within, and to be filled with God alone. It is, in the expressive language of Plotinus, the "flight of the alone to the Alone," of the spirit divested of all finitude to the absolute One.[1]

The flight
the alone
the Alone

In Plotinus then we see in an extreme form the religious inversion of man's ordinary consciousness. Our ordinary consciousness rests, indeed, as all intelligence must rest, on a presupposed unity, but it seldom makes that unity the direct object of thought, still less separates it from all other objects, as that which is central, all-inclusive and all-transcending. Nor does religion at first altogether change, though it may modify, this ordinary way of thinking. Rather, in spite of occasional movements of feeling, in which the infinite, as it were, breaks in upon the finite, it on the whole remains a secular consciousness, for which the world is a collection of independent things and beings, and the good of man's life still seems to lie in a number of separate interests—of which religion is only one, though it may be one of the most important. God is not yet represented

[1] VI, 9, 11.

as the absolute One, in whom we and all things "live and move and have their being." Thus we seem to move from one thing to another, from one interest to another, while the all-encompassing circle, within which all objects and interests are comprehended, can hardly be said to exist for us. Our thought rests on difference as the primary fact—on the difference of one thing from another and of the self from the not-self—and, if the unity be recognised at all, it is as a unity of external relation or synthesis. It is a great step in advance, nay, it is like a rending of the veil under which the meaning of life is hid, when it is realised that all the differences of our consciousness presuppose its unity. And it is not unnatural that when this consciousness first arises, it should appear in a one-sided and exclusive form. Mysticism, as it is expressed by Plotinus, represents the first overpowering realisation of this idea, in which no place, or at least no logical place, is left for any other thought. We can, therefore, understand how it is that he dwells so much upon the conception that the One is always with us and within us, though we seldom realise its nearness. But, just because we do not realise this, our life, he contends, is disorganised and at discord with itself, or rather with a principle in it which is deeper even than the self. We look outward instead of looking inward, and we look inward instead of looking upward. Our

[margin note: ife is ganised discord]

[margin note: ook out-d, instead inward]

first is that which ought to be last, and our last is that which ought to be first.

The only way, therefore, in which we can put ourselves in harmony with the truth of things and of our own being, is by an entire inversion of the usual attitude of our consciousness. "A soul that knows itself," he declares, "must know that the proper direction of its energy is not outwards in a straight line," that is, out from itself to an object, "but that it moves in that way only by external influence; while the movement that really conforms to its nature is round about a centre, a centre which is not without but within it. In this, its true movement, then, it will circle round that principle from which it derives its life, and will attach itself to the same centre to which all souls ought to cling. To that centre the gods always move, and it is because they so move that they are gods; for that which is closely attached to the central principle is divine; while a soul that withdraws itself from that centre sinks into a man with his complex and animal nature." [1] Yet Plotinus bids us remember that all this is merely an analogy; for the soul is not a circular figure in space, nor does it move in a circular course, and what is expressed by this metaphor is a relation of spiritual nearness and dependence. We have therefore to use

[1] An allusion to the θηρίον ποικίλον καὶ πολυκέφαλον of Plato (*Rep.* 588 c). Cf. *Phaedrus*, 230 A.

the analogy without forgetting its difference from the
thing illustrated.   For " bodies by their nature cannot
enter into real communion with other bodies, but
incorporeal things are not kept apart by corporeal
obstructions.   If they are separated from each other
it is not by place but by difference and antagonism of
nature, and when this disappears they are immediately
present to each other.   Now the One, having no difference in it, is, therefore, omnipresent; and we are
always present to it, except in so far as we alienate
ourselves from it.   It, indeed, cannot make us its aim
or centre, but it is itself our true aim and centre.
Thus we are always gathered around it, though we do
not always turn towards it.   We may compare ourselves to a chorus which is placed round a Choragus,
but which sings out of tune so long as it directs its
attention away from him to external things; but when
it turns to him, it sings in perfect harmony, deriving
its inspiration from him.   So it is with us: we are
always gathered around the divine centre of our being ;
and, indeed, if we could withdraw from it, our being
would at once be dissolved away, and we should cease
to exist at all.   But, near as it is to us, often we do
not direct our eyes to it.   When, however, we do so
direct our gaze, we attain to the end of our desires
and to the rest of our souls, and our song is no more
a discord, but, circling round our centre, we pour forth
a divinely inspired chorale.   And in the choral dance

we behold the source of our life, the fountain of our intelligence, the primal good, the root of the soul." [1]

This passage is a good illustration of the way in which Plotinus becomes possessed with a sacred enthusiasm which turns his words into poetry, whenever he tries to express the relation of the soul to God. I quote them, however, for another purpose, namely, as expressing very clearly his view that the usual attitude of the soul is essentially perverted. In the ordinary consciousness, we take shadows for realities, and realities for shadows; we are equally blind to our own nature and to the nature of the things around us. The beginning of wisdom for us, therefore, is to renounce all that from this false point of view we seem to know. Still, even when we do make this renunciation, we are at first like men who turn from the reflexions of light in other things to the sun, and who, though they are looking at pure light, are so dazzled by it that they can see nothing at all. So, in turning our souls to the unity, which is the presupposition of all our consciousness of other things, we lose sight of every image of sense or imagination, and we are even carried beyond all the definite thought by which we distinguish one object from another. We are, so to speak, in perfect light, where we can see as little as in perfect darkness. For all definite thought of objects or of ourselves is got by

[1] VI, 9, 8.

distinction of elements within the whole, and when we turn our thoughts to the unity of the whole itself, we can find nothing by which to characterise it. Even the attempt to characterise it by negation, as we have seen, is self-contradictory : for that which is negatively related to the finite, is still finite. Thus the inmost experience of our being is an experience which can never be uttered, or which becomes self-contradictory whenever it is uttered.

This is the difficulty with which Plotinus is ever struggling, and we might say passionately struggling, using all the resources of intellect and imagination in the effort to exhibit and overcome it. To this he returns again and again from new points of view, as if driven by the pressure of a consciousness which masters him, which by its very nature can never get itself uttered, but which yet he cannot help striving to utter. He pursues it with all the weapons of a subtle dialectic, endeavouring to find some distinction which will fix it for his readers, and he is endlessly fertile in metaphors and symbols by which he seeks to flash some new light upon it. Yet in all this struggle and almost agony of effort after expression, he is well aware that he can never find the last conclusive word for it; and he has to fall back on the thought that it is unspeakable, and that his words can only be useful if they stimulate the hearer to make the experience for himself. "God," says Plotinus, "is neither to be expressed in speech nor in written discourse; but we speak and write in order to direct the soul to him, and to stimulate it to rise from thought to vision, like one who points the upward road which they who would behold him have to traverse. Our teaching reaches so far only as to indicate the way in which they should go, but the vision itself must be their own achievement." [1] In other words, we can stimulate men and set them in the way to realise what is the inmost fact of their being; but we cannot reveal to them what everyone must discover for himself, because it lies beyond sense, beyond imagination, and even beyond intelligence, and can only be realised in an ecstasy of unutterable feeling.

There is, however, a certain ambiguity about such expressions, which it is important for us to clear up before we go further. For, up to a certain point, the language of Mysticism and the language of Pantheism are identical with each other, or separated only by subtle differences which it requires some discrimination to detect. Thus the words of Tennyson—

"That which we dare invoke to bless,
    Our dearest faith, our ghastliest doubt,
    He, They, One, All, Within, Without,
    The Power in darkness whom we guess"—

might seem to express only that mingled certitude and despair with which Plotinus approaches the ultimate

[1] VI, 9, 4.

secret of spiritual life ; but they really indicate something more.   They are the utterance of one who seeks
God *in* the world and not *out of* it, though in the
failure of language to express the fulness of his consciousness of the Infinite in the finite, he is forced
to borrow the language of an Agnostic.   The positive
meaning, however, is perceptible through the negation,
though Tennyson is still something of a mystic.

But hear another voice in which the Pantheistic
note rings out more clearly.   When in Goethe's *Faust*
Gretchen questions the hero of the play whether
he believes in God or no, the answer is : " Who may
name him, or who can venture to declare ' I believe
in him ? '   Who can feel him, and who can dare
to say : ' I believe in him not ? '   The All-embracer,
the All-sustainer, does He not embrace and sustain
thee, me, himself ?   Does not the heaven arch over
us and the earth stand firm beneath ?   And do not
the eternal stars arise and look down upon us as with
the eyes of a friend ?   Do not I see eye to eye with
thee, and do not all things at once press home upon
thy heart and brain, and weave themselves together
in eternal mystery, visibly, invisibly, around thee ?
Fill thy heart full with it, and when thou art entirely
wrapt up in the bliss of feeling, call it what thou
wilt, call it joy, heart, love, God.   I have no name
for it : feeling is all in all ; names are but noise and
smoke clouding the glow of heaven."

All this seems at first closely akin to the ecstasy of Plotinus, but there is an essential difference which reveals itself when we look more closely. We have passed with Goethe from the transcendent God of Mysticism to the immanent God of Pantheism, from Plotinus to Spinoza. But the likeness and difference of the two systems is such that it may be useful to dwell for a short time upon the comparison of them.

Spinoza, like Plotinus, rises to the assertion of the one substance by negation of all that is finite, and for him all that is determined is finite. It is his doctrine that '*determinatio est negatio*,' and that, therefore, to get rid of all negation we must drop all determination. But thus the ultimate reality will be absolutely indeterminate, and in seeking for a purely positive or affirmative being, a substance which is beyond all limitations, we seem to be landed in the most abstract of all negations. Spinoza, however, immediately identifies the idea of the *indeterminate* with that of the self-determined, the *causa sui*, which is perfectly determined by itself, and, therefore, receives no determination from without, but is rather the source of the determination of all other things. And, on this basis, he proceeds to treat the one substance as manifesting itself in an infinity of attributes and modes. It is, indeed, an important question, whether in this second process he does not contradict the first or, in other words, whether, in the movement downwards, he can consistently reassert the reality of that which in his movement upwards he has denied to be real. But for my present purpose I need not farther explain or criticise the logic of his system. I need not ask whether Spinoza has justified his transition from the indeterminate to the self-determined, or whether, in his negation of the limits of the finite, he still leaves it open to himself to admit a reality in finite things, which is *not* negated: whether, in other words, he has a right on his own principles to conceive of the absolute substance as manifesting itself in attributes and modes. In any case it is very clear that he does so conceive it, and that for all those finite things, which he treats as negative and illusory in themselves, he finds in God a ground of reality, of a self-assertive, self-determining, self-maintaining being, which can as little be destroyed or annihilated as the divine substance itself. Nay, we may even say that for Spinoza the divine substance is not, except as it is in them. Spinoza's philosophy is, therefore, a true pantheism. Everything is lost in God, yet in a sense everything is again found in him. And God, as is indicated in the oft-quoted phrase *Deus sive Natura*, is conceived as the immanent principle of the universe; or perhaps we should rather say the universe is conceived as immanent in God. When, therefore, it is said that Spinoza is 'not an Atheist but an Akosmist,' in other words, that he denies the reality of the world but not of God, this, if it be the truth, is not the whole truth. For to Spinoza both movements of thought—the movement by which he dissolves the finite in the infinite, and the movement by which he finds the finite again in the infinite—are equally essential. If for him the world be nothing apart from God, on the other hand, God is nothing apart from his realisation in the world.

Now this Spinozistic solution of the difficulty is not possible for Plotinus. With him the *via negativa* involves a negation of the finite or determinate in all its forms, which makes it impossible to find the finite again in the infinite. The Absolute One decisively repels the many, and cannot in any way admit difference or multiplicity into itself. Its unity, therefore, must be conceived not as immanent but as transcendent. And if it be still connected with the determinate and manifold, it must be only as its external cause or source, and not as a principle which manifests itself therein. The One must, indeed, be the fountain from which all being springs, but it cannot be the reality into which all other existence is taken up and absorbed. Plotinus is, therefore, not a pantheist but a mystic; and though he refers everything to God, yet he cannot, like Spinoza, treat either the material or the spiritual world, either extension or

[margin note:] Plotinus (not find finite in infinite

[margin note:] Plotinus : not a pa but a my

thought, as the attributes of God. Hence, if in the upward movement of his logic, Plotinus distinctly leaves behind every order of being, even the intelligence, and in a sense condemns them all as unreal, yet this with him is no merging of all or any form of finitude in the infinite. Thus we have the strange paradox that the Being who is absolute, is yet conceived as in a sense *external* to the relative and finite, and that He leaves the relative and finite in a kind of unreal independence, an independence which has no value, and yet from which it as finite cannot escape. These words, indeed, as we shall see afterwards, do not express the exact thought of Plotinus, but they may serve sufficiently to indicate that aspect of his system which I am trying to illustrate, namely, that while he thinks the true attitude of the soul to be one in which the light of reason is extinguished in the ecstasy of union with God, he at the same time regards the spiritual world as in some way coming out from God, and even as repelled into difference from him. The soul seeks to lay down the burden of its finitude, to escape from the body and to rise above all the interests of its finite life; even of its very consciousness of self it would divest itself, as of something that still shuts it out from God. But this last barrier is so strong that the soul cannot, except for a few favoured moments, forget its separate existence. Thus we have, on the one side, a life which is nothing apart from God, and which, nevertheless, can never be united to him, except as it loses itself altogether; and, on the other side, an Absolute, which yet is not immanent in the life which it originates, but abides in transcendent separation from it. It is this contradiction which gives a kind of troubled intensity to the writings of Plotinus and makes them the supreme expression of Mysticism.

LECTURE TWENTY-THIRD.

THE PLACE OF PLOTINUS IN THE DEVELOPMENT OF GREEK PHILOSOPHY.

In the last lecture I tried to define the position of Plotinus as the great representative of Mysticism. I showed that up to a certain point the logic of Mysticism and that of Pantheism were alike. Both point to an absolute unity which is presupposed in all existence and in all knowledge; and both regard it as essential to a true view of things that the consciousness of this unity should be awakened, and that it should be treated as the basis of everything else, the principle upon which all other truth depends. Both, therefore, follow the *via negativa*, and regard our ordinary view of finite things as one that must be abandoned, and even inverted, by him who would know the reality which is hid beneath appearance. But here the similarity ends. For, in the first place, the Pantheist—at least if we take Spinoza as representing Pantheism in its most characteristic form—is one who thinks it possible to have knowledge and, indeed, scientific knowledge of the Absolute; while for Plotinus the Absolute is beyond knowledge, and can only be apprehended in an ecstasy in which all distinct thought is swallowed up and lost. And, in the second place, Spinoza, though he agrees with Plotinus in maintaining that we must transcend our immediate consciousness of things in order to reach the Absolute, yet contends that neither the ideas of matter and mind, nor even those of individual minds and bodies, are in this process finally negated and abolished. On the contrary, they are taken up into our thought of the Absolute and reproduced from it. If, therefore, all things, as represented in our immediate experience, are treated as illusory and unreal, yet it is held that there is a higher point of view from which we can see all things in God, and that, as so seen, they have a divine reality. On the other hand, though Plotinus holds that all things and all minds presuppose the absolute unity, and that we can understand neither the world nor ourselves except in relation to it, he cannot admit that it is immanent in them or they in it. Rather he conceives the One as complete in itself apart altogether from the natural, and even from the spiritual world; nor will he admit that either sense or intelligence can apprehend God in his essential being. Hence the universe is for Plotinus a hierarchy of powers stretching up from the darkness of matter to the light of pure intelligence; and even the highest of these powers is regarded only as a product of the Absolute and not as in organic unity with it. These powers, indeed, to use a favourite metaphor of Plotinus, are at best but the images placed outside the temple, which cannot express or represent the perfect beauty of the God within. As for the Hebrew religion there was a Holy of Holies, into which the High Priest could enter only once a year, so for Plotinus the One is a God that hides himself, and can only be apprehended by the spirit in the rare moments when it has stripped itself of all finite conditions, and even of its conscious intelligence.

Now at first it might seem impossible to explain this view of Plotinus without falling back on some eastern influence. When we consider how Plato regarded the vision of the poet and the prophet as, indeed, inspired, but an inspired madness—in other words, as a kind of intuitive perception which could give no intelligible account of itself, and was therefore far lower than the reflective insight of the philosopher, it seems absurd that Plotinus should appeal to *him*, as the founder of a philosophy which maintains that we approach nearest to the divine in an ecstatic state of feeling in which all definite thought is lost. When, also, we remember how Plato exalted the dialectical process, as enabling us to reach a comprehension of the universe, not as a bare unity nor as a collection of separate elements, but as an organic system, in which the whole should be known through the distinction and relation of all the parts, it seems strange that Plotinus should attribute to him a theory which separates the highest unity from all difference and regards the world not as an organism, but as a hierarchy of degrees of reality, rising up to an Absolute which transcends them all. Still less, it might be thought, can we find anything like the Mysticism of Plotinus in the definite conceptions and clearly articulated logic of Aristotle, whose God is self-conscious reason, and whose interest is so far from being absorbed by theology, that it extends to every form of finite existence. And, if in the Post-Aristotelian schools we find a narrowing of such interests and a tendency to concentrate on the subjective life of the individual, yet a system like that of the Stoics, which laid such emphasis on the unity of all things, and especially on the ultimate identity of mind and matter, and which regarded God as immanent in the universe, could hardly be supposed to have much affinity with a philosophy which separated the material from the spiritual, and withdrew God altogether from the world. Looking at the history of Greek philosophy in this way, we might be disposed to regard the Mysticism of Plotinus, not as the culminating phase of Greek thought, but rather as a complete transformation of it by some powerful influence from the East.

A closer view of the facts, however, enables us to see that the philosophy of Plotinus was no product of the East, but the legitimate outcome of the previous history of Greek speculation; and that, however Eastern influences may have affected it, they acted only as favourable conditions for its own development. It may, I think, be shown that the idea of the transcendent and unknowable unity of the Absolute is simply the final expression of that dualistic tendency, which had been working in Greek philosophy from the time of Anaxagoras.

The first step in this direction is taken in the *Philebus* and *Timaeus* in which the intelligible world of ideas, which is eternal, unchanging, and in perfect unity with itself, is set in opposition to the world of sense which exists in time and space, and is therefore essentially manifold, ever in conflict with itself and perpetually changing. Further, while this intelligible world in its unity is identified with the divine intelligence, the world of sense is regarded as having its basis or substratum in an infinite or indefinite something which Plato seems to identify with space or with that which gives to phenomena their spatial and temporal character. And, in connexion with this, Plato already gives expression to an idea which was to play a great part in Plotinus, the idea that the sensible world is a mere image or semblance of the ideal world, and that matter is the quasi-substance in which this image is reflected, and in which it takes its peculiar form. Lastly, Plato maintains that, while the intelligible world is the object of pure intelligence, the sensible world is apprehensible only by sense and opinion. We are not, therefore, to take the world of sense and opinion as objectively identical with the intelligible world, or the intelligible world as only the world of sense perfectly understood. On the contrary, it is his view that the sensible world cannot be apprehended by the pure reason, for it has in it a material element which can be grasped only by a kind of 'spurious intelligence'; in other words, we can only explain it by imperfect analogies borrowed from the relations of things in the sensible world itself, such as the clay used by the artist to mould his figures, or the passive mirror in which reflexions are cast from without. Hence it follows that the sensible world in its spatial and temporal existence, its self-externality and change, has something which permanently baffles conception and definition.

This contrast reappears in an even stronger form in the philosophy of Aristotle. It is true that from one point of view Aristotle corrects the negative

conception of the world of sense to which Plato
tended. He refuses to give that world up to opinion
and reclaims it for science, which can, he holds,
grasp the inmost nature of each of the substances
which belong to it, and determine their essential
attributes. He holds further, that, even when such
demonstrative science is not possible, we can still
trace out the effects of the action and reaction
of substances upon each other either universally
or in the generality of cases. Even in the sphere
of human conduct, where contingency takes the
largest place, we can find law and order. What
is even more important, Aristotle, stimulated probably by his biological studies, shows a tendency
in some passages to do away with the fundamental
contrast between form and matter, or to reduce it
to an opposition of elements which are correlative
with each other. He is, however, unable to maintain
this point of view or to work out an organic conception either of the world in general or of the
nature of man. And the very fact that he has
given to matter a more positive character than it
had from Plato, in the end lands him in a more
pronounced and definite dualism. This is shown
both in his conception of the relation of reason to
the other elements of human nature, and in his
view of the nature of God and of his connexion
with the world. For reason in man is conceived

as an absolute intuitive power, which yet has to
realise itself in and through the sensitive nature
which belongs to him as an animal; and all the
speculative power of Aristotle is taxed to bring
together these irreconcilable elements. In like
manner, the pure self-consciousness of God, in which
subject and object and the activity that relates
them to each other—νοῦς, νοητόν and νόησις—are
perfectly unified and which, therefore, is complete
in itself without reference to any other object,
cannot logically be conceived as going beyond itself
to create the finite world of movement and change.
For though the latter involves the former as that
on which it depends for its existence, the former
cannot be regarded as involving the latter, or as in
any way essentially related to it. The world in
time and space is a realisation of the pure unity
of thought in a matter in which it can never be
perfectly realised; but the existence of such matter
seems in no way to be accounted for by the purely
ideal principle of thought. Thus we are obliged
to refer the world to God, but God seems by his
nature to have no need of the world, and, indeed,
to be incapable of acting upon it. In short, there
seems to be no reason for the existence of the
world at all—except the presupposed matter, which,
if it exists, cannot but come under the dominion of
the universal principle in so far as its nature admits.

When, however, philosophy has reached this point a further regress becomes necessary. If we can abstract from the relations of the pure self-consciousness of God to the world in space and time, this means that we can break away the self from the not-self, the pure unity of self-conscious thought from the manifoldness and externality of the objective world. And this step was taken in the Post-Aristotelian philosophy. In particular, the Stoics sought to fortify the individual against all the chances and changes of the world by teaching him to retire into himself, and to treat everything that was not in his own power as unnecessary and without value for him. It is true that the Stoic conceived himself as in his inmost being one with the Universal Reason, and therefore with God as the principle of the Universe, and that in this unity all distinctions, even the distinction of mind and matter, seemed to be transcended. But as his conception of God was not less abstract than his conception of the self, the idea of unity with God could add nothing to the idea of unity with self. To live in harmony with nature, both with the nature of the world without and with the nature of the self within, meant, therefore, nothing more than to treat every particular object and end as indifferent, and to fall back upon the simple ' I am I ' of self-consciousness as complete in itself and self-sufficient.

But this immediately suggests another question and prepares the way for a further regress. If we confine self-consciousness to itself and treat it as a complete whole, which needs nothing else for its fulfilment, must we not carry our abstraction further? It was simply by reason of the division and opposition, the vicissitude and change, which are the characteristics of the world in space and time, that Plato and Aristotle regarded it as an imperfect world, a world that does not conform to the demands of the intelligence, and cannot, therefore, be regarded as altogether real. But can we escape such division and antagonism, vicissitude and change, by confining ourselves to the pure intelligence and its κόσμος νοητός? Does not self-consciousness itself involve division and opposition between the subject-self and the object-self—a division and opposition which is no doubt immediately transcended in the perception of the identity of the two factors, but which must exist in order to be transcended? If such difference and opposition can exist, and yet be overcome and brought to unity, why might not the same be conceived to be possible in the case of the difference and opposition of the world in space and time? If, on the other hand, it cannot be overcome in the latter case, why should we expect to find the problem more easy to solve in the case of the intelligence itself?

In one aspect of it, the antagonism between the subject and the object in self-consciousness is not the easiest, but the most difficult, of all antagonisms to reconcile, just because the opposites are not external to each other, but brought together in the essential unity of one life. Is not the greatest of all divisions our division against ourselves, the most violent of all conflicts the battle we have to wage with ourselves? What are the struggles of opposing forces in the outward world to the struggle of the solitary spirit with itself? When the soul withdraws itself from its conflict with the world, does it not often find a worse enemy within, than it had ever to face without? If we take self-consciousness in its concrete form, we soon discover that in it the universal or spiritual nature of man is at war with the special feelings and desires of the individual. If, on the other hand, we endeavour with the Stoic to purge self-consciousness from all that is particular, to raise it above all the perceptions and desires that belong to the individual as such, and to identify it with a universal reason which seeks to know and to realise nothing but reason itself, we find that it becomes emptied of all content or meaning whatsoever, except that which it derives from the very particular consciousness it rejects. Hence by a necessary dialectical transition the Stoic's pride or consciousness of inward strength passes into its own opposite and becomes a consciousness of absolute weakness and dependence on that which is beyond itself. Thus, as we have already seen, the spiritual bankruptcy of Scepticism is the necessary result of the recoil upon the abstract self which cuts it off from every external support. With the Stoic the soul was raised to an absolute pinnacle of self-confidence by the denial of value to every particular object or interest that could influence it. But such self-confidence is close upon self-despair; and it becomes self-despair so soon as the subject, thus isolated in its subjectivity, begins to comprehend its own isolation. The Sceptic needs only to realise what he means by his own admission, that the negation of knowledge applies to the subject as well as to the object, and what we may call the comedy of Scepticism turns into tragedy. The spectator who stood aloof and watched the process of self-contradiction in which all opinions and dogmas, all objective truth and reality, were dissolved, is himself drawn upon the stage to experience the fate of the puppets he was watching. If the world we behold without is an " insubstantial pageant," we ourselves to whom it appears must be " such stuff as dreams are made on."

Now it might be said that if the consciousness of the pure subject as such be found to have no completeness or reality in itself, any more than the consciousness of the object, the true resource is to regard them both as factors in a unity, which lose their meaning when torn away from each other, but have their value restored to them, when they are brought together as elements in one whole. According to this view, it is just by rising to the consciousness of the absolute reality of the one principle which is present both in object and in subject, both in the world and in the mind that knows it, that we learn to estimate aright the relative reality of these elements.

We may illustrate this point by reference to a controversy which has arisen in our own time in reference to the *Logic* of Hegel and its connexion with the other parts of his philosophy, especially the philosophy of Nature. That *Logic* ends with the conception of a pure self-consciousness in which all the differences of the object and the subject have become transparent, or are seen to be the essential differentiation and manifestation of the unity of the self. And the next step taken by Hegel in the beginning of his philosophy of Nature is to set up the opposite of this ideal unity, namely, the conception of the objective world determined as in space, and therefore as existing in limitless self-externality.

Now this step has often been objected to by critics of Hegel as involving a *mauvais pas*, that is, as an attempt to pass from thought to reality by a transition which has no logical rationale. In reality, however, this step is only one, and perhaps the most obvious, of the results of the Hegelian principle of dialectic, by which the complement of an imperfect conception is sought in its opposite; and the idea that such a step is illegitimate is closely akin to the fundamental error of the Greek dualism. In truth, we cannot separate the pure unity of self-consciousness from its correlate, the world in space and time; any more than we can conceive unity without multiplicity or the positive without the negative. Either the whole conception of the nature of thought, as it is expressed in the Hegelian *Logic*, must be rejected, or this step must be taken as one of the most luminous and natural illustrations of it. In other words, the whole process of Hegel's philosophy is a movement from the abstract to the concrete: it is a process in which the statement and solution of the simpler differences and antagonisms of thought gradually leads to a deeper, more complex and comprehensive view of the subject. It is, therefore, quite in accordance with his usual method that, when he reaches the idea of self-consciousness as purely and transparently one with itself in all the diversity of its subjective and objective aspects, he should at once proceed to that which is obviously the opposite counterpart of this, the continuous self-externality of the world in space and time. And the whole further course of Hegel's speculation is just an attempt to show that even this greatest of all antagonisms cannot be understood, except as based upon a still more complex and concrete unity: in other words, that the consciousness of self and the consciousness of the not-self cannot be made intelligible, unless they are both referred back to that which is deeper and more comprehensive than either, the consciousness of God.

To this point I shall have to return. For the present I refer to it only to illustrate by contrast the process of thought by which the Stoic gave rise to the Neo-Platonic philosophy. For the movement of speculation in Greece took a course directly opposed to that of the dialectic of Hegel. In other words, the progress of Greek philosophy was not from the abstract to the concrete, but rather from the concrete to the abstract. In the Post-Aristotelian philosophies it made a regress from the object upon the abstract subject, and endeavoured to treat the life of that subject as complete in itself. And when in turn the bare self of the subject was shown to be, in its isolation, insufficient for itself and self-contradictory, the Neo-Platonist sought to find truth by a still further regress upon the unity that is presupposed in the duality of the life of the subject, the bare One, which is beyond all difference and division. The One was, therefore, taken in its abstraction, as having in it no difference or division, not even that of the pure self-consciousness. Yet at the same time, this unity had to be conceived as the source of all things and therefore as containing them virtually or potentially in itself. Hence we have the strange contradiction in the Mysticism of Plotinus, of which I have already spoken. For, on the one hand, Plotinus isolates the Absolute from everything and refers it to itself alone, and prohibits us from regarding it as requiring the existence of anything else than itself, or even as having any relation to such existence. From this point of view, therefore, we have to think of it as so self-contained and complete in itself that our consciousness of it falls entirely outside of it. Thus we cannot properly attach any name to it, cannot call it even 'the *One*' or 'the *Good*,' lest we should bring it down into relation with that which is other than itself. Yet, on the other hand, it is the very dependence of all other things on something beyond them that has made us assert *its* transcendent being; and we are obliged to think of it in relation to them, in order to regard it as absolute. Hence, from this point of view, we have to take the names by which we call it as expressing its true nature; we have to regard it as really the *One*, the beginning or first principle from which everything else springs, and as really the *Good*, the end to which everything else tends. We have seen a modern philosopher, Mr. Spencer, driven into the same *impasse*, just because he is compelled to treat the Unknowable, to which he refers back all things, as also the creative force which manifests itself in all things.   And, indeed, the difficulty is one which is familiar to us in some phases of ordinary religion, which refers all things to God, and yet is afraid to speak of any necessity in God's nature to reveal himself in and to the world, lest such necessity should seem to make him dependent on that which is not himself.

What, however, we have here specially to notice is that the peculiar form taken by the philosophy of Plotinus is due just to its being a kind of summary, or concentrated expression, of the whole movement of Greek philosophy.   Plotinus represents the universe as distributed into a series of stages or degrees of reality, reaching up from matter to God; and in these different stages we have, as it were in an abbreviated form, the different stages in the development of Greek thought.   In particular, we have to notice that he reaches his Mysticism not directly but through a previous Idealism, and we may add, through a previous Spiritualism.   He is first of all an idealist who, like Plato and Aristotle, maintains the supreme reality of form as opposed to matter, of the intelligible essences or principles of things as opposed to the contingency of their particular manifestations.   But farther, already in Plato and still more distinctly in

Aristotle, these universal forms are conceived as gathered up and concentrated in the intelligence, as the principle of the intelligible world, which is eternally realised in God and capable of being realised in all rational creatures and therefore in man. Aristotle, indeed, did not especially connect his view of reason in man with his conception of the divine reason. But the Stoics, who regarded reason as at once a universal principle and as constituting the self of every individual, familiarised the world with the idea of a *civitas deorum et hominum*, in which each member is an independent, self-determining being. And Plotinus, as he enters into the inheritance of Greek philosophy, accepts the Stoic doctrine of the supreme reality of spirit, while he breaks entirely with the simple identification of spirit and matter, by which the Stoics attempted to escape from dualism. He falls back, therefore, upon the spiritualism of Plato's later philosophy, and maintains the reality of the intelligence and the intelligible world, as above and beyond the world of appearance and sense, and as the source and end of all its life: and also, like Plato, he finds in the soul of the world and the soul of man a mediating principle which connects the former with the latter.

But, again, while he thus takes up the position of an idealist or spiritualist as against materialism, and in the sharpest way opposes the pure intelligence, which abides in itself and is eternally in unity with itself, to the world of spatial externality and temporal change, which is ever in conflict with itself, he has learnt from the development of Post-Aristotelian philosophy to regard the regress upon thought, upon intelligence, upon subjectivity, as only a stage on the way to a still deeper reality, to an Absolute which in its unity is beyond even the difference of self-consciousness. Hence, while he develops the thought of Plato and Aristotle, and gives to their idealistic and spiritualistic system a sharper and fuller expression than it had found in their own writings; while he gives new definiteness to that substitution of the unity of the intelligence for the unity of ideas which is suggested in Plato's later works; and while he works out the hints of Aristotle as to the opposition between the intuitive and the discursive intelligence much more fully than is done in the *Metaphysic* and the *De Anima*, he is not content with these results, but hastens on to what seems to him a still higher point of view, and, after turning Idealism and Spiritualism against Materialism, he ends by turning Mysticism against both.

Yet none of these points of view is so insisted upon as altogether to set aside the others; and even the material world, though reduced to a world of shadow and appearance, is still left as a distinct stage of being, outside the spiritual world; while the spiritual world and the Spirit that includes all other spirits in itself, are also maintained as a distinct sphere of being, from which finally we climb up to the One which is above being and above knowledge, and which in one way excludes and in another way includes everything else.

This account of the genesis and nature of the system of Plotinus at once suggests a special difficulty, for which he was bound to find some kind of solution. We have seen that his upward progress depended upon a negative logic, like that of Spinoza, by which all difference and determination were gradually removed as involving something finite and defective. At each successive stage, therefore, the process was supposed to get rid of an element of unreality and dependence; for, while the lower always has need of the higher, the higher is regarded as having no need of the lower to support or manifest it. Hence, when we arrive at the highest, it is treated as having no need of anything but itself. Such a process, however, is one which cannot be reversed, and it seems as if in ascending, Plotinus had drawn up the ladder after him and left himself no possibility of descending again. Yet as the existence of the lower forms of being is not denied, and the highest as absolute is that from which every other form of being must be derived, some way downward has to be found. The One, as complete in itself, has no need to create; nay, it seems as if it would be a contradiction to its essential nature that it should create. Yet it has created, and Plotinus is bound in some way to account for the fact, and to cut the knot if he cannot untie it. And it is all the more necessary for him to do so, because the same problem repeats itself at every step of the way downwards.

Now a full explanation of the views of Plotinus on this subject would carry us beyond the point we can reach in this lecture; but one remark may be made by way of preparation, namely, that the *logical* movement of Plotinus, the movement in which he is guided by definite and explicit thought, is always upwards; while, in describing the movement downwards, he has to take refuge in metaphors and analogies, the full meaning of which is never explicitly stated or realised. These metaphors and analogies, indeed, often involve a quite different principle from that which is expressed in his account of the way upwards. To put this point more definitely. In the upward process we have, as has been indicated in the last lecture, simply the ordinary dialectic of the finite—that dialectical movement of thought which is initiated, whenever it is discerned that finite things are fleeting and unreal in themselves; or, in other words, that every definite form of existence or thought, when taken as a *res completa,* becomes self-contradictory and forces us to look beyond itself for a deeper principle of reality. Further, this dialectical movement is taken by Plotinus in a purely

negative sense; and it is not suspected by him that
what, in one aspect, is negated, must in another be
taken up into that higher reality which is reached
by negation of it. Consequently, the end which
Plotinus ultimately reaches is the absence of all
determination; it is that to which we cannot even
give the name of the One, except by opposition to
the multiplicity which is set aside.

On the other hand, when Plotinus attempts to
show how the infinite One gives forth the successive
phases or degrees of reality down to the lowest, his
idea of its completeness in itself seems to prevent
his achieving his purpose or conceiving it as in any
way going beyond itself to them. And in defect of
any logical transition, he is obliged to have recourse
to images which, if they mean anything, imply that
the One is *not* the self-centred Absolute which it
was described as being. "The Good or the One,"
says Plotinus, "cannot look to anything but itself:
yet it is the fountain of all actualities and makes
them like itself, yet without any activity directed
toward them." How, then, are we to throw light
on the conception of such an inactive principle
which yet is the fountain of all activity? Plotinus
objects to the Gnostic idea of emanation as involving that the One goes beyond itself; but yet he
tells us that it, "as it were, overflows, owing to its
excessive fulness of reality, and so produces another

than itself."[1] More frequently he compares it to the sun which, he asserts, gives forth light and heat without in any degree losing by its radiation. There is a " radiance that shines out around it while it abides in itself, as the sun has a bright halo round it, which it continually produces, though itself remaining undiminished."[2] And he even goes on to set it forth as a general law that everything that exists must beget some other existence which is dependent on it as an image on the original. "Thus fire produces heat, and snow does not retain its cold in itself. And above all, things that are sweet-smelling are an evidence of this; for, as long as they exist, they send forth a scent into the surrounding air which is enjoyed by all beings that are in the neighbourhood. Everything in its perfection generates another, and that which is eternally perfect has an eternal generation, producing ever something lower than itself."

Now it is at once evident that such metaphors either prove nothing at all, or they prove the reverse of what Plotinus seeks to establish. For, in the first place, I need hardly say that no material thing can act and send forth an influence without *ipso facto* exhausting some of its latent energy; and the idea that the sun pours forth light and heat without any diminution of its resources, only shows the immature

[1] V, 2, 1.　　[2] V, 1, 6.

state of physical science in the time of Plotinus. But, even overlooking this point, there is a false abstraction in the attempt to divide between what a thing is and does in relation to itself, and what it is and does in relation to other things. What is indicated by such metaphors, is not that anything has an outgoing or *transeunt* activity which is altogether different and separable from the im- manent activity that constitutes its real being ; but rather the reverse, namely, that nothing exists except as it manifests itself, and that the very idea of a self-directed activity, which only accidentally produces an external effect, is irrational and baseless. Least of all can we think of the Absolute as having an external effect which is not necessarily involved in its own nature. The metaphors of Plotinus, therefore, so far as they show anything, seem to show that an absolutely self-centred and self-directed activity is impossible, or possible only so far as the Being to whom it belongs includes all other being in his own. In any case, they give us no real ex- planation of the problem they are intended to solve, namely, how God, who is absolutely complete in himself, can yet be the source of existences which are external to him and not included in the process of his own life.

LECTURE TWENTY-FOURTH.

THE WORLD-SOUL AS MEDIATOR BETWEEN THE SENSIBLE AND INTELLIGIBLE WORLDS.

IN the last lecture we were considering the way in which Plotinus deals with the Absolute One as an exclusive unity to which we rise by negation of all finitude and difference, and which, from this point of view, is opposed to everything else, while yet it has to be conceived as the source from which everything else flows. And I pointed out that these two aspects of the One, as an all-exclusive unity and yet as the fountain of all existence, are not reconciled by Plotinus, but that he hides from others and from himself the difficulty of reconciling them, by alternating between the language of exact thought and the language of imagination, generally using the former when he is following the way upwards from the worlds of sense and intelligence to the One, and the latter when he is seeking to throw light on the process downwards from the One to the intelligible and sensible worlds. This formal difference in the mode of expression only imperfectly conceals the contradiction which arises, when the Absolute, to which all being and thought are related, is yet conceived as not in any sense relating itself to them. We have here in an intensified form a difficulty which had already risen in the Aristotelian philosophy, when God was defined as a purely contemplative activity, while yet He was at the same time conceived as the beginning and end, the first and final cause, of the universe. In Plotinus, this difficulty is doubled; for he regards God, the supreme unity, as lifted above even the contemplative activity of pure intelligence; while at the same time he has to explain how the Absolute Being, whose activity, so far as it is active, has no object but itself, should yet be the centre from which all being and thought are radiated. Further, we have to remember that this difficulty repeats itself at every stage of the hierarchy of existence. For while Plotinus always upholds the principle that a thing, so far as it is perfect, occupies itself only with itself or with that which is above itself, yet he equally maintains that it is just through this self-directed activity that it gives rise to a lower kind of being, which is its image or imperfect copy. To understand Plotinus is in great measure to discern the reasons which made him maintain this apparently contradictory doctrine.

Now I have already indicated how it is that he is
so anxious to maintain the isolation of the divine
unity, and to deny that it can have any outwardly
directed activity. As the last great exponent of
Greek dualism, he finds himself unable to think of
any outgoing or *transeunt* activity of God, because
in his view such activity would involve want and
imperfection in God. He is ready, indeed, to repeat
Plato's words that the Divine Being can have no
envy in him, which should prevent the good that is
in himself from flowing out to his creatures :[1] but
it is impossible for Plotinus to admit that God is
occupied with *them*, or with anything but himself.
Hence for want of the conception of God as a self-
revealing spirit, Plotinus is obliged to fall back upon
the unexplained necessity, of which I have already
spoken, that the highest being should produce an
image or imperfect copy of itself, which again in
its turn gives rise to a still less perfect image,
until at last we reach the lowest and most unreal
of all existences.

Frequently this relation of the higher to the lower
is represented as one of *form to matter*. From this
point of view the first external product of the One
is said to be an ideal matter in the shape of a
potential intelligence ; and this, by turning to the One
that is its source, becomes developed into an active or

[1] V, 4, 1.

actual intelligence.   Thus, to take one passage for many, Plotinus says:[1] "The first genesis of being is this.   The One, being perfect so that it seeks and needs nothing, yet through its very perfection overflows, and its superabundance produces another than itself : but that which is produced turns itself towards the One, and, being fulfilled by it and contemplating it, it becomes intelligence.   Thus, while its permanent relation to the One gives it being, its contemplation of the One gives it intelligence.   Standing, therefore, in relation to the One so as to behold it, it becomes at once being and intelligence."   Thus the intelligence, as one with the intelligible world, forms the first stage in the hierarchy of 'degrees of reality,' which surround the divine unity.

But, in the second place, the pure intelligence, with the intelligible world which is its object, is declared to be too perfect not to produce another like itself, though inferior to it, namely, the world-soul; and here also the production is described as primarily the genesis of a potentiality, a soul in *posse*, which by turning to the intelligence becomes formed and realised.   This world-soul is the lowest stage of the ideal or spiritual world, and it is distinguished from the intelligence in so far as in it the difference of one idea from another is more definitely actualised.   In other words, instead of

[1] V, 2, 1.

dwelling, like the intelligence, in one unbroken intuition of the whole, the world-soul moves from one idea to another, though still keeping up their unity with each other and overcoming or transcending the distinctions and divisions which it produces. This completes the Trinity of Plotinus, which, like that which appears in the theology of Origen, is a Trinity of subordination. But the process of descent still goes on, and the world-soul in turn produces the world of matter and change, into which individual souls are conceived as falling when they assume a mortal body.

In this material world, again, we find life showing itself in a descending scale which reaches down to plants and to inorganic things that have no life in them, and therefore no farther power of production. Yet even in relation to the inorganic also, Plotinus maintains the same contrast of matter and form; for he declares that in it, as in the higher degrees of reality, what first comes into being is something formless, and that this something receives a form by turning to that which has produced it. Only there is this difference, that what is produced in this lowest grade of being is no longer a kind of soul, but is lifeless and indefinite. In other words, what is produced at this stage is primarily pure matter, which becomes some kind of inorganic substance when it receives a form from that which is above it. Thus

matter in itself, according to the Aristotelian conception, is only a potentiality and cannot be conceived
to exist by itself; but still it is viewed as a substratum for images received from above, from that
which has a higher degree of reality. Even this
formless matter, however, is explained by Plotinus
as owing its existence to the infinity of the divine
power which carries its radiation to the utmost verge
of unreality. In this, Plotinus makes a change
in the earlier dualism of Greece: for, while still
maintaining the division of form and matter, he
refers the matter as well as the form to the One,
or, what is the same thing, to some kind of being
that springs from the One. Still, subject to this
change, we have in Plotinus, as in Plato and Aristotle,
the conception of a form realising itself in a matter
which is inadequate to it, an ideal principle determining something other than itself, and therefore
failing to realise its own ideal nature.

The most important difference of Plotinus from the
earlier idealists is, however, this, that he carries up
the distinction of form and matter into the ideal
world itself,[1] and thus is led to look for a higher
principle of activity than even the intelligence; though
the ideal matter of the intelligence is not conceived

[1] This ideal matter may have been suggested by the νοητὴ ὕλη of
Aristotle. But Aristotle does not conceive *his* intelligible matter
as entering into the objects of pure intuitive reason. Cf. Vol. I,
p. 336.

as interfering with its unity in the same way that
the matter of the sensible world interferes with the
unity of that world. Even for this, however, he finds
a verbal support in the language of Plato, who had
spoken of the idea of Good as "beyond being" and
"above knowledge." In so expressing himself, indeed,
Plato did not mean to point to any transcendent unintelligible unity, except in the sense that the principle
which is manifested in thought and reality alike, is
beyond either taken abstractly. Still, we are obliged
to admit that this last regress of Plotinus is only
the legitimate result of the movement of thought
by which, in Plato and Aristotle, the ideal world
and the pure intelligence whose object it is, are
separated from the phenomenal world in time and
space, and even from the soul through which in that
world the intelligence realises itself. For, if once we
admit that the phenomenal world cannot be explained
on purely ideal principles, and cannot therefore be
apprehended in intuitive, but only in discursive
thought, we must soon discover that even intuitive
thought contains traces of difference and change, of a
movement out of itself and a return into itself: and
thus a further regress becomes necessary, in order to
reach that pure identity in which alone, *ex hypothesi*,
the mind can be satisfied. The fundamental error lies
already in the first regress, namely, in regarding intuitive
thought as capable of being separated from discursive

thought, or self-consciousness from the consciousness of the world in space and time; for, when once this error has been committed, the farther error, of seeking for the absolute unity in something that transcends even the distinction of self-consciousness, is a necessary consequence. And out of this, again, springs the whole system of subordination described above, in which Plotinus begins with the absolute One, proceeds from it to the pure intelligence, and ends with the *anima mundi* which, as the lowest grade of the intelligible world, has to discharge the function of connecting it with the phenomenal world in time and space.

It appears, then, that the fivefold hierarchy of Plotinus with the unknowable Absolute at the top, and the unknowable matter at the bottom of it—the one above and the other below knowledge—is the necessary consequence of the failure of Greek idealism to recognise that, in rising above the opposition of the pure intelligence and the consciousness of the world in space and time, what we are really seeking is not some ultimate abstraction in which all difference disappears, but rather a principle of unity which transcends and explains that difference. Such a principle is represented in the philosophy of Plotinus, as in that of Plato, by the *world-soul*. This, however, is regarded by them both, not as an expression of the essential unity between the ideal and the phenomenal worlds, but simply as a kind of bridge to connect two terms which it is impossible really to unite. But no such bridge is needed, if the absolute principle of unity be regarded not as an abstract One, which is complete in itself apart from the world, but as a unity which realises itself in all the differences of that world. Or, to put the same thought in a theological way, the true solution of the difficulty is that God should be conceived not as the head of a hierarchy of powers by the lowest of which He is connected with the finite world, but as a self-manifesting Spirit which realises and reveals itself in nature and in man.

Now if this be true, it is just in the excessive recoil of the Neo-Platonist from the materialism of the Stoics, as in the excessive recoil of Plato and Aristotle from the materialism of their day, that we find the reason why the idealism of Greece remained imperfect and unfruitful. For, in turning away from the material world as incapable of being idealised, they practically raised matter into the place of an independent substance. This result Plotinus, no doubt, attempted to escape by treating matter in itself as purely negative or non-existent, and by reducing the material world to a semblance—an image of being cast upon the darkness of not-being. But this expedient only reproduces the original error in another form; for, inevitably and in spite of all his reluctance, he has to treat this purely negative being as the positive cause of the corporeal conditions under which the soul realises itself in the world of sense, and of all the imperfection and evil which arise in that world. And, on the other hand, the ideal reality, just because it excludes such imperfection and evil, has to be regarded by him as something purely affirmative, which escapes all negation only by excluding all determination. In other words, it is reduced to an empty abstraction.

After what has been said, we may gather the peculiarities of the system of Plotinus under three heads: first, it develops to its extremest form the Greek dualism of form and matter, of the ideal and the sensible, of the pure and permanent unity of intelligence and the divided and changing world of sense: secondly, it thereby reduces the mediation between the two by the *anima mundi* into an external and therefore accidental connexion : and lastly, in consequence of the inadequacy of this mediation, it is obliged to seek its highest principle not in that soul, but in a transcendent Absolute, which has no connexion with anything but itself, although, *as* the highest principle, it must be conceived to be the first and the final cause of all things.

As to the first point, I have said that Plotinus develops to its extremest form the Platonic antagonism between the ideal and the phenomenal world, and this is true both as regards their content and their form. As regards the *form*, it is noticeable that Plotinus devotes much attention to the question of the categories, and that he is the first to draw a broad distinction between the categories of the intelligible and those of the phenomenal world.[1] As to the categories of the intelligible world, Plotinus derives his list of them from the *Sophist*, where Plato discusses the relations of the ideas of being and not-being, identity and difference, permanence and motion.[2] Plotinus, however, makes two changes in the scheme of Plato. In the first place, he omits the category of 'not-being' as not properly applying to the intelligible world, and puts in its place, as the category contrasted with 'being,' the notion of 'thought' or 'intelligence' ($\nu o \hat{v} s$). In the second place, he takes the six categories not as separate conceptions but as correlated pairs of opposites which are essentially united to each other. The categories of the intelligible world are thus in reality only three in number, and they express respectively the *unity of identity and difference*, the *unity of permanence and motion*, and the

[1] The subject of the Categories is discussed by Plotinus in the first three books of the sixth *Ennead*, which really form a connected treatise. His views are explained and criticised with much insight and clearness by von Hartmann in his *Geschichte der Metaphysik*. See especially Vol. I, p. 135 *seq.*

[2] $\sigma \tau \alpha \sigma \iota s$ and $\kappa \iota \nu \eta \sigma \iota s$. Plotinus adopts the terminology of Plato by whom $\kappa \iota \nu \eta \sigma \iota s$ is used in a general sense for all change or activity (see Vol. I, p. 213). Rest and motion in the proper sense are for Plotinus categories of the sensible world.

unity of intelligence and reality. They represent different aspects of that organic or super-organic nature which Plotinus attributes to the intelligible world, as a system in which the whole is present in every part, and in every part is conscious only of itself. Thus the pure intelligence is viewed as one with itself through all the differences of its objects, differences which, therefore, are no hindrance to its transparent unity. Again, its self-determined life combines rest with motion, or rather absolute permanence with unceasing activity, because it is an activity that never goes beyond itself. And this, finally, involves the complete relativity of the distinction between thought and reality ; for the object, as intelligible, cannot be severed from the intelligence, nor can the self-consciousness of the intelligence be divorced from the consciousness of the intelligible world. By working out the unity of all these pairs of opposites Plotinus brings before us in the most forcible way that perfect interpenetration which he conceives as the essential characteristic of all the members or organs which partake in the unity of spiritual life. The perfect inwardness of intelligence in all its differences, as opposed to the reciprocal externality and exclusiveness of material objects, was never more vividly expressed. Here we have that idea of spirit by which St. Augustine was enabled to free himself from the materialistic conceptions of his earlier Manichaeism; and he who would realise its extraordinary religious power has only to read the *Confessions*, in which St. Augustine constantly returns to the language of Plotinus whenever he has to speak of the all-pervading presence of God.

So much for the form of the intelligible world, but what of its content? The intelligence, Plotinus answers, contains all things in their ultimate ideas. It thus contains in itself a real difference and multiplicity, which yet, because of its ideal character, offers no hindrance to the unity of its life. We find in it all the manifold kinds of being, each showing its distinctive quality, yet maintaining such perfect relativity to the rest, that they all are seen to be organs in one great organism. This conception of the transparent unity or perfect interpenetration of the ideal forms that constitute the intelligible world is anticipated by Plato; but what is characteristic of Plotinus is that this world is regarded not merely as a system of ideas or forms or even such a system as related to one mind, but rather as a system of *minds*, all of them embraced and contained in one supreme mind.[1] The infinite Spirit is thus the living principle of an organic world of spirits, who 'live and move and have their being' in him: and while each of these spirits maintains its separate identity, they are all

[1] This was suggested by Plato, as we have seen (Vol. I. p. 217 *seq.*), but it is in Plotinus only that it is fully developed.

forms of the life of one great intelligence and, as such, each of them is transparent to all the others, knowing as he is known by an immediate intuitive vision. For, says Plotinus, "light is manifest to light."[1] It is as in Dante's heaven, where all the blessed read each others' thoughts in God without any need of words. In fact, the medieval conception of the hosts of angels and spirits of the redeemed, dwelling in a Paradise of pure light and harmony and enjoying the undisturbed vision of God,

> "In regions mild of calm and serene air,
>   Above the smoke and stir of this dim spot,
>   Which men call earth,"

is only a somewhat sensuous reproduction of the Neo-Platonic idea of the intelligible world. It is a conception of one life ever pouring itself into diverse organs, yet never giving rise to any collision or conflict, because the unity of each with all and of all with each is never for one moment lost or obscured. In all this, however, Plotinus is only working out the idea suggested by Aristotle's account of God as a purely contemplative being, in whom the highest activity, as it is purely an immanent activity and has for its object only itself, is at the same time perfect rest, an ἐνέργεια ἀκινησίας. The great difference is that Plotinus answers a question which Aristotle

[1] V, 8, 4. Cf. Whitaker, *The Neo-Platonists*, p. 63. See also p. 194, where the parallel conceptions of Dante are referred to.

leaves unanswered as to the relation of the pure intelligence in us to the divine self-consciousness, by making the life of God include and sustain the life of all the intelligences of which He is the centre; so that, instead of one solitary self-contemplative Being, we have a world of spirits.

The opposite counterpart of this pure unchanging heaven of intelligence is for Plotinus the material world, a world of beings which have no substantial permanence but are in perpetual flux from one mode of existence to another. For that which here takes the place of substance is matter, and that not the ideal matter of the higher world which gives rise only to differences that are transparent, but the baser matter which is ever in essential difference from itself and can never, except externally, be made one. This matter is conceived, indeed, in the first instance, as that which is purely receptive, which receives any image but retains none, a mere *substratum* in which one quality succeeds another without permanently determining it as this rather than that. As realised in such matter, the sensible world in a way repeats or imitates the spiritual world and has in it an image or semblance of each of its attributes. But the different aspects which in the intelligible world are in perfect unity with each other, become here separated and opposed. Thus a material body has a kind of unity through all its differences, but the unity is merely the continuity of extended parts each of which is outside of the others, and the differences appear as disparate qualities which are not connected with each other by any necessary bond. It has motion and rest, but its rest is merely a certain limited resistance to extraneous influences and its motion is a change in which it ceases to be one with itself, and turns into a quite different kind of body. Thus while the ideal substance is complete in itself and has no activity except in relation to itself, the material substance is essentially incomplete and can only exist in acting on something else or being reacted on by it. Its being is a continual becoming, a continual striving after that which it is not, and its life is a process to death. Again, while the ideal substance is essentially one with itself and eternal, the material substance exists in time and space, is external to everything else and even to itself. It is, therefore, in continual conflict with itself as with other things and beings, continually destroying and being destroyed by them. Thus the sensible world is supposed to be an imperfect image of the intelligible world, and every characteristic of the latter is reflected in the former in a broken and distorted way. All these deficiencies are supposed to arise from the fact that the form of the sensible world is external to its matter, and that its matter is absolutely indeterminate in itself, and communicates its indeterminateness to the form which is impressed upon it.

It might seem, indeed, that the dispersion, separation, and opposition which thus overtake the ideal forms as realised in matter imply in matter itself a positive power of changing and corrupting the forms, which is inconsistent with the purely negative and passive nature attributed to it. But Plotinus prefers to think of these characteristics as arising from the incapacity of matter to hold the forms in their original unity. Because matter has no form of its own to hold it together, it lets the forms imposed on it fall asunder into local separation and qualitative opposition. Moreover, this incapacity or negative nature of matter makes it incapable of being known. Matter is in itself essential unreality and evil, and it can only be grasped by the intelligence in the same sense in which we can say that we see darkness, or as we dimly recognise an indefinite something as lying beneath all our determinations.[1] Our mind, indeed, shrinks from such an ἄπειρον, and feels a kind of *horror vacui* as it approaches it, as if it were drawn beyond the borders of being, and forced to contemplate absolute unreality and untruth. Yet we cannot escape, Plotinus holds, from the necessity of admitting its existence as the basis of sensible phenomena, as a mirror is necessary for the existence of images. And to it we are forced ultimately to attribute all change and decay, all evil and discord both

[1] I, 8, 4.

in the material world itself and in the souls of men, in so far as they are immersed in the darkness of such a world.

Plotinus thus develops to the utmost sharpness of antagonism the Platonic opposition of the ideal and the material worlds. But he also tries, as I have already indicated, to work out Plato's doctrine of the soul as the mediator or link of connexion between the two. The world-soul, according to Plotinus, belongs to the ideal world, but it has also to take the place of a *tertium quid* or middle term between the unity of the self-complete intelligence, and the dispersion and change of the sensible world. Let us consider how he describes this mediating function of the soul. " On the one hand," he declares, " there are existences which are essentially divisible and capable of endless dispersion. They are those in which no part is identical with another part or with the whole, and in which each part is necessarily less than the whole. Such are all sensible *quanta* that have corporeal mass ; for each of them is confined to its own place, and none of them is capable of retaining its identity and yet occupying several places at once. Again, there is a substance which is entirely opposed in nature to those that have just been described, a substance which is undivided and admits of no division, and which is not capable even in thought of having its constituents separated from each other. This substance

cannot be circumscribed in place or contained in anything else, either in part or wholly; for it is, as it
were, incumbent upon all things, not as being sus-
tained thereby, but because other things cannot exist
without it. Again, it is always identical with itself;
and in relation to all other things it is like the centre
of a circle from which all the radii extend to the circumference, leaving the centre to abide in itself and
yet deriving from it their origin and existence. Thus,
although the radii diverge from the centre, they ever
maintain connexion with it; and although they are
divisible, their beginning or principle lies in the
indivisible."

"Now, between this substance which is altogether
indivisible and occupies the first rank in the intelligible world and that sensible existence which is
altogether divisible, there is a third nature which is
not primarily divisible like material bodies, but which
yet becomes divisible through its relation to them.
Consequently, when such bodies are divided, the form
which is immanent in them becomes divided also, yet
in such a way that, while thus becoming manifold, it
remains whole in all its parts, in spite of their separation from each other. We might illustrate this by the
case of colours and other qualities and forms which
communicate their whole being to many elements at
the same time, yet so that each of them is affected
in a different way; and which, therefore, must be

regarded as falling under the head of divisible things."

"We see, then, that in close connexion with that which is altogether indivisible, there is another nature which derives from it the character of indivisibility, but which, as it diverges from its original, is carried away towards the opposite extreme, and so comes to hold a mediating position between that which is indivisible and that which is corporeal and divisible. The illustration used above, however, is not altogether adequate; for the identity of this nature is not like that of a colour or any other quality which is repeated in many different extended objects; for in that case the quality in one of these objects is altogether cut off from the similar quality in another, just as extended objects are themselves separated. But such identity of quality cannot produce a real community or sympathy between the quite different things that partake in it; or, in other words, what we have in such a case is only a similarity of affections or modes and the substances remain different. But, on the other hand, the nature that comes next to the indivisible being, that is, the soul, maintains a permanent and substantial unity with itself, though it unites itself with bodies and so accidentally partakes in their division. Thus it is *divisible*, in so far as it animates every part of the bodies in which it is, and yet *indivisible*, because it is whole in all of these bodies and in each of them severally."

"He who thus considers the greatness of the soul and its powers, will recognise how wonderful and divine it is, and to what a superior order of being it belongs : how, without having any extension, it is present in all extension, and how it occupies a place without being excluded from other places. Thus it is divided yet undivided, or rather it never really is or becomes divided ; for it abides complete in itself, and is divided only in relation to bodies which, in virtue of their divisible nature, are not able to receive it indivisibly. Thus the division belongs really to the bodies, and cannot be attributed to the soul itself."[1]

The world-soul, then, appears to Plotinus as a *tertium quid* which connects the intelligible with the sensible world, though it is conceived as belonging to the former, and only in a secondary way acquiring the qualities of the latter, in so far as it has to manifest its powers through material bodies. Thus, it is out of space and time, and it acquires both spatial and temporal characteristics only as it acts on the material world, and maintains its constant cycle of change. Yet we have to remember, on the other hand, that the material world itself, and the matter which is its potentiality, are conceived as necessary products of the soul. In itself, the world-soul is all but iden-

[1] IV, 2, 1.

tified with the intelligence which it is conceived as continually contemplating; and its action upon the sensible world is not regarded as interfering with its purely ideal life. Further, just because it acts on the whole material world, and is not specially concerned with any particular part of it, the world-soul is free in its activity from all the opposition and conflict of that world; for there is nothing outside the universe which could destroy or in any way affect it. And even the particular souls which are included in the world-soul (just as all intelligences are included in the supreme intelligence), so long as they maintain their unity with the world-soul, are conceived as sharing in its own blessed life. At the same time, as particular souls, they are regarded as capable of falling away from it, and becoming bound up with special bodies, as Plato had already suggested in the *Phaedrus*; and then, though they cannot altogether lose their connexion with the soul of the whole, yet they become involved in all the vicissitudes of the body with which they have become identified. Their good seems to them to be one with the welfare of their particular bodies, and they are thus brought into conflict with other embodied souls which are filled with similar desires.

In this way the individuality of the particular souls seems to carry with it a possibility of evil, which becomes realised in so far as they are drawn down into connexion with particular bodies, and so are caused to forget their own universal nature. And in this association even that universal nature, which they cannot entirely lose, becomes perverted; and their very innate love of the One and craving for union with it, turns into an insatiable greed and a gigantic selfishness which makes them seek to drag everything to themselves. On the other hand, looking at this process from the opposite side, the fall by which particular souls are brought into connexion with material bodies, is also the process whereby these bodies are drawn up into a higher existence than properly belongs to them, and become the organs of human, or animal, or, at the lowest, plant life. For Plotinus follows Plato in maintaining that all forms of life are ultimately identical. The higher principle of soul is in them all, and the distinction merely means that the particular soul has had a less or greater fall, and has sunk into less or more forgetfulness of its divine origin. But such forgetfulness is never final, and it is possible for every soul gradually to retrace the process of its descent, and to rise from the lowest to the highest stage of finite existence. Nay, it is possible for it finally to become delivered from the body altogether and to be restored to its unity with the universal soul, with the universal intelligence, and finally with the Absolute One itself.

It is at once obvious that in this view of the soul we have a concentration of all the difficulties of the system of Plotinus. The soul comes in, as with Plato, to reconnect the material with the spiritual worlds, which have been set in such antagonism that they cannot be directly united. But, if it is to bind the two worlds, it must have something of the nature of both. The possibility of such mediation, however, is itself inconsistent with the absolute opposition of the terms to be united, and the link of combination itself tends to break into two. For the soul, after all, belongs to the higher world; and even when, by the aid of the general principle that the higher form of being always produces a lower copy of itself, we have supposed it to give rise to a material universe upon which it impresses the likeness of its own unity, we need also the supposition of a fall of the particular souls, ere we can bring them into the material world or conceive them as identifying themselves with particular parts of it. And this fall has again itself to be explained by something defective in the nature of these particular souls, which made it impossible for them to maintain themselves in the intelligible world to which they originally belonged—a defect which it is altogether impossible to explain, if the intelligible world is as absolutely separated from the material world as Plotinus maintains it to be. Or, if we adopt the other alternative, and refer the defect to a pre-existing matter which, if it exists, must be invaded by powers derived from the spiritual world, this only throws the difficulty a step farther back, and forces us to ask *why* matter itself must exist, and *why* perfection must produce imperfection. Why, if the One be complete in itself and perfect, need there be anything else besides the One ? Or why, even supposing that the One must manifest itself in an intelligence and an intelligible world, must that intelligence go on to produce a lower manifestation of itself, which involves as a condition of its realisation the existence of matter—matter being essentially evil and producing evil in everything into which it enters as a constituent element ?

The difficulty in which Plotinus is involved, as has already been indicated, was in itself insoluble ; for it was impossible on his principles to discover any logical connexion between the material and intelligible worlds. He had insisted with such one-sided emphasis upon the opposition of these two terms that he was not able to discern the necessary relation that binds them to each other. The pure unity of the self-conscious intelligence is, indeed, as Plotinus saw, the opposite of the dispersion and self-externality of the world in space and time ; but it is its opposite counterpart and cannot therefore in thought be separated from it. Hence they do not need any *tertium quid* to bring them into connexion with each

other. Or, putting it otherwise, their difference and
relation involve that they are complementary elements
in one whole, and the unity of that whole is the only
tertium quid required. It is the usual expedient
of dualism to try to bridge the gulf it has made
by putting some intermediate nature between the
opposites which cannot be directly brought together;
but, if the gulf really exists, such a middle term
will contain in itself both the contradictory elements
and will need another middle term to combine
them. The only possibility of mediation for such
an antagonism is that the opposites should be recognised as essentially related, and, therefore, as the
differentiation of a higher unity. On the other hand,
if the opposites be not regarded as related, except
externally and through an intermediary, a farther
division and abstraction becomes necessary. If we
have, on the one side, the pure unity of self-consciousness maintaining itself through the difference
of subject and object, and, on the other side, the
essential difference and self-externality of the material
world in space and time; and if these two be not
regarded as necessarily united, we are driven in both
cases to explain the combination of unity and difference in both worlds by the matter in which the
unity is realised. Nor does it make any essential
distinction that, in the intelligible world, we have an
ideal matter which produces only a transparent

difference, and in the sensible world a real matter which is capable only of an external synthesis.

The result of this failure of the mediation of the soul is that in the Plotinian scheme we have at the one extreme bare unity, and at the other bare difference, connected by a threefold mediation. In other words, just because Plotinus does not conceive the soul as the unity of the intelligence with the material world, but as a *tertium quid* that partakes of both, he is obliged on the one side to deny that the absolute unity is a unity of differences, or that it ever goes out of itself into the difference of self-consciousness; and he is obliged to deny, on the other side, that matter is ever really brought into subjection by the unifying principle in the material world. What he gives us, therefore, is a *subordination-system*, in which the attempt is made by many intermediates, to overcome the separation of absolute opposites, which cannot be brought into any intelligible relation with each other. And the assertion that the One is above, and matter is below existence and knowledge, only shows that the very idea of an intelligible world is destroyed by dualism, that is, by a theory which divides the world between absolute opposites and refuses to carry them back to any ultimate unity. Thus, to hold that there is, at the one extreme, a positive unity which is completely separated from difference, and which is not capable of being differentiated or determined even by itself, although it is somehow regarded as the source of all the fulness and multiplicity of existence, and, at the other extreme, an essentially negative manifold which cannot be unified, and yet which is somehow externally brought under the unity of ideal forms, is to heap contradiction upon contradiction. Yet all this is not more than the necessary result of the first step towards dualism which was taken by Plato. And, what is still more important, all this is the necessary result of the logic of Mysticism, in so far as Mysticism with one of its voices refers all reality to God, and yet with the other represents the finite existence which is thus negated as somehow subsisting apart from God, even if it be only in order to deny itself. For Mysticism, as we have seen, differs from Pantheism in this, that it does not follow its negative movement to the end; and, just because it fails to do so, it is unable to get beyond its negations to a new positive. In its intense religious concentration it would seem to claim everything for God and leave nothing to his creatures; yet it never loses the consciousness of their independent reality in that of their relation to him. Or rather, perhaps, we should say, that it is so afraid of lowering the divine by connecting it with the finite, that it gives to the finite a kind of independent, though shadowy and illusory existence, which is separate from the divine.

This attitude of mind reaches its extreme expression, and, we might even say, its explanation, in the theory that all moral and natural evils are to be referred to something which in itself is purely negative and unreal, but which yet, as an element in the life of the creatures, turns into the positive opposite of God. Mysticism is a religious experience in which the feeling of God is at its maximum of intensity, an intensity which defeats itself, because it absolutely refuses to expand into a consciousness of God in the world. To it God seems to be at once nothing and all things: *nothing*, because He transcends every definite form of reality, and *all things*, because nothing can be apart from him. Thus every word which it utters has instantly to be retracted on account of its inadequacy. Some of the finest expressions of this attitude of the soul—in which it seems to itself to be ever alone with God without any world between, and is alternately attracted and annihilated by his presence—may be found in the *Confessions* of St. Augustine. But when St. Augustine expresses his deepest religious feelings, we find that he repeats the thoughts and almost the very words of Plotinus. Thus in that great passage in which Augustine gives an account of his last conversation with his mother, Monica, about the life of the redeemed in heaven, he tells us how at first their thoughts tried to climb by means of images derived from the

highest things in the natural world to some idea of
the bliss of perfect union with God, and how, as
they talked and expressed to each other their longing
for it, they seemed for a moment " to reach out to it
with the whole force of their hearts." And he tells
us how, after this moment of ecstatic feeling, words
came again, and they tried to express what they
had felt; and what they said to themselves was this:
"Suppose all the tumult of the flesh in us were
hushed for ever, and all sensible images of earth
and sea and air were put to silence: suppose
the heavens were still, and even the soul spoke no
words to itself, but passed beyond all thought of
itself: suppose all dreams and revelations of
imagination were hushed with every word and sign
and everything that belongs to this transitory world:
suppose they were all silenced—though, if they speak
to one who hears, what they say is: 'We made not
ourselves, but He made us who abides for ever'—yet
suppose they only uttered this, and then were silent,
when they had turned the ears of the hearer to
Him who made them, leaving him to speak alone,
not through them but through himself, so that we
could hear his words, not through any tongue of
flesh nor by the voice of an angel, nor in thunder,
nor in any likeness that hides what it reveals;
suppose, then, that the God whom through such manifestations we have learnt to love, were to be revealed

to us directly without any such mediation—just as, but now, we reached out of ourselves and touched by a flash of insight the eternal wisdom that abides above all; suppose, lastly, that this vision of God were to be prolonged for ever, and all other inferior modes of vision were to be taken away, so that this alone should ravish and absorb the beholder, and entrance him in mystic joy, and our life were for ever like the moment of clear insight and inspiration to which we rose—is not this just what is meant by the words 'Enter thou into the joy of thy Lord?'"

How deeply Neo-Platonism must have sunk into the spirit of St. Augustine, when, in describing the highest moment of his religious experience, he adopts almost verbally the language in which Plotinus tries to depict the mystic ecstasy of the individual soul as it enters into communion with the soul of the world![1]

[1] V, 1, 2.

LECTURE TWENTY-FIFTH.

THE NATURE OF MAN AND HIS RELATION TO GOD.

THE subordination-system of Plotinus described in the last lecture is closely connected with his view of man: for man is a microcosm in which all the grades of reality are repeated, as it were on a reduced scale. His nature reaches up to the Absolute, and down to the animal and the plant. His soul, bound up though it is with the existence, and occupied with the care, of a particular body, yet derives its life from a universal intelligence, which in its turn rests on the absolute unity. He is dependent on the sensations of his physical organism for the material of his thought, and he is therefore liable to be enslaved by the appetites of the animal, and even by obscure instincts that spring out of the nature he has in common with the plants: yet he is capable, like Plato's philosopher, of becoming a 'spectator of all time and existence,' and even of

rising beyond the life of intelligence into immediate
contact with the divine. He is thus a sort of
amphibious being who belongs to both worlds, and
who therefore can climb up to the highest and sink to
the lowest. His peculiar sphere, however, lies in the
middle region between sense and intelligence, the
region of discursive thought, which receives contribu-
tions from both.[1] By virtue of this discursive reason
he, on the one hand, makes judgments and inferences,
in which he distinguishes and connects the images
derived from sense, while, on the other hand, he takes
cognisance of ideas coming to him from above, from
the pure intelligence; and he is able to recognise the
agreement or disagreement of the former with the
latter—a process which Plato called reminiscence.
"Thus when sense apprehends the image of a man
and supplies this image to discursive reason, discursive reason may simply accept the image for what
it is: or if the individual has been formerly met with,
it may ask itself 'Who is this?' and it may answer
by the aid of memory that 'It is Socrates': or it may
go on to evolve the content of the image and distinguish the different elements in it. Or, again, going
beyond all this, it may raise the question whether
Socrates is good, and then, though sense may furnish

[1] This view is closely connected with the ideas of Aristotle expressed in the *De Anima* (see Vol. I, p. 283 *seq.*). The first book
of the first *Ennead* is almost a commentary on the *De Anima*.

the subject matter, or object of thought, it is from itself that the soul derives the criterion of goodness which it uses in its answer. And if it be asked whence it gets this criterion, we must say that it has in itself the form of good, and that the light of intelligence which shines upon it gives it the power of grasping such forms; for this part of the soul is pure, and therefore receives into itself the impressions of the intuitive reason. . . . It appears, then, that *we* are identified not with the intuitive, but with the discursive reason, while the products of the activity of the intuitive reason come to us from above and those of sense from beneath; and that which constitutes our self is the predominant part of the soul, which stands midway between the two powers, the higher and the lower, both of which we may call 'ours' but must not identify with our self."[1]

Yet, on the other hand, we have to remember that this identification of the self with the discursive reason merely represents the ordinary or average self-consciousness of man, in which he is not aware either of the heights or of the depths of his own being. Dwelling in this sphere of thought, man is conscious of himself as a particular individual in relation to, and distinction from other individuals who appear to be external to him and to each other; and his mind moves from one to another of these particular things

[1] V, 3, 3.

or beings, determining them severally, or in relation
to each other, by the categories of the finite. As so
conscious of himself in his finite individuality, man
regards himself as one with a particular bodily
organism; and he is immersed in cares for its preservation, so that it is hard for him to raise his eyes above
the immediate concerns of his earthly life, or to realise
that he has a higher nature than the things of sense
to which his attention is directed. Hence he is
unable to recognise that *they* are but appearances which
come and go with the passing hour, while *he* has
the roots of his being in that which is eternal. He
is, as it were, imprisoned in his individual life, and
subjected to the conditions of time and space, like
the objects he perceives around him; and his love
of himself takes the form of a desire to assert himself
against all others, to prevail over them in the struggle
for existence, and to gain for himself the greatest
amount of satisfaction for his sensuous appetites or
his earthly ambition.

Plotinus contends, however, that this narrow and
limited existence is not due to the essential nature
of the soul; it is the result of a fall from its
original estate. Moreover, it is the act of the
soul itself that has separated it from the universal
life of reason and imprisoned it in mortality. In
its self-will, it has sought to be something for
itself; and it is just this self-seeking which has

confined it to a particular finite form of existence
and identified it with an animal body, and thus
shut it out from the universal or divine life in
which there is no 'mine' and 'thine,' but everyone
possesses the whole and is possessed by it. The
soul has chosen the unrest of time in place of the
peace of eternity; it has chosen spatial division and
externality in place of that presence of all to all
and in all which is the characteristic of the life of
spirit. For "what," asks Plotinus, "has made the
soul forget its divine Father? How is it that
being of a divine nature and born of God, it has
come to be ignorant of itself as well as of him?
The beginning of evil was its audacious revolt,
its fall into the region of becoming and difference,
its desire to be something for itself. When it has
once tasted of the pleasures of self-will, it makes
large use of its power of determining itself as it
pleases; and thus is carried so far away from the
principle of its being that it loses all consciousness
of its original. Such souls are like children torn
away from their parents and brought up in a
foreign country, till they have forgotten what they
themselves are, and who are their parents. Thus
seeing neither God nor themselves, they are degraded
by ignorance of their kinship. They have learnt,
indeed, to honour everything rather than themselves, to spend all wonder and reverence and

affection upon external things, and to break, so far as they can, all the ties that bound them to the divine. Their ignorance of God is bound up with their admiration of such things, and with their contempt for themselves. For he who pursues and admires that which is alien to himself, *ipso facto* confesses his own inferiority; and believing himself to be lower than the things of this world, he regards himself as the most degraded and transitory of all the creatures that come into being and pass away, and the thought of the nature and power of God is entirely banished from his mind." [1]

Our ordinary consciousness of self, then, is the consciousness of being one among many others, external to them as they are to us, and in constant rivalry with them for the limited satisfactions of appetite and ambition; but this is not a consciousness of the real self, and hence it is not a consciousness of God, who is, so to speak, the deepest ground of the self. It is the consciousness of one who in seeking to save his life has lost it, in seeking to be an independent self-sustained being has become divorced not only from God but from himself. But, according to Plotinus, this descent into finitude—this identification of the soul with a particular individuality, and with the bodily

[1] V, 1, 1.

organism, which is its expression—is never complete.
In descending, the soul 'always leaves something
of itself above.'[1]

In this way Plotinus expresses the idea that the
universal nature of the soul is not extinguished, and
that, however much it is forgotten, it is possible for
us to become conscious of it again.   For, after all,
the discursive reason derives all the principles by
the aid of which it judges and reasons, from the
intuitive; and just in so far as we become conscious
of these principles, we lift ourselves above the point
of view of discursive reason.   In other words, in
grasping the principles that enable us to connect
one thing with another, we grasp the unity which is
presupposed in these principles.   We thus realise
that there is a unity of the intelligence with itself
which is beyond the difference of subject and object,
and for which that distinction, like all others, becomes
transparent.   In this unity of the intelligence, therefore, we now find our real self, and, in doing so,
we detach ourselves from all the interests of the
phenomenal world, even from the interest in our self as
one particular object in it.   This movement of thought
is closely akin to that which we observed in the
Stoic philosophy, with only the difference that
Plotinus realised, as the Stoics did not, that the
point of view thus reached is one which excludes

[1] IV, 8, 8.

all the activities of the practical life. For when the distinction of the subject and the object is transcended, nothing is left but the purely contemplative consciousness which Aristotle ascribed to God, and which in the *De Anima* he declared to be a consciousness of all things in their forms, *i.e.* in that ideal reality that is beyond all change.

" In this way," says Plotinus, " we and all that is ours are carried back into real Being. We rise to it, as that from which originally we sprang. We think intelligible objects and not merely their images or impressions, and in thinking them, we are identified with them. Thus we participate in true knowledge, being made one with its objects, not receiving them into ourselves, but rather being taken up into them. And the same is the case with the other souls as with our own. Hence, if we are in unity with the intelligence, we are in unity with each other, and so we are all one. When, on the other hand, we carry our view outside of the principle on which we depend, we lose consciousness of our unity and become like a number of faces which are turned outwards, though inwardly they are attached to one head. But if one of us, like one of these faces, could turn round either by his own effort or by the aid of Athene, he would behold at once God, himself and the whole. At first, indeed, he might not be able to see himself as one with the whole; but soon he would find that there was no boundary he could fix for his separate self. He would, therefore, cease to draw lines of division between himself and the universe: and he would attain to the absolute whole, not by going forward to another place, but by abiding in that principle on which the whole universe is based."[1]

Plotinus, then, like Aristotle, regards discursive thought, which takes things in their separation and connects them externally with each other, as a limited and imperfect manifestation of the intelligence under the conditions of our finite existence. We cannot explain discursive reason, any more than we can explain intuitive reason, as a mere product or property of the bodily organism; but it is because a spiritual being is 'in the body' that he is obliged to think through images, and therefore to conceive things as externally related to each other in time and space. In like manner Plotinus thinks of all the impulses of our individual life, whether of θυμός or of ἐπιθυμία, as closely connected with our physical nature. When, therefore, we rise to the principle on which the discursive intelligence rests, when we become aware of the unity that underlies all our consciousness of particular things, even of our own particular existence, we are already beginning to emancipate ourselves from the body and from the limits of finite individuality that are

[1] VI, 5, 7.

connected therewith. We are rising into a region in which the barriers that divide us from objects, and especially from other beings like ourselves, are thrown down, and in which each intelligence, in knowing itself, at once and intuitively knows all things. We are making a regress upon the universal self, whose consciousness of self is in organic correlation with the consciousness of the not-self. We, therefore, transcend the difference of self and not-self, at least in the form in which that difference at first presents itself, as well as all the other differences that are subordinate to this. Further, as the intuitive unity of all things becomes consciously recognised, the discursive intelligence and its object, the world of time and space, gradually disappear from our view. We are raised into a world of pure light and harmony, into a region like the heaven of Dante, from which all darkness, confusion, and antagonism are excluded, because the whole is present in every part, and every part is transparent to all the others. We have thus found the reality of things in finding our true self, and the partial and distorted images of both which were due to their reflexion upon matter, vanish from our sight.

But, as we have seen, there is a still higher height which we may attain, and in which we may transcend even the transparent division of the intuitive self-consciousness. For as the discursive rests upon the intuitive intelligence, so the intuitive intelligence rests upon an absolute unity, which maintains itself through all the assertion and negation of difference which are essential to self-consciousness; and of this unity we must become conscious, if we would truly know ourselves. Unfortunately in attempting thus to turn back on its own ultimate presupposition, the mind finds itself engaged in what seems a self-contradictory task; for, the very effort of thought to realise its own principle, separates it from that principle, and produces a new division, which seems incapable of being referred to the unity which it is trying to grasp. We thus appear to be repelled from the unity by the very effort we make to approach it; for we are seeking to reach an identity above all difference by means of an intelligence to which the difference of subject and object is essential. To reach that unity, therefore, we must transcend even self-consciousness, and become nothing in order that we may find all things in God. For, in this case also, Plotinus will not allow that we can attain to the higher, if we carry anything of the lower with us, and our intelligence must expire in the love with which it grasps its object. His words are these: " When the soul becomes intelligence it possesses and thinks the intelligible, but when it has intuition of God it abandons everything else. It is like a visitor introduced into a lordly dwelling, who for a while is content to gaze upon its varied beauties, but who forgets them all when the master of the house presents himself; for the master, he finds, is no mere statue or ornament for a moment's wonder, but a presence that demands all attention for himself alone. Upon him, therefore, the visitor will steadfastly fix his eyes till, in the continuous intensity of his contemplation, he no longer sees the object he contemplates, but his vision becomes, as it were, incorporate therewith. Thus, what was at first a mere object of sight, becomes an inward seeing which shuts out even the memory of everything else he has ever seen. In order, however, to make the simile exact we must think of the master of the house not as a man, but as a God, and, again, we must think of this God as not merely appearing to the eyes of the visitor, but as filling his soul: for this alone will fitly illustrate the difference between that lower power of intelligence by which it contemplates what is in itself and that higher power by which, in a flash of intuition and inspiration, it grasps that which is beyond itself, first seeing it, and then becoming one with what it sees. And, while the former is the vision of an intelligence which still is in possession of itself, the latter is the intuition of an intelligence which is transported beyond itself by love. For it is just when it has drunk of this nectar which deprives it of understanding, that it is reduced by love to that simple unity of being which is the perfect satisfaction of our souls." [1]

[1] VI, 7, 35.

Observe further that, while Plotinus speaks of the soul divesting itself of all that divides it from God, even of thought, he does not hold that in doing so it is going out of itself to something strange or foreign; for God, in his view, is not 'far from any one of us,' but on the contrary, we truly come to ourselves only as we lose ourselves in him. "God," says Plotinus, "is external to nothing and to no one, but is present even with those who do not know him: though they escape out of him, or rather out of themselves, and, therefore, are not able to see him from whom they have exiled themselves. Having thus lost themselves, how can they find another being? A child who is frenzied and out of his mind will not know his father. But he who has learnt to know himself, will know also the Being from whom he comes."[1] Hence it is only needful to remove the division we have ourselves produced in order to be at one with God. In an earlier lecture, I quoted the passage of Plotinus where he compares men to a chorus, which, though it encircles the choragus, yet sings out of tune when it turns away from him and looks outward to other things, but which, when it turns to him, sings in perfect harmony because it makes him its centre. God is our centre, from whom to separate ourselves is to be in discord with ourselves and with all things; while to be in direct

[1] VI, 9, 7.

communion with him is to attain perfect harmony and peace with ourselves and with the universe. The result, then, is that the ascent of man, as Plotinus describes it, is not an ascent into some region from which he was at first entirely separated : it is his ascent into himself, into self-consciousness, and, finally, into a consciousness of, or rather a contact with God, as that unity of our being which is even deeper than the self.

On this we may remark, in the first place, that Plotinus clearly recognises the distinction between what is potential in man and what is actually realised in him ; and, secondly, that in the main, though not entirely, this distinction coincides with the distinction between the unconscious and the conscious—between that which man is and that which he realises himself to be. Up to a certain point at least, what is actualised in man is what he is *for himself*; and when we speak of anything in him of which he is not conscious, we are pointing rather to what he may become, than to what he actually is. From this point of view, we cannot give him credit, or at least full credit, for anything that goes beyond his own view of himself, and of the world to which he is related. He *is* what he thinks himself, and thinks himself what he *is*. Hence Plotinus maintains that men, as men, are identified with the discursive reason and its products, meaning that in their ordinary consciousness they know themselves and others only as beings who are external to each other in space and changing in time; and that, therefore, if we regard their actual attainments in this stage, we must look upon them as beings who are limited to this kind of existence and this kind of consciousness. Yet Plotinus holds equally that they have in them, involved in this very consciousness, a higher potentiality, and that to realise *it*, they do not need to be transformed, but only to be developed. They do not need to go *out of* themselves, but rather, so to speak, *into* themselves, or, in other words, to become conscious of their own real nature. Or, rather, if we are to put it exactly as Plotinus puts it, the process is not a development of something new, but rather a recovery of what they have lost. Their rise to something better is a return to their native origin; it is deliverance from a yoke to which they have subjected themselves; it is the removal of an illusion which hides them from their own eyes.

On the other hand, while the way upward for man is the way to a deeper consciousness of himself than that which he at first possesses, there is open to him also a way downward which involves the gradual darkening and extinction of that consciousness of himself which, as man, he still retains. The soul, by indulgence in sensuous passions, may immerse itself more and more completely in the material body, till the light of discursive reason dies out into the obscure sensations and instincts of the animal, and till even these are lost in the unconscious movements of the nutritive and reproductive life of the plant. For Plotinus—as against the view of Aristotle that each soul is relative to a particular organism—recurs to the Pythagorean or Platonic idea of transmigration. The soul, he argues, *is* everything potentially, and, therefore, can *become* anything. It can pass through all the grades of being from the lowest to the highest: it can ascend up to the absolute One, and it can descend till all consciousness, even in the form of sensitive feeling, is extinguished in it.

So far the ascent of man seems to be the development of a clearer self-consciousness, and his descent the obscuration of the self-consciousness he possesses. But this, in the view of Plotinus, holds good only within very narrow limits. For, in the first place, even the rise to what Plotinus describes as the purer self-consciousness of intelligence seems to involve the disappearance of self-consciousness in the ordinary sense of the word; since in the pure intuition of reason all memory and imagination, as well as all discourse of reason, are lost. The remembrance of the events of the earthly life of the individual and all circumstances attaching to his transitory individuality, must vanish from the consciousness that sees all things *sub specie aeternitatis*. Nor, indeed, can there remain in it any thought of the particular self as such. Hence the self of which the pure intelligence is conscious is simply the pure subjective unity of thought to which all objects are referred; and in this sphere objects are known only through the changeless ideas that are realised in them. The objects of such a pure intellectual consciousness are not the things of the immediate experience of the finite individual; and the self of which it is conscious in apprehending them is not the empirical self. Plotinus, indeed, asserts that in this pure consciousness the individuality of every particular intelligence is still preserved. But it is hard to see what this can mean. For, even at this stage the movement of ascent seems to be, not the rise to a higher self-consciousness—in which all that was present in the lower sphere is reasserted, though with a new light thrown upon it—but the recoil upon a simple intuition in which all that concerns the limited individual life is left out. It is a movement towards a more abstract, and not towards a fuller and more concrete, view of things.

And this holds still more obviously of the last movement of ascent to the immediate experience of the absolute One. Plotinus himself confesses that this, if it be in one sense a progress to a deeper experience, is yet a movement away from all definite consciousness either of the self or of its objects; and he even goes so far as to compare the indefinable and indeterminate nature of matter which is below knowledge with the equally indefinable nature of the One which is above it. "As it is asserted of matter that it must have none of the qualities of things in itself, if it is to receive equally the impressions of them all, so and in a much more absolute way, must the soul become formless, if nothing is to hinder it from being filled and enlightened by the nature which is before all others."[1] Are we then to say that the whole process of spiritual ascent is not a movement to a more full and concrete consciousness of reality, but simply a movement of abstraction, in which, one after another, every feature of the world we know disappears till nothing is left? And is the "presence deeper than knowledge" in which it ends only another name for the disappearance of the soul and all its contents in the absolute unity?

On this point two things have to be said. The first is, that the religious man's realisation of the deepest truth often takes a form which might without much inaccuracy be described as a "presence deeper than knowledge," or at least deeper than *his* knowledge. In other words, in contrast with his ordinary dispersed and changing experience of finite things, the religious man has an immediate consciousness of a permanent power and presence of the divine, on which he rests, but which he is unable

[1] VI, 9, 7.

to measure. And when he tries to define what he experiences, expression seems to fail him. Sometimes, like a Hebrew prophet, he uses the highest images he can think of, only to declare their inadequacy; at other times he takes refuge in negatives to get rid of the apparent limitation of every affirmation. As in Dante's vision the whole universe was gathered round a central point in God, who yet at the same time was conceived as an infinite circumference embracing all things, so in the worshipper's heart God contains, and yet transcends, everything; and the double aspect of God as the One in whom all is lost, and yet the One in whom all is found, seems to be expressible only by asserting the failure of all expression. Thus what is really the deepest and fullest of all our experiences is apt to adopt the language of Agnosticism, in order to convey a meaning that seems too great for any form of words.

But, in the second place, we have to observe, that when the man who is thus inspired by "thoughts beyond the reaches of this soul," declares that he knows nothing, he means the very opposite of what he says. He does not mean that his mind is empty, but that it is too full; and his revolt against the idea of knowledge is caused by his realising a deeper unity, and so a greater completeness of being, than that which is consciously present to

him in what he ordinarily calls knowledge. He seems,
therefore, to leave such knowledge behind him, as
having no relation to the higher object that fills his
soul.   Nor does he realise that it is from the common
consciousness of things and experience that he starts,
and that his highest vision or intuitive feeling would
have no meaning if it did not reflect back its light on
the ordinary world of experience, and enable him,
however imperfectly, to reconstitute his view of that
world in accordance with " the pattern showed him in
the Mount." For it is, after all, with materials
derived from the world of sense that we must build
up our New Jerusalem; and the Divine Being whom
we oppose to everything else, would be a mere
abstraction, if we did not somehow refer all that is
finite to him.

If once this truth be realised, it comes to be
seen that the religious movement upwards cannot
be a mere movement of abstraction; and that, if it
be in one aspect a *via negativa*, yet its negations
always have a positive behind them.   The defect of
Mysticism, and especially of the Mysticism of
Plotinus, is that it does not discern this; and that,
therefore—if we follow out its characteristic way of
thought to the logical result—it ends in a false isolation
at once of the God worshipped and of the spirits
that worship him.   For the whole way upwards is
described as one in which the spirit divests itself of

one element of its life after another in order to adapt
itself to the nature of the object with which it seeks
to be united. In this sense, Plotinus compares the
true mystic to one who, before entering into a shrine,
has to purify himself from all the defilements of the
world, and even to strip off all his garments, that he
may leave behind him whatever is unworthy of or
alien to the god. So must man in his upward progress divest himself of everything finite, even of
things which in the lower plane of finite life were
good and useful. Thus practical morality is regarded by Plotinus as simply a process of purification
($\kappa\acute{a}\theta\alpha\rho\sigma\iota\varsigma$), by which the body and its passions are
got rid of; and when once the cleansing is complete,
the ethical life with all its virtues is to be left
behind. Thus the practical gives way to the
contemplative life, which, as we have seen, is
emptied of all reference to the experience of the
individual in this world. And, finally, even the contemplative life itself has to make way for an ecstasy,
in which the soul is stripped of everything except the
bare feeling of the divine. The ultimate result is a
religion which, just because it has substituted itself for
all other interests, has ceased to be the consecration of
all action and all knowledge, and which, in being
set against both, loses all its value even as a religion.

From this it appears where the error of Plotinus lies.
It lies, not in the regressive dialectic by which he

reaches higher and higher points of view, but in the fact that the higher point of view is taken at each regress to exclude the lower and not to enable us to correct the results won from it.   It may give some additional force to this criticism, if we remark that the successive steps of the ascending movement of the thought of Plotinus have a close analogy to the stages in the development of the idealistic philosophy of Germany—an analogy which, however, conceals a profound difference of method.   Thus both these movements begin in a perception of the defects of the ordinary consciousness, in so far as it conceives all objects as externally related to each other, and takes even the self as one particular object among others.   And they both seek to correct this defect by calling attention to the universality of the self, to which in knowledge all objects are referred.   When, therefore, Plotinus referred back the discursive to the intuitive reason, he was making the same kind of reflective regress upon the conditions of experience as that which was afterwards made by Kant when he brought to light what he called the *Transcendental Unity of Apperception*—when, in other words, he showed how the unity of the self is implied in all determination of objects as such. We may add that Kant made substantially the same mistake as Plotinus, when he regarded that relation of the world of experience to the self as showing that the world of experience is merely phenomenal. For thus Kant was led to isolate the bare unity of thought with itself from the unity of experience which depends upon it, in the same way that Plotinus severs the intuitive from the discursive reason.

The true lesson, as was shown by Kant's idealistic successors, was simply that we must not view any object as complete in itself apart from the mind that knows it. Hence, as Fichte already contended, the world of experience—which we at first take as a world of independent individual things conditioned by time and space and acting externally upon each other, a world whose elements are bound to each other only by external necessity—must ultimately be regarded as an organic system, which is so essentially related to the intelligence that all its parts and changes are phases in the self-determined life of that intelligence. In like manner, if Plotinus were right in regarding the perfect unity of intuitive reason as the presupposition of even our discursive knowledge of the world of sense, the inference is that the idea of the former must be taken, not as excluding the idea of the latter, but as enabling us to reinterpret it. In other words, the spiritual world must be regarded, not as another world to which we ascend by leaving the natural world behind us, but as simply the natural world viewed in relation to its principle.

Lastly, the regress of Plotinus upon the One viewed as an absolute unity—transcending even the division of subject and object which is found in the pure intelligence—is very similar to the step which Schelling took when he rose above the subjective Absolute of Fichte's earlier philosophy. For as soon as it had been proved that there is a real correlation between subject and object so that the consciousness of each implies the other, it became necessary to conceive the unity, to which the world is referred, as transcending the opposition between them. And the analogy may be carried farther. For Schelling, at least in his earlier writings, seemed to regard that unity as a centre of indifference, an Absolute of which nothing could be said, though it is the source both of the ideal and the real world, both of spirit and nature. It, however, soon became visible to Hegel, if not to Schelling himself, that the unity cannot thus be separated from the difference which presupposes it, but that both the real and the ideal process must be reinterpreted from the higher point of view of that unity. In other words, the idea of God would lose all meaning, if He were taken as simply a unity transcending all finite and particular existence, and not as a Being who realises himself in the whole process of nature and spirit.

It thus appears that modern philosophy has retraced the ascending path of Plotinus, and indeed, of the whole ancient philosophy which gathers to a climax in him. But the result is different, because in each step of this ascent the endeavour of modern philosophy has been, not to set the higher view of things in opposition to the lower, but rather to reconstitute the latter by means of the former. In other words, the ultimate tendency of modern philosophy has been not to separate spirit from nature, and God from both, but to see God as the principle from whom both come, of whom both in their difference and relation are the manifestation, and to whom through the whole process of their existence they return.

It appears, then, that the movement of Greek philosophy toward a deeper and deeper self-consciousness, ends, owing to the method of abstraction it follows, in the absolute negation of all consciousness. In other words, it is just because it separates the higher from the lower point of view instead of using the former to correct the latter, that, ultimately, it empties the higher point of view of all its positive meaning. For, when the intuitive unity of self-consciousness, with its ideal difference of the subject and the object self, is torn away from the discourse of reason with its external synthesis, and when the unity beyond the difference of self-consciousness in its turn is torn away even from *its* transparent difference, the ascent is made in such a way that the path of descent is absolutely barred. The πρῶτον ψεῦδος of this method may be already

detected in Aristotle's conception of the purely contemplative life of God from which all essential
reference to the world was excluded. But, while
Aristotle was content to take the world for granted,
Plotinus was forced to face the difficulty of its origin.
And, as we have seen, he could find no ground for the
existence of anything other than God, except in the idea
of a natural necessity by which the higher, though its
activity is and can only be directed to itself, produces
some lower copy of its own nature. But, in thus
making the universe an accident, produced, indeed, by
the divine, yet not because God is essentially self-
manifesting, but only because it is somehow necessary,
Plotinus practically revives the old Greek doctrine
which puts fate above the gods. In other words, he
escapes making matter independent of God, only to
subject God to a natural law which is independent of
himself. Thus Plotinus implicitly denies, what he
seeks above all to affirm, that God is all in all, the
source and end of all things.

And we must further note what is at least one of
his motives for this denial. He is solicitous to guard
against attributing deliberation or design to God in
the creation of the world, because this would throw
upon God the responsibility for all the evils and
imperfections that are found in it. God creates
because He cannot be and not create, and, therefore,
the universe may be described as eternally begotten.

Moreover, when it is begotten, it is not God that seeks it, but it that seeks God; κινεῖ ὡς ἐρώμενον, as Aristotle had said.[1] Thus Plotinus involves himself in more than all the difficulties of the Aristotelian doctrine, which transfers the cause of motion from the object of love to the lover.   Nor can the difficulty be removed by conceiving such love as a mere want, which is satisfied by the influence coming from its object. Love, indeed, is a want, but it is also a principle of activity that reaches beyond the want to its satisfaction; and the being in whom it is has a principle of movement in himself, and cannot be conceived as a mere matter for a form that comes from without.   *A fortiori* the Being who is the ultimate source as well as the object of all love cannot be conceived as having no love in himself. Thus God must be regarded not simply as creating beings other than himself, but as realising *himself* in his creatures; for if not, their relation to him will be accidental and external, and He will not be *their* God.   Thus the philosophy of Plotinus is the condemnation of the Greek dualism, just because it is he who carries it to its utmost point.   It is the proof that we cannot so emphasise the *transcendence* of God in relation to his universe as to deny his

---

[1] In VI, 8, 15, Plotinus says, ἐράσμιον καὶ ἔρως ὁ αὐτὸς καὶ αὑτοῦ ἔρως, but in this passage he is avowedly using language which he admits to be not strictly accurate.

immanence therein, without ultimately being led to the absolute denial that He is *its God* at all. Or, to put the same truth in its particular application, we cannot deny that God is essentially related to man, without also denying that man is essentially related to God.

Now, it may, I think, be shown that the doctrine which finds the universe, and especially the doctrine which finds humanity, *in* God, was implicit in Christianity from the first, and that it found expression in the development of Christian doctrine. At the same time, as it was by the aid of Greek philosophy, and especially of Neo-Platonism, that that doctrine was developed, it was impossible that the dualism which was so deeply rooted in Greek philosophy should not greatly influence that development. And we find, as a matter of fact, that this was so, and that, as a consequence, the very doctrine of reconciliation became itself the parent of a new dualism which deeply affected Christianity all through the middle ages, and has not ceased to affect it down to the present day.

Into this, however, as it lies beyond our present subject, we cannot yet enter. But it may help to deepen our view of the difficulty if, in the next lecture, we examine the way in which Plotinus deals with the problem of evil, and how, in doing so, he and his followers were brought into collision with the Christian Church.

LECTURE TWENTY-SIXTH.

THE CONTROVERSY BETWEEN PLOTINUS AND THE GNOSTICS.

THE period of the activity of Plotinus as a teacher at Rome lasts from 244 to 262 A.D., a period in which there was great activity of thought in the Church, and much controversy with the Gnostics and other heretics, who sought to introduce into its doctrine many elements borrowed from Eastern religion and Western philosophy. Nor can there be any doubt that Plotinus was brought into close contact with such speculations, and that he had to maintain his ground against them in the discussions of his school. The Neo-Platonist system was, as we have seen, the concentrated result of Greek philosophy, and its disciples were the natural representatives of the principles of that philosophy in the defensive war of ancient culture against the new ideas that were invading the world. The echo of these controversies is discernible not only in the one directly polemical work of Plotinus against the Gnostics, but also in many of his later writings, particularly in his discourses upon Providence.[1] From these we can gather that Plotinus had to meet an attack upon his doctrines from two sides, both from those who represented a deeper Pessimism and from those who represented a higher Optimism than his own. And, indeed, these two attacks sometimes merged in one, in so far as the Gnostics, who carried the dualism of Greece to a form more extreme than Plotinus, at the same time maintained in a somewhat imperfect form, the Christian doctrine of the redemption of the lost and degraded.

It is curious to notice the intensity of passion with which Plotinus threw himself into the defence of both aspects of his own doctrine, and insisted upon the necessity of the exact compromise by which he attempted to reconcile them with each other. From the nature of the case, he had to maintain a balance between opposites. He had, to put it shortly, to prove that the world is relatively good, or rather that it is the best of all possible worlds, because the One, which is also the Good, is its source and its end. Yet, on the other hand, he had also to contend that, as a material world, it is evil and opposed to the divine, and that the great object and purpose of the moral and religious life is to escape from it. In the effort

[1] III, 1-3.

to maintain at once these two opposite positions,
his philosophy is, as it were, torn asunder. We
cannot say that he was ever shaken in the conviction
of the truth of his own system; but there are passages
in his later works which show how deeply he felt
the stress of upholding it against its assailants. And
while, even in these works, there are chapters full of
the glow of passionate faith, yet I think it is true
that, as his dialectic becomes more subtle and com-
plicated, the movement of his thought becomes less
spontaneous and less vividly imaginative. On the
whole, it is in his earlier writings that we find the
finest expressions of sublime religious enthusiasm.
And the reason seems to be that his thought, through
all the first period of his teaching, dwells mainly
on the soul's ascent from grade to grade in the
spiritual world, or, in other words, on the ways in
which it may escape from matter and sense, and
return into union with the divine. Love of beauty,
dialectic, and the practice of moral virtue are described
as different means by which it can purify itself and
prepare for true final deliverance ; and the various
orders of being are represented as stages which the
soul has to traverse on its upward way to God, in
whom alone it can find rest and blessedness. The
climax is found in the ninth book of the sixth
Ennead, in which Plotinus devotes his highest powers
of imaginative expression to describe the flight of the

'lonely soul,' the soul that has freed itself from all difference and finitude, to the 'lonely One,' φυγὴ μόνου πρὸς μόνον. It had not yet occurred to Plotinus to deal seriously with the difficulties which arise when we consider that all these lower stages of being, with all the evils they contain, must owe their existence to that divine or absolute Being, who alone is conceived as perfectly good.

Now these difficulties were first brought before Plotinus in an effective way by certain members of the Gnostic schools, who maintained that the sensible and material world was produced by an evil *Demiurgus* or Creator; that the spirits of men, in so far as they belong to that world, are subject to darkening and polluting influences; and, finally, that they, or rather the elect among them, are to be delivered from such influences by a Redeemer emanating from the higher spiritual world, who should descend into the world of sense to break the chains by which they are bound. Plotinus had made the world-soul the lowest grade in his Trinity of the spiritual world, and had treated it as the mediating principle through which the higher grades communicate with the world of sense and matter. But the idea that the material world is essentially evil, was abhorrent to him; and if he was obliged to admit—if, indeed, it were necessarily involved in his philosophical principles—that that world has evil in it, yet he is eager to maintain that

it is as good as it can be, and even that it is in essence
good, and only accidentally evil. This world-despising
mystic, therefore, when he encounters the coarser and
more pronounced dualism of the Gnostics—which not
only condemns the material as such, but gives over the
present world to the evil one, and regards it as
essentially the kingdom of Satan—remembers that he is
a Greek, and that sensible beauty is for him, if not the
perfect manifestation, yet the reflexion and product of
a still higher ideal beauty. From this point of view,
therefore, he is fain to glorify that very phenomenal
world from which, in his mystic mood, he had turned
away almost with loathing, as the best of all possible
material worlds. As a material world, it is a ' shadow
of good things, and not the perfect image of them'; but,
at the worst, it provides the first stepping-stone from
which, and by means of which, we can ascend to a
higher order of being. Hence he is roused to anger
against those who would destroy the fine balance of
the Platonic spirit, in which the aspiring idealism that
seeks to emancipate the intelligence from the bondage
of sense is so perfectly poised against the artistic
feeling that clings to the sensible, as the manifestation
of the ideal. And he does not reflect that this fine
balance has already been destroyed by his own
mysticism.

Urged by such motives Plotinus, in his discourse
against the Gnostics, endeavours to go as far in the

direction of Optimism as his general principles will allow him. This world is, indeed, he allows, only a reflexion or copy of the higher world, and, as a reflexion, it cannot be equal to its original; but it comes as near to that original as a reflexion can do. We are not to say that this world is evil, though there are many untoward things in it; it would be too much to expect that it should have all the perfection of the intelligible world. But, he asks, allowing that it is only an image, "what more beautiful image could there be? After the fire of the intelligible world, what better image of it could there be than our fire? What earth, outside of the intelligible earth, could be better than ours? After the self-centred unity of the intelligible world, what sphere could be more perfect or more regular in its revolution than the sphere of our heavens? Or, again, if we set aside the sun of the intelligible world, what other sun could shine more brightly than ours?"[1] That contempt of the world of sense, which the Gnostics regarded as a proof of the elevation of their spirits, is rather, Plotinus contends, a proof of the opposite; for he who despises the beauty he has seen, must be one in whom it does not awake the reminiscence of the higher beauty from which it is derived. "For what musician, who has perceived the harmony of the intelligible world, will

[1] II, 9, 4.

(margin notes:)
...orld, tho' a copy, comes near to the ...al as a ...y can.

not evil: not perfect.

Gnostic con-...t for the ...d of sense

...ho despises ...auty he has ...must be in whom it ...kens no rem-...ence of the ...ir beauty from ...t came

listen without emotion to the harmonies of sensible sound? Or what scientific man, who possesses the knowledge of geometry or arithmetic, will not rejoice to recognise the symmetry and proportion and order of the objects that are presented to his eyes? Even one who looks at a picture can hardly be said to see it, unless he recognises in it a visible imitation of ideal beauty, and unless it carries him out of himself and awakens a reminiscence of the truth it imitates. It is this reminiscence, indeed, which is the beginning of love. If, then, he who sees beauty well represented in the face of a man, be carried beyond it to the intelligible, can anyone be so inert and insensible of soul as to behold all the beauties of the material world with all its symmetry and order, and all the glory of form which shows itself in the heavenly bodies, far off as they are, and yet not to take all this to heart and reflect with reverence what they are, and from what original they come? He who can do so, hath truly beheld neither the one nor the other."[1]

Above all, the supposition that the general system of the world is evil, and that no good is to be found in it except in the souls of those men whom the Gnostic called spiritual, strikes Plotinus as an absolute inversion of the truth. To him, as an inheritor of the tradition of Plato and Aristotle, the principle

[1] II, 9, 16.

seems axiomatic that Providence looks to the whole
rather than to the parts, and that the world-soul
participates in good in a higher degree than the
souls of individuals. In particular he holds to the
peculiarly Greek idea (which Philosophy adopted from
mythology), that the heavenly bodies, the sun and the
stars, are in a special sense the organs of the divine, and
are lifted by their perfect order and regularity of movement far above the change and contingency of the life of
man. "It is absurd," he declares, "that they (*i.e.* the
Gnostics), who have bodies like other men and are
subject to sensuous desire, and to fear and anger,
should form such a high idea of their own capacity,
and should assert that *they* can attain to the intelligible, while they will not concede to the sun, which is
far less exposed to passion and disorder and change, a
greater wisdom than belongs to us men, who are
the creatures of a day and who are kept back from
the truth by so many illusions. Yet they assert that
their own souls, yea, and the souls of the meanest of
men, are immortal and divine, while the whole
heaven and all its stars, composed as they are of
nobler and purer elements, have no part in immortality; and this, though they see the perfect order
and symmetry that prevails in tho heavens, and
tho disorders of our earthly life. It is as if
they supposed that the soul, which is immortal,
of set purpose chose the worse place for itself, and

surrendered the better place to the souls of mortal men." [1]

The world of sense, then, is for Plotinus as good as it can be, and we see its goodness the more, the more we look to the whole or to those parts of it which, like the heavenly bodies, partake in its eternity, and the less we look to the changing lot of mortal creatures upon earth. Man occupies a middle rank and partakes at once of immortality and of mortality, and for him, therefore, we may expect a mingled and checkered life, corresponding to his double nature. Somewhere in the hierarchy of being there must be such a creature as man, and the defect of his nature

---

[1] II, 9, 5. We cannot say with certainty that these words were directed against Christianity, but no language could more clearly bring out the opposition between the spirit of intellectual aristocracy that still clings to Neo-Platonism and the levelling Universalism of the Christian faith, with its uncompromising claim of the highest for the most degraded of men. It reminds us of the striking passage in the *Confessions* of St. Augustine, in which he tells us what he found and what he did not find in Neo-Platonism, and how, therefore, he could attain no final satisfaction in it, but only in the Christian faith. He found in Neo-Platonism a conception of the spirituality of God, which freed him from the materialistic tendencies of his earlier Manichaeism; but he did not find in it that doctrine of the Word made flesh, which showed that all humanity is sacred, even in its utmost degradation, which humbled man with the sense of his unworthiness, yet at the same time revealed to him an infinite hope. *Ubi erat illa aedificans caritas a fundamento humilitatis, quod est Christus Jesus? . . . Non habuit illae paginae vultum pietatis hujus: lacrimas confessionis, sacrificium tuum, spiritum contribulatum, cor contritum et humiliatum, populi salutem, sponsem, civitatem, arrham spiritus sancti, poculum pretii nostri. Conf.* VII, ch. 20, 21.

shows itself in a weakness of will, which makes him incapable of sustaining himself in the intelligible world.   Yet we are not to suppose that this original defect is a fixed limit to man's soul.   He can by experience of evil learn to choose what is good, and the way upward as well as the way downward is open to him.   As Plato said, " Virtue owns no control but its own," and by his conduct in one life man chooses the δαίμων that is to rule him in the next.   We might be disposed to refer this idea of transmigration and of the possibility of an ultimate deliverance from the necessity of being born again into the world of sense, to influences derived from the East, and especially from India, where the doctrine prevails to this day ; for we know that Plotinus accompanied the Emperor Gordian in his campaign in the East, and he might there have come into contact with some representatives of the Indian pantheism.   But his language shows that he is merely developing the ideas of Plato.

Plotinus has several ways of explaining evil which seem to run into, or alternate with each other.   In the first place, he refers it to the free choice of the individual.   He is specially earnest in denouncing the idea of fate, in the sense of an external necessity which determines all individual things and beings. Indeed, he points out that such an idea, if universalised, is self-contradictory.   "This necessity," he

declares, " by its very excess destroys itself and does
away with the enchainment or continuous connexion
of causes.   For it would be absurd to say that our
different members are fatally moved, because they are
moved by the directing principle of our will—seeing it
is not one thing that gives and another that receives
the impulse, but there is one principle present in all
our members determining them to move and be moved
by each other.   So, in like manner, if in the whole
universe there be one principle which is common to
that which acts and to that which is acted on, and the
movement of one part cannot be referred to that of
another, we should express the truth best by saying,
not that all things happen through the causation of
one by another, but that all things are one.   On this
hypothesis, then, we could not even say that we are
ourselves, or that any action is ours, but all our
counsels and resolves must be referred to the determination of another.   In that case, to say that *we* act
would be like saying that our feet kick, when we kick
by means of them.   We must, therefore, maintain for
each individual his own individuality, and we must
give to each the credit of his own acts and thoughts,
whether they be good or bad.   And especially we
must not attribute our deeds to the whole, least of all
our evil deeds." [1]

In this way Plotinus shows that a thorough-going

[1] III, 1, 4.

system of necessity is inconsistent with the attribution to the individual of an independent will or even of a self; for the idea of necessity presupposes relatively independent things or beings, one of which determines the other, but if the determination of one by the other is absolute, there will be no independent things or beings. We must, on that hypothesis, treat not only freewill but even self-consciousness as an illusion; for an ego or self can only exist on condition that we are entitled to refer actions and thoughts to it as apart from all other things or beings. And the same holds with all individuality, whether self-conscious or not. Fate, therefore, is a self-contradictory conception; for if the principle of the whole never gives, nor can give, an independent individuality to the parts, it cannot of course take it away. This, no doubt, is an important thought, and the consideration of it may suggest an answer to an objection commonly brought against the idea of freedom. It is often said that, if we regard the universe as a whole and refer it to one principle, which, as the principle of the whole, must be absolute and infinite, we cannot admit anything like freedom or independence in any of the parts. But to this it may be answered that, if we adopt such an argument, we are really limiting that very principle, which at the same time we are declaring to be absolute and infinite; in other words, we are maintaining that an infinite Being cannot go beyond itself or give rise to any creature even relatively independent of itself. Thus we seem to be driven to the conclusion that, if there be any ultimate unity at all, it must be a Pantheistic unity, in which all difference is so completely lost that even the illusive appearance of it becomes inexplicable. In the language of Plotinus, the doctrine of necessity carried to the extreme contains the negation of itself; for the many existences, which are connected by links of necessity, must collapse into one, and to say that the one Being who includes all is necessary, has no meaning.

So far, the argument of Plotinus is irresistible; but how does he himself escape the difficulty? He also holds that the Absolute One does not go beyond itself, and that its activity, so far as we can ascribe to it activity, is directed only to itself. He holds, to put it broadly, that *it* is not responsible for the existence of those lower forms of being, which nevertheless must be allowed to spring from it, and to owe their existence to it. But how then can they exist at all, if the Absolute does not realise itself in them? Plotinus, as we have seen, is obliged to fall back on the strange supposition of an action of the Absolute which is accidental, or has only an external necessity. The inexplicable law that the higher form of being always produces a lower form, though without any action directed to the lower, is used by Plotinus at once to account for the existence of the lower, and yet to save the higher from any responsibility for it. Hence we have a descending scale of degrees of reality, each of which produces the imperfect image of itself in that which follows it, till ultimately we are carried beyond the intelligible world into the region of matter, in which defect turns into physical and moral evil. Thus God is saved from being the cause of evil by a twofold expedient: first, by the interposition of a number of intermediate beings between the highest and the lowest; and secondly, by the idea that the production of the lower is an accidental result, and not the aim or object of the activity of the higher.

But it is obvious that this is no satisfactory solution of the difficulty. For, in the first place, the very idea of an accidental operation of the Absolute is self-contradictory, as it implies that the Absolute in its outgoing activity is subjected to a law which is not involved in its own nature as absolute. And, in the second place, the interposition of the pure intelligence and the world-soul between the absolute One and the region of matter, only distributes the problem of evil over the different grades of reality, without doing anything towards the solution of it. Plotinus, indeed, seems to maintain that, though the intelligence and the world-soul are defective as compared with the

One, yet there is, strictly speaking, no evil, till we reach the material world. But this contradicts the doctrine of Plotinus himself, that evil lies essentially in defect, in the negative as such. It also contradicts another of his doctrines, according to which the reason for the descent of an individual soul into the material world must lie in something defective in its nature as a soul, or even as an intelligence. For, as we have seen, Plotinus repeatedly refers this fall to the self-will of the soul, which withdraws itself from the whole, and seeks to be something for itself. In one passage, indeed, he seems to find a reason for the fall in the need of the soul to learn by experience of evil that 'good is best.'[1] But this, again, would imply that the soul in the intelligible world is a mere possibility or potentiality, and that it requires to pass through the trial and discipline of this world, in order to become developed. Such a conception, however, involving, as it does, that existence in the material world may itself be regarded as a necessary stage in the development of the spirit,

[1] In IV, 8, 5, Plotinus says that "if the soul soon escapes from the world of sense, it has suffered no loss by entering it, but, on the contrary, has gained the knowledge of evil, and learned to recognise its essential nature; it has become conscious of its own powers and manifested them in action, powers which would never have come into exercise if it had remained in the intelligible world. Thus the soul could never have known its own possessions; for only the actual exercise shows the capacity, which would otherwise remain unknown, and could not even be said to exist in any true sense."

would necessitate, if it were worked out to its consequences, a complete transformation of the whole
view of Plotinus as to the relation of the two worlds.
Finally, when Plotinus refers all evil to matter, he
makes it inexplicable how the soul should ever
descend or enter into connexion with matter; or how,
if by some external necessity it does so descend, the
responsibility for the evils to which that fall gives
rise, should ever attach to the soul itself.

In his discourses upon Providence, the principal
aim of which is to maintain that God is not responsible for evil, Plotinus adopts another and a more
promising line of argument.   He compares the course
of the world to a drama in which there is much
conflict between the *dramatis personae*, yet in which
such conflict is always subordinated to the unity of
the whole.   And, in connexion with this metaphor,
he goes on to maintain that the nature of the
universe will be more rational and perfect if it
allows room, not only for difference, but also for
antagonism between its separate parts; indeed, he
even seems to suggest the idea that the highest unity
is that which admits and overcomes the greatest
antagonisms within itself.   Now in the intelligible
world there is a perfect organic unity overcoming all
its difference; but in the world of sense, which is its
copy, this difference changes into a conflict of opposites
which can never be completely overcome or reconciled;

and in this world, therefore, the parts are continually warring against each other and even destroying each other. Here, then, we have a continual process of generation and decay, a mixture of good and evil which cannot either be separated or reconciled. Yet, through all this checkered existence a certain providential order is maintained in the rise and fall of individuals and the interchange of existence. Thus, though evil exists in the world, it is continually subordinated to good. Justice is ever being done, in so far as it is the character of individuals that determines their fate; and the movement of the whole system is an imitation on a lower plane of the perfectly organic constitution and process of the intelligible world. And if it be objected that in this world we often see the wicked triumphing and the good depressed, Plotinus bids us remember that suffering and death are little things to an immortal being. The conflicts and wars of the phenomenal world, we are to consider, are after all rather a dramatic exhibition than a real battle ; and the *dramatis personæ* who have been slain on the stage, as soon as the curtain is down, rise up to begin a new play, in which the parts are distributed anew, according to the goodness or badness of their acting in the first piece.

" A rich life," says Plotinus, " manifests itself in the universe, which creates all beings, giving manifold variety to their existence, and unceasingly producing beautiful forms to be, as it were, its living playthings. And when we contemplate the battles of mortal men and the weapons they use when, ranked in graceful order, they fight against each other, it appears to us like a Pyrrhic dance; and it suggests to our minds the thought that the serious business of mankind is nothing but play, and that death is not at all to be feared; for, after all, those who die in battle only anticipate by a short time that which would happen to them in age, and those who depart soonest from the earth will the sooner come back. Again, if men be deprived of their property, they may easily compute with themselves that it was not really their own beforehand, and that the robbers have gained no serious possession in that of which they will soon themselves be robbed; for, we may even say, to keep *such* goods is worse than to lose them. We must, then, regard all that befals us like actions upon a stage, and we must consider that the murders, the various kinds of death, the conquest and plundering of cities, are but changes of scene and character, and theatrical imitations of tears and lamentation. For here, as in all the vicissitudes of life, it is not the inner soul but the outward shadow of humanity which laments and complains and bewails itself when, with the whole earth as stage, men make their manifold exits and entrances. Such, indeed, are the doings of those who understand only how to live the lower and outer life, and have not discovered that all its sorrows, and even its most serious interests, are only play. For none but the man who knows the real earnest of life is called upon to be in earnest; while play is seriously treated only by those who do not know what earnest means, and who are themselves but playthings. But if a really earnest man takes part with them in the game and undergoes the vicissitudes which they undergo, he will know that he has lighted upon the plays of children and will take off his mask. Even a Socrates may play, but he plays only with the external Socrates. We should, therefore, keep in mind that weeping and lamentation are not to be taken as proofs of the presence of real evils; for children also weep and lament when no ill has befallen them." [1]

In this attempt to explain, or explain away, evil, we see Plotinus wavering between a justification of it as a necessary means to a greater good, and the denial of its reality except as a transient appearance of the phenomenal world; and it is obviously just because he is not able to carry out the former principle successfully, that he is obliged to resort to the latter. The idea that the highest unity is that which manifests itself in the greatest differences and antagonisms and overcomes them, is, as we have seen,

[1] III, 2, 15.

suggested by Plotinus; but in his view of the sensible world he practically gives it up. Yet it really contains the solution of many of his difficulties. For it carries with it the consequence that the Absolute must be conceived, not as excluding, but as including, all differences and oppositions. If we adopt this principle, however, we must regard the Absolute not as an abstract unity, but as a unity in which all difference is embraced. We must raise the pure intelligence above the One to which Plotinus subordinates it, while conceiving it with Plotinus as a conscious self, a self whose self-consciousness implies and includes the consciousness of the intelligible world. Farther, we must conceive the intelligible world, not as a world of pure forms or abstract intelligences, but as simply the external world under all the conditions of time and space; and we must recognise this world of externality and of change, as the opposite counterpart, and therefore as the necessary correlate, of the pure unity and transparent difference of self-consciousness. Finally, we must represent this divided and finite world as yet a world in which spiritual life is realised, not in one but in many spirits who, in spite of their finitude and change, or by means of it, are having developed in them the same principle of self-consciousness in which the whole system finds its beginning. For the idea that the highest unity is the unity of the greatest differences

leads, not only to the conception of that unity as
spiritual, but also to the conclusion that God can
realise himself only in a kingdom of spirits, to whom
he has given the same independent selfhood which
constitutes his own nature; for

> " God is chiefly God by going forth
> To an individualism of the infinite
> Eterne, profuse, intense." [1]

If it be true that the Absolute is not a self-
contained, but a self-manifesting spirit, He must also
be a Father of spirits. In the striking words of
Schelling, He can only give *himself* to his creatures as
he gives a *self* to them, and with it the capacity of
participating in his own life. On such a view, his
infinity will not be, as Pantheism would make it, the
negation of their independent life, but the very reason
and source of its freedom.

Now it is a stroke of insight on the part of
Plotinus to discern that spiritual life, at least in
creatures who are under the conditions of the sensible
world, must itself become the source of greater
division and strife than could exist among creatures
who do not partake in reason, a division and strife
which rise even to internecine war. Thus, after
stating that " the reason of the world, in order to be
perfect, must produce in itself not only difference,
but contrariety," he goes on to say that, if reason

---

[1] I cannot find the reference for this quotation.

has this character in itself it will show it still more in its products, in so far as these are further separated from each other. " Now the sensible world has less unity with itself than that higher world which is its reason or principle Consequently, it is more manifold and admits greater antagonism in the members of it. Hence also their desire to maintain their own life, and their impulse to compel all things into unity with themselves, is greater ; and, in the egoistic effort to seek their own good, by their very love they destroy the objects of their love, when these are perishable ; for the part, in its endeavour to attain the whole, drags to itself all that it can. Thus the good and the evil are thrown into opposition, as when the same art of dancing compels the many members of a chorus to make opposite and contrasted movements ; for, though we call one part good and the other bad, yet the combination must be pronounced excellent. It might, indeed, be objected that this way of looking at the matter involves that there is no badness at all ; but the answer is that it does not involve the denial of the badness of individuals, but only that their badness is to be attributed to any one but themselves." [1]

Plotinus, then, goes on to show how the divine Being may give to the evil and the good their appropriate parts in the drama of existence, according

[1] III, 2, 67.

to the characters which may have so far developed in themselves; and how their playing of these parts may be itself a further step in the evolution of their characters, which will be rewarded in their next incarnation, as actors who play their part well may receive a higher rôle in the next piece, and those who play it ill may be degraded. The doctrine of transmigration is thus used as a means of escape from some of the difficulties connected with the imperfect evolution of individual character in the short life of man.

The doctrine thus stated is not without ambiguity, but it seems to contain a principle which would go farther to explain the origin and limit of evil than the theory which Plotinus generally advocates. For what on that theory Plotinus seeks is to free all the powers of the intelligible world (to which on different grounds he gives the name of God) from responsibility for evil, simply by denying that their activity is primarily directed to the sensible world, which nevertheless they produce. In the passage just quoted, however, it seems to be suggested that the highest unity *must* realise itself in the extremest division;[1] from which it would follow that God cannot be a mere self-contemplative reason, but must be regarded as realising himself in a world of spirits who, as

[1] Of course, Plotinus saves his consistency, in appearance at least, by taking the greater division of the sensible world for granted.

such, are conscious of a universal life, a life which is centred in itself. Evil may thus be explained as springing from good and from God, in so far as it arises from the conditions of the development of finite spirits in whom the germ of a divine life is implanted. For, as possessing such a life, they must be independent, not only in relation to men, but even in a sense in relation to God.

Further, as Plotinus points out, this selfhood of finite spirits shows itself at first in the greatness of their claims, in what Hobbes calls their "natural right to all things" that sets them in rivalry and antagonism to each other. For, as Carlyle often reminds us, a self-conscious being is one who cannot be satisfied unless he has the universe to himself; and yet actually he is at the same time but one individual, an insignificant part of this partial world, and he necessarily comes into internecine conflict with others, so soon as he attempts to realise the claim which his selfhood makes him set up. This enormous contrast of actuality and possibility, of individuality and universality, of a narrowly limited existence under conditions of time and space and an infinite want claiming to be satisfied, is the essential problem of human life, the problem which finds expression in the writings of Marcus Aurelius and St. Augustine, of Pascal and Rousseau, in all the writers who have penetrated deeply into the secrets of the

inner life.   It is the same antithesis which is involved
in the Platonic doctrine that man always seeks the
absolute good and can be satisfied with nothing less:
from which it seems to follow that his actual life as an
individual can bring to him nothing but a series of
disappointments.   For if he seeks an absolute good
in anything finite, he must be disappointed; yet at
first there seems to be nothing else in which he can
seek it.   The source of his evil, therefore, is his ignorance of that which he is seeking.   And if it be asked
how he can be seeking what he does not know, the
answer is that what he seeks is a complete satisfaction
of the self, and that he has not yet learnt that the
self must be lost ere it can be saved.   He cannot be
satisfied with anything short of the life of God, but
he has not yet discovered that the life of God is a life
of giving and not of taking, and that he who would
participate in it must accept its principle.   Yet even
in this his independence is maintained; for, as he is a
self, he must learn from his own experience to accept
that principle, and no power can make him accept it,
except as the result of his own life and experience.

Now, if this view be true, the difficulties as to evil
which beset Plotinus lose at least a part of their force.
For, in the first place, evil, as a subjective experience,
cannot be absolute, cannot be other than the perversion or imperfect development of a nature which is
rooted in good.   It can be nothing but the seeking of

the finite as if it were infinite; and its fundamental characteristic must be ignorance—the self-contradiction of a being who knows not what he really is, and, therefore, seeks his good where it is not to be found. On the other hand, as an objective fact, evil can exist only as the collision of individual selves who by such self-ignorance are brought into conflict with each other.   We only hesitate to call it ignorance, and to generalise the saying of Christ that those who do evil 'know not what they do,' because the term ignorance rather suggests the absence of some particular piece of knowledge, and not the whole attitude of a self-conscious being towards himself and towards others. Further, we have to observe that the conflict of self-conscious beings with each other, which includes almost everything we call evil, is itself part of the discipline by which the selfishness and self-will that causes it may be overcome.   For it is only through the experience of the evil of self-seeking in oneself and others, that a clear consciousness of the good to be found in self-surrender can be developed.

From this point of view, the error of Plotinus is that he *does* practically admit the existence of absolute evil, that is to say, of a matter that cannot in any way be made a means to good.   But, in a passage already quoted, he partly corrects this error when he refers the fall not to matter but to egoism, to the wish of finite spirits to be something for themselves; and when he explains this egoism as itself a result of that desire for the good which, when it becomes developed and enlightened, is turned into the love of God. In this he shows a true insight into the fact that evil is a self-contradictory state of the will of a rational being. The correlative truth would be, that such a will does not need to be rooted out, but only to be brought into harmony with itself; for the change from selfishness to love is not the extinction of the self, but rather the opening up of the way to its true realisation. Plotinus, however, is too deeply imbued with the conception of evil as a purely negative element, introduced into the soul by its connexion with the body, to adopt any view of the process of its purification and conversion to good, except that it is an escape from this defiling contact. He is unable, therefore, to work out the consequences of his alternative idea of evil as consisting in self-will and self-seeking. And, though he protests against the Gnostic conception of the world as evil, and as the creation of an evil *Demiurgus*, he cannot get rid of the dualistic assumption which is at the bottom of that conception. All we can say for him is, that he gives us the means of correcting the defects of his own view, when he suggests that the highest unity is that which overcomes and reconciles the greatest antagonism; when he recognises that this greatest of antagonisms is to be found in the conflict of self-conscious beings with each other ; and above all, when he shows that this antagonism, though in itself the very essence of evil, arises from the fact that, as self-conscious, they must seek the highest good for themselves.

Turning to the other main difficulty of the subject, the difficulty either of referring or of not referring the origin of evil to God, who is the principle of all things, we see that Plotinus adopted a very lame solution of it, when he regarded matter as the utmost result of the *transeunt* activity of the One, as an effect of its overpowering energy, which yet has no connexion with its inner nature. It was the last refuge of Greek Dualism to think of the Absolute as subjected to a foreign necessity. And this Plotinus at times is near admitting when he maintains with Plato the absence of envy in God ; when he speaks of the creative activity as, for that reason, essential to God and even of the sensible world as a manifestation of him ; and above all when he declares that the descent of the soul of man into this world is necessary to its own spiritual development. If, indeed, we reject the false opposition of an *immanent* and a *transeunt* operation of God, and conceive of him as essentially self-manifesting, and as capable of fully manifesting himself only in and to spiritual beings to whom he imparts the principle of his own life, we can see our way to the solution of the difficulty which Plotinus is seeking. In other words, we can see how the divine Being may be regarded as the principle or first cause of all his creatures and yet not in the strict sense the cause of evil as such.   For, if the root of evil lies in the self-will of creatures, who, in seeking themselves, divorce themselves from the life of God and become the rivals and enemies of each other, yet, on the other hand, such self-will is a necessary element in the inchoate consciousness of self, and it is only by passing through it and overcoming it that the consciousness of a self which is at one with man and with God can be developed.   A self-conscious being cannot possibly be, or become, good by the determination of another; and in this sense we may say that it is impossible even for God to create a good spirit, a spirit which is good apart from its own will, or good except by the overcoming of evil within and without it.   For the very consciousness of self carries with it the assertion of self and the seeking of self; and in a finite being such self-assertion and self-seeking have in them the germ of all that is evil.   Such a being has by its own experience to discover that it can be one with itself only as it is one with God, and it must discover this *for itself*. From this point of view we can say that evil is essentially involved in the existence of finite spirits, and that even divine power could not prevent it, if God was to be the Father of spirits who could share in his own life.   For a spiritual kingdom is necessarily a kingdom of freedom, and this means a kingdom of those who have realised for themselves their membership in it. Thus it may be seen that the Christian idea of God as self-revealing suggests, or contains implicitly in it, the solution of the problem which Plotinus vainly endeavoured to solve by distinguishing the *immanent* from the *transeunt* or outgoing operation of the Divine Being.

This idea, however, was at first only implicitly contained in Christianity, and its full evolution is to be found only in the history of the development of Christian doctrine and of the philosophy which arose out of it.

LECTURE TWENTY-SEVENTH.

THE INFLUENCE OF GREEK PHILOSOPHY UPON CHRISTIAN THEOLOGY.

In the last lecture we were dealing with the Neo-Platonic treatment of the critical question as to the nature of evil and its relation to the absolute Being who is called *par excellence* the Good. In arguing this question against the Gnostics, and perhaps against the Christians, Plotinus is brought into considerable difficulties, because he has to face those who from one point of view are greater pessimists, and from another point of view greater optimists than himself. On the one hand, the Christian Church had inherited the Jewish antagonism to all nature-worship, and even something of those darker views which the Jews had derived from Persia, according to which this present world was regarded as given over, for a time at least, to Satan and the powers of evil. And this way of thinking was exaggerated by some of the Gnostics—and obviously by those with whom

Plotinus was brought into contact—into the belief that the world was created by an evil *Demiurgus*. In these Gnostics, indeed, the dualistic or pessimistic tendency was carried to an extreme by a combination of eastern with western elements, of the Jewish belief in demoniac possession with the Greek abhorrence of matter. Even the Christian church, though it rejected Gnostic extravagancies, was in the time of Plotinus becoming every day more ascetic and less inclined to regard this world as anything but a place in which to prepare for the next. As against such antagonists, Plotinus, in spite of the ascetic and mystic tendencies of his own philosophy, was constrained to maintain the Platonic view of natural beauty as a stepping-stone to the higher beauty of the intelligible world: and, inheriting the traditions of a religion and philosophy which had treated the heavenly bodies as of a diviner nature than men or any of the other creatures of the phenomenal world, he was particularly scandalised at the idea that the former should be regarded as the work of an evil power. For him, this world, though in a sense a world of shadow and semblance, was an image or copy of the intelligible world; and from this point of view he was obliged to palliate its evils, and to treat its existence as a good and its defects as merely the necessary drawbacks that go along with that good.

On the other hand, in Christianity and even in

Gnosticism, there were elements of a deeper optimism, which were equally obnoxious to Plotinus. For apparently, in spite of their dualism, some Christian ideas as to a 'new earth' and a bodily resurrection of the blessed had appeared in the Gnostic writings; and these were at once rejected by Plotinus as conflicting with his conception that perfect bliss is to be found, not in any change of the material world, but in a complete escape from it. And with still more decision did he repudiate the doctrine that humanity is in itself divine, and that the highest good can be attained even by the commonest of men without ceasing to be human. The idea that union with the supreme God is for the élite of humanity, and that it can be realised only by the way of philosophic contemplation, makes him revolt against the universalism of Christianity.

Christianity then, as I have indicated, contained at once a deeper pessimism and a higher optimism than is to be found in the system of Plotinus, and just because of this, it could admit no dualism nor any of the compromises that dualism necessarily brings with it. Realising, as Plotinus on the whole refused to do, that the seat of evil is in the consciousness and will of the rational being as such, Christianity could be content with nothing less than its complete eradication; nor could it admit that there was anything in the world or in humanity that was essentially evil, or in which good could not be realised. It was a doctrine of conversion, redemption, regeneration, reconciliation: and it could not without inconsistency allow that there was anything outside of the circle of the divine life, least of all any human being, who, as such, must be made in the image of God. Yet as little was it inclined to minimise the actual facts of the division of men from God and from each other. In recognising evil as rooted in consciousness and will, it deepened very greatly the conception of its antagonism to good, at the same time that it made it possible that that antagonism should be completely overcome. What is more, it made even the existence of evil explicable, as a necessary step in the development of the finite spirit to a consciousness of the divine principle which is realising itself in and through its finitude.

When, however, we say that all this was implicit in Christianity, we must make a distinction. It was clear from the beginning that Christianity involved a new conception of the relation of God and man, but this conception was at first an undeveloped germ, a germ of which the whole history of thought from that time has been the development. Presented at once as a doctrine embodied in an individual life, Christianity seemed from the beginning to be fully concrete and real; yet, just because it was so presented, it was really at first undefined and unexplained, a fruitful principle rather than a developed system. It was the idea of God as revealed in man, and the idea of man as by a supreme act of self-surrender finding the perfect realisation of himself as the son and servant of God. It was this as embodied in an individual to whom others might attach themselves, and by this attachment participate in the same life. It was man losing himself to find himself again in God, and God manifest in the flesh to draw all mankind to himself. It is this divine dialectic, as we might call it, which was directly expressed in the words of Christ as they are recorded in the Synoptic Gospels; and this also was the lesson which St. Paul generalised from the life and, above all, from the death of Christ. It was the same solution of the difficulties of life which had been suggested to the prophets by the sufferings of the people of Israel, trodden under feet of other nations, and yet conscious of itself as the people of God. And it also contained implicitly the key to all the antagonisms of thought that had been developed in Greek philosophy—the antagonism of the material and the spiritual, the antagonism of the phenomenal and the ideal or intelligible world, the antagonism of the finite and the infinite, the antagonism of the temporal and the eternal. In a word, it contained in itself the principle of an optimism which faces and overcomes the deepest pessimism, of an idealism which has room in itself for the most realistic consciousness of all the distinctions and relations of the finite.

But it contained all this only *in principle*, and even that principle was not distinctly expressed, but was at first wrapped up in the conscious relation of the individual to One in whom it seemed once for all to be embodied. And though there is a truth in the assertion that relation to an individual person often contains, for those who experience it, a deeper meaning than they could have received or appreciated in any other form, yet, just for that reason, they can hardly be said to understand or possess the truth by which they are thus influenced; rather we should say that it possesses them, and carries them on to results which they cannot foresee. Thus, while an ideal, apprehended in an individual form, may be significant, and even infinitely significant, its significance is always to a great extent hidden even from him who feels it, and the more closely hidden, the greater that significance is. Admiration and love often anticipate the intelligence, and the heart may obscurely realise the presence of a power which the mind cannot measure. But such realisation is a dim foretaste, an obscure anticipation, of the truth; and it may require a long process of development ere it can pass into the intelligent appropriation and conscious appreciation of the principle involved in that which is admired and loved.

And there is, again, a long way to traverse between such acceptance of a principle and the recognition of all its consequences.

This will become clearer, if we bear in mind the novelty of an individualistic consciousness of God, such as that age was seeking, and such as it found in Christianity. The religion, like the morality, of earlier times was essentially social, mediated by the organisation of the community or national society, as a member of which, and only as a member of which, the individual was conscious of rights and duties in relation to other men, as well as of an ideal relation to God which consecrated both. But, as we have seen, the conquests of Rome put an end to all this. The Roman empire was the embodied negation of all such civic and national bonds, and, as such, it conquered at once the nations and their gods. But philosophy with the Greeks and Romans, and prophecy with the Jews, had provided a refuge for the religious consciousness, in the idea of a direct relation of the individual man to God, altogether independent of his relation to others as members of one political society. Already in the philosophical schools of the Greeks, and in the synagogues of the Jews, there had begun to exist what we may call a *Church*,[1] a bond of human beings as all directly related to God, and only through God related to each other. And this bond was by

[1] Cf. Wellhausen, *Israelitische and Jüdische Geschichte*, Chap. XV.

its very nature altogether independent of the unity of the State, which indeed, in the Roman empire, had ceased to be an ethical organisation of life, and had become only the maintainer of outward order.

Now, the consciousness of a relation to Christ, as the personality in whom the unity of God with man was consummated and manifested, while it gave a new life to this purely spiritual organisation, could not make it more than a Church; it could not raise it to that community of all interests secular and sacred, which had formerly been embodied in the civic or national State. The brotherhood of Christ was a union of abstract charity, which united men as religious beings, without making them the members of a political society. The Catholic Church was Catholic, because it included all Christians *as individuals* in virtue of their universal or spiritual nature; but it separated the concerns of that nature from all the secular affairs of life, and even when it did not seek to isolate the individual from these affairs, it could not do more than put an external limitation upon them. It could not unite flesh with spirit, the particular impulses of the finite life with the highest aspirations of the religious consciousness, in such a harmony as had been in large measure achieved in some of the political societies of the ancient world.

St. Paul, indeed, gives us a picture of the Church as a body, in which each member has a special office, and yet all members contribute to one life; but the actual Church, by the very fact that it excluded from its direct purview all the secular interests of life, could not possibly realise that ideal. It could not organise men into a real social whole by means of their particular tendencies and capacities. It could produce a collective unity of individuals through one supreme interest, but it could not mould them into a real social organism, since it excluded or at least did not directly include, their other interests. In fact, it could deal with those other interests directly only by treating them as of no account, and so creating not a State but a monastery. This fundamental weakness inevitably forced it, almost in spite of itself, in spite of the idea of the essential unity of the human with the divine on which it was based, into the path of asceticism. As a consequence, it tended more and more to obscure that idea, or to give a transcendent interpretation to it as a unity of God with men which was realised only in the person of Christ, and could not in the same sense be participated in by his followers. Thus the very dualism of human and divine, which Christ seemed to have come to terminate, began to reappear in a new form, in so far as the idea of their union was, as it were, lifted into the skies, into the region of abstract dogma as to the nature of the divinity.   And as this change was consummated, Christianity tended to become a religion of other-worldliness, a religion in which the life of this world was viewed merely as a preparation for another.

This tendency was at first resisted by the conception of Christ as the Jewish Messiah.   For though the early Christians had learnt to regard Christ as a Messiah who conquers by suffering and death, and to look upon the world, in which this is the lot of supreme goodness, as in a sense given over to the power of evil, yet they did not despair of an earthly victory over such evil.   On the contrary, it was their hope and belief that the struggle of a few years would bring about a renewal of all things, and that the church, by the return of its Lord, would be changed into a divine State, or kingdom of God upon earth. As, however, the days went on, and the ' promise of Christ's coming' seemed to fail, this hope passed away. The Church resigned itself to be only a church, and the world seemed to be finally given over to other powers. And, as a necessary consequence, the divine kingdom, for which the teaching and discipline of the Church was a preparation, transferred itself to another world. The Christian was a pilgrim and a stranger in this world, and his *patria*, the native land of his soul, where alone he could be a citizen, was to be found

only in heaven.   And with this transference of the
realisation of Christianity beyond death and time,
the elevation of humanity into unity with the
divine through union with Christ inevitably took the
aspect of an unrealisable ideal, unrealisable at least
on earth ; and, as a natural consequence, the Church
was set in perennial antagonism to the State.

There was, however, a still more important influence
which acted in the same direction, namely, the influence
of Greek, and in particular of Neo-Platonic, philosophy.
This influence had already done much to modify
Jewish religion at the beginning of the Christian
era, as is shown by the writings of Philo, and it
could not but be felt still more powerfully in the
Christian Church.   For, as soon as the Messianic
idea left Jewish soil, it had to find an equivalent or
substitute among the conceptions of the classical
nations, and no idea could seem so appropriate as
that of the *Logos* which had already been adopted
by Philo.   But with this change all the limitations,
which in the Jewish mind were connected with
the Messianic idea, were at once thrown off.
Already in the writings of St. Paul the conception
of the Christ as 'the first-born of many brethren,'
who had been raised from the dead by God as an
evidence of his universal mission to men, seems to rise
above every condition of finite life ; and in the later
Epistles he is declared to be the ' image of the invisible

God,' the Being who 'is before all things,' and by whom 'all things consist.'[1] And there was a danger that the Neo-Platonic idea of the *Logos* should be carried so far as to reduce the whole human life of Christ to a mere illusive appearance of one who was not a real human being at all. Even the Gospel of St. John might seem to give some countenance to such a view; for while the writer protests against it, and even dwells with special force and vehemence on its opposite, speaking of 'that which our eyes have seen and our hands have handled of the word of life,'[2] and denouncing as the worst of heresies the idea that Christ had not 'come in the flesh'; yet he himself throughout his narrative is continually insisting on the supernatural aspects of the life of Christ. It was, in fact, just because the Son of Man was so much lost in the Son of God that the assertion of his real humanity had become absolutely necessary. In the protests of St. John, therefore, we see the beginning of those controversies as to the relation of the divine to the human in Christ, which were to vex the Church through all the centuries in which it was occupied in the formulation of its creed. The two terms, God and man, were here for the first time brought together with a full consciousness of all that tends to divide

---

[1] Col. I, 16, 17.

[2] If the first Epistle be by the same writer as the Gospel.

and oppose them; and it was impossible that the Church should rest until the difficulties of their difference and unity should be fought out to some decided issue. It was, therefore, by no avoidable accident that these controversies arose in the Church. For so soon as the meaning of the life of Christ, and of the attitude of perfect surrender to God and unity with him, which Jesus Christ maintained both in his life and in his death, began to be realised—and this could not be long delayed in an age when Greek thought had made men so fully alive to the antagonistic elements involved in the question—it was inevitable that this problem should become all-important. Nor was it possible that the Church should rest with complete assurance in its faith, till all the various aspects of it were considered, and till the controversy regarding them was brought to a definite issue.

Now there are many writers, and not only sceptical writers, but Christian theologians—including, indeed, the most important school of German theology in recent times—who hold that the great controversies of the early Church about the Trinity and the Incarnation were controversies about words, or at best about subtilties introduced by Greek philosophy into the Christian religion, which have no real significance for later times. They are, in the language of Harnack, parts of that secularisation of the Christian faith by which it was drawn down into the sphere of an unchristian system of thought. Or, as others have held, they are meaningless attempts to define the incomprehensible, from which no satisfaction to the intelligence of man can be drawn. Such a view seems to me to show a want of the power to recognise that the controversies of an earlier time have a real meaning, though the problems discussed are not exactly *our* problems, and the language used in the debate has become unfamiliar. If, however, we can get over this appearance of strangeness, we shall be little inclined to the superficial view that the human mind wrestled for centuries over the difference between verbal definitions of the Unknowable. I do not believe that controversies about words ever occupy a great space in human history, although it is true that the controversies of the past often seem to us mere controversies about words. But this is simply because we have not realised what the issues really meant to those who contended so strenuously about them. In the present case we have only to go a little below the surface to discern the vital relation which the controversies of the early Christian centuries have to those which occupy our minds in the present day.

The truth is that the question of the early Christian centuries was simply the great problem as to the relation of the human to the divine, of the spirits of men to the absolute Being, which is the greatest

theme of modern philosophy ; but in that age the
opposing views could only take the form of different
conceptions of the person of Christ.   Can God reveal
himself to and in man ?   Can man be the organ and
manifestation of God ?   Such is the perennial issue
which the Christian Church has had to face; but in
that age it had to face it only in relation to him, in
whom the consciousness of sonship to God had shown
itself in its first and most immediate form.   Admitting that Christ was such a being, and that in
him and to him God was revealed, could he be regarded as a real man ?   Was it not a degradation
for him to be brought into contact with mortality,
and must not his appearance be regarded as a mere
semblance which was necessary for the purpose of his
mission ?   On the other hand, if his appearance as
man were such a semblance or illusion, how could he
reveal the reality ?   How could a mediator, who was
not man, unite man to God ?   Must not the two
terms break asunder and require some new middle
term to unite them, unless Christ were at once very
man and very God ?   This was the circle within
which the controversy turned during the first five
centuries of the Christian era.   The ultimate result
of the conflict was the assertion of the unity of
divinity and humanity in Christ; but at the same
time this result was in two ways deprived of a great
part of its meaning.   In the first place, it was

confined to Christ alone; and in the second place, the unity was regarded as, so to speak, rather a static than a dynamic unity, that is, not as a unity realised in the process of the Christian life, the process of self-surrender and self-sacrifice through which humanity becomes—what potentially it is—the highest organ of the divine self-manifestation, but as a unity that exists independently of any process whatsoever.

Now the imperfection of this result is partly explained by the necessity that the *principle* of the unity of the divine and the human should be asserted, ere it could be worked out to any farther consequences. Christ was the one crucial instance which, if it could be maintained as real, must inevitably determine the whole issue. If one man, living such a life of self-sacrifice for mankind, were in perfect unity with God, so that his consciousness of himself could be taken as the divine self-consciousness, then must not the same be true of all who followed in his footsteps? If so, then the highest goodness was shown to be only the realisation of an ideal which every human soul, as such, bears within it. God is manifested in man under the ordinary conditions of human life, whenever man gives himself up to God. The power that builds and holds the universe together is shown, in a higher form than by any creative act, in every man that lives not for himself, but as an organ and minister of divine love to men.

But this result could not be seen at first. In the early centuries the idea could not be realised except in relation to its first pure manifestation. Christianity had, indeed, revealed God in man, but at first only in *the* Man, who was 'the first-born of many brethren.' And the whole movement of thought was at first concentrated on the effort to realise this unity of humanity and divinity in the person of him, who was presented as at once the Son of Man and the Son of God. Christ must be 'lifted up' ere he could draw all men to him. In other men, this unity was a 'far off divine event,' which had to be realised by a self-conquest that could never be quite complete. Thus Christianity had cast man down, in order to raise him up; and the negative aspect of this revelation must necessarily show itself before the positive.[1] This was the inner necessity of the situation. But there was also an outward necessity corresponding to it. Greek philosophy supplied the form in which the reflective thought of the time was cast, the intellectual weapons with which it worked, the categories or general conceptions by means of which it sought to deal with any new matter that was brought to it. And this philosophy was, as we have seen, profoundly dualistic, and the efforts of Neo-Platonism to overcome the dualism had only brought it into a more startling form. Its hierarchy

---

[1] Cf. *Evolution of Religion*, II, Lect. 10.

of powers reaching up to the absolute One and down to formless matter, showed at once the *need* of mediation, and the *impossibility* of attaining it in consistency with the presuppositions from which the system started. For in a true mediation the middle term cannot be a mere intermediate, but must transcend, and comprehend in one, the two terms that are opposed. A reflexion which was guided by the ideals of such a philosophy was apt to bring division into the nature of the object to which it was applied, or, at least, to bring into active manifestation any tendency to division that belonged to it. Now, as we have seen, Christianity had in it from the first a negative side. Its essential moral idea was that of self-realisation through self-sacrifice. "Except a corn of wheat fall into the ground and die, it abideth alone." In such words Christ showed his confidence, that a new and a richer life would arise out of the death or sacrifice of the immediate natural existence ; but he demanded that the old life should perish ere the new life could arise. These two elements, the negative and the positive, are held in perfect balance in the consciousness of Christ, as it is expressed in the Synoptic Gospels, with its perfect self-surrender even to death, its absolute trust in God, and its confident reading of the divine goodness in all nature and providence, in the face of the fiercest manifestations of evil passion. In Christ, we might say, optimism emerges serene and triumphant from everything that could be brought to prove its opposite. Perfect idealism shows itself stronger than all the materialism of the world. *Das Ernst des Negativen*, the reality of sin and misery, has full justice done to it, but the positive overreaches it, and transforms it into good. The prayer " Father forgive them, for they know not what they do," with its reduction of evil to ignorance, is perhaps the most victorious assertion of the relativity of evil that ever has been made.

But it was hardly possible that this balance should be preserved, and the very exigencies of the prolonged struggle of the Church with the world tended to bring the negative aspect of its doctrines into greater and greater prominence. Moreover, modes of thought derived from Greek philosophy were constantly aiding this tendency, and even at times threatening to break up the unity of the Christian consciousness altogether. Through the more educated of the converts to the Christian faith, through the Gnostics and the Christian Fathers—who opposed the Gnostics, but in doing so received a strong reactive influence from Gnosticism—through the Alexandrian school of theology, especially as represented by Clement and Origen, and at a later date by Augustine, the ideas of Neo-Platonism invaded the Christian theology. And wherever they came,

they tended to emphasise the negative and to
weaken the positive elements of the Christian
faith. The result was somewhat ambiguous. The
fundamental idea of Christianity could not be lost;
but it was, so to speak, driven back to its last
entrenchment in the consciousness of Christ, and all
the outworks were surrendered to the enemy. To
put the matter more clearly, Christianity could not
give up its central idea of the unity of the human
with the divine, nor could it give up the faith that
men in some sense are capable of being participators
in the divine nature. But, under the influence of
Neo-Platonic modes of thought, the gulf between Christ
and other men tended to widen. The heresy that
reduced the humanity of Christ to an illusive appearance was defeated in its direct aim, but it was
victorious in so far as the glorified Christ was
absolutely separated from and raised above all his
fellows, till it became almost a paradox to say that
"he was in all points tempted like as we are." The
strong language of St. John's Gospel, "that they may
be one, even as we are one," had to be explained
away. And though St. Athanasius could still say,
that "He became man that we might be made gods," [1]
it was inevitable that such words should come to seem
too daring.

---

[1] αὐτὸς, γὰρ ἐνηνθρώπησεν, ἵνα ἡμεῖς θεοποιηθῶμεν. *De Incarn. Verbi*,
§ 54.

The change which passed over the doctrine of the Trinity is another indication in the same direction. In earlier writers and in St. Athanasius it is immediately connected with the doctrine of the Incarnation ; it is essentially an attempt to deal with the great question of the unity of God and man. But with St. Augustine, who was deeply under the influence of the Neo-Platonists, and from whom the Athanasian creed with its mysterious antithetic utterances is derived, it becomes an almost unintelligible account of the inner nature of the Deity.[1]   It might fairly be said that a change passed over the idea of the God-man very like that which passed over the idea of the world-soul between Plato and Plotinus, by which the very link between the intelligence and the matter was itself taken up into the intelligible world.   And the mediation of the Virgin and the saints had to be brought in to fill up the breach thus made in the unity of the human and the divine.   At the same time, the Christian view of life had to be modified in conformity with the new conception of the relation of man to God.   The possibility of the realisation

[1] St. Augustine, indeed, still tries to illustrate the idea of the Trinity by several analogies, *e.g*, the unity of *memoria, intelligentia*, and *voluntas* in one consciousness ; but otherwise he seems to lose the meaning of the distinction of Persons in the *inseparabilis operatio*. The Divinity, in fact, becomes with him a mystery, rather than what the doctrine first sought to be, an explanation.   And this change is manifestly due to Neo-Platonic influences.

of the life of Christ in other men was not and could
not be denied, but it was referred to another world,
for which this was regarded merely as a preparation.
Millennial anticipations of a regenerated earth were
exchanged for the conception of the earthly life as a
trial and discipline for a better world. And if the
ascetic ideal could not absolutely triumph in a religion
that proclaimed the resurrection of the body, if the
natural feelings and affections of humanity could not
be declared essentially impure, because connected
with sense and matter, yet the discredit of following
a lower ideal was attached to the life of the family
and the State. In short, it may fairly be argued that
through this whole period the development of
Christianity was one-sided, and that, though it could
not altogether surrender its essential character as a
doctrine of reconciliation, as the revelation of a unity
of human and divine that underlies their difference and overcomes it, yet it was drawn in the
direction of dualism as far as was possible consistently with its retaining any hold of the life of
Christ. And if it be said that this dualistic movement was itself a necessary stage in the development
of the Christian idea, yet, on the other hand, we
cannot doubt that the main agency by which it was
accomplished was the Greek, and in particular the
Neo-Platonic philosophy. In this case, even more
clearly than in the case of the empire of Rome,

we can see that conquered Greece laid spiritual fetters on its victor. Greece provided Christianity with the weapons of culture which enabled it to subdue the minds of its opponents, but at the same time it did much to determine the main bias and direction of the religious consciousness which was established by its means. It gave its own form to the life and doctrine of the Church, at least down to the time when, by a new reaction, the spirit of Christianity began to free itself from the tutelage that was necessary to its earlier development.

These remarks on the influence of Greek philosophy, especially in its Neo-Platonic form, upon the development of Christian doctrine, are of course not intended to be exhaustive. They are intended merely to indicate the great effect of the movement of Greek thought upon the theology of the Christian Church. In different ways Greek philosophy may be regarded as the germ out of which Christian theology sprang, or as the great adverse force which it had to combat. It was the former, if we consider that in Neo-Platonism Greek philosophy was struggling with the ideas of the antagonism between the divine and the human, and at the same time of the necessity of their relation. The problem which Christianity had to solve, reached its most definite and decisive expression in the Neo-Platonic philosophy. And we must remember that he who puts such a problem distinctly before the human mind, has already done much to help towards its solution. On the other hand, Neo-Platonism itself was not able to reach such a solution. It set the two terms in such absolute opposition that a true synthesis or reconciliation of them was impossible. It altogether separated the Infinite from the finite; or, if it tried to mediate between them by means of the intelligence and the world-soul, yet as it regarded even the world-soul as belonging entirely to the intelligible world, it could not conceive it as descending into the world of sense and matter, or as reconciling the world of sense and matter with the divine. Its last word was escape, not reconciliation, the deliverance of the soul from the bonds of finitude, and not the conversion of the finite itself into the organ and manifestation of the infinite. Hence, when brought in relation to Christianity, Neo-Platonism became an influence in favour of dualism. It tended to break the unity of life and thought which Christianity sought to establish, or at least to limit and make imperfect the reconciliation which Christianity sought to attain.

Yet, even so, it discharged a very useful office. In the region of spirit a victory won too easily is of little value. An optimism established without any difficulty becomes worse than any pessimism: an idealism that has not entered into all the differences and antagonisms of the real is futile. Even Christianity has tended to become an ignoring rather than a healing of the evils of life when it has not been based on the deepest consciousness of those evils. Hence we must regard as a friend in disguise the enemy which again and again has forced the church and the world to recognise, how imperfectly the spiritual object of Christianity has been attained, how far the actual is from the ideal, how secular and profane the life of even the most Christian of men still is, how far the kingdoms of this world are from realising the idea of the kingdom of God. As a 'facile Monism' is the grave of any true and comprehensive attempt to discover the ideal meaning of the universe, so the idea of the unity of God and man may itself become the most shallow of illusions, if that unity be taken as a static identity, and, if it be not recognised that the realisation of it involves the overcoming of the deepest of all antagonisms.

Now, modern philosophy from the time of the Renaissance has sought to emphasise the positive rather than the negative aspect of ethics and religion, almost as decisively as the Middle Ages emphasised their negative aspect. Sometimes, indeed, it has gone so far in this direction as to forget the negative altogether. Even where it has not proclaimed Hedonism as the principle of morals, it has tended to exalt self-development to the exclusion of self-sacrifice, and it has sought the divine in nature rather than beyond it. And a Pantheism that speaks of *Deus sive Natura* leaves it at least ambiguous whether nature is taken up into God, or God is merged in nature. If this tendency had gained absolute predominance, the modern world would have forgotten its Christianity, and gone back—as Heine at one time wished it to go back—to a kind of aesthetic paganism. It is essential to Christianity to maintain—in the face of all the positive tendencies of the modern spirit—that a true self-development can be attained only through self-sacrifice, and that, if God reveals himself in man, it is only as man gives himself up, to be the servant and organ of a divine purpose in humanity. Hence there is much still to be learnt from a philosophy that keeps before us the depth of the antagonism between the natural and the spiritual, between the real and the ideal, between man and God. And we may regard Greek philosophy, in spite of the negative character of its ultimate result, and perhaps because of it, as, in itself and in its influence upon Christian thought, contributing an invaluable element to theological thought.

INDEX.

GLASGOW : PRINTED AT THE UNIVERSITY PRESS BY ROBERT MACLEHOSE AND CO.